SHADOW TRAFFIC'S

NEW YORK
SHORTCUTS
AND TRAFFIC TIPS

BY GRIDLOCK SAM

Fodor's Travel Publications, Inc.
New York • Toronto • London • Sydney • Auckland

**In Memory of Diane Gellman,
the keeper of the "traffic numbers," 1946–1993**

ISBN 0-679-02482-4
First Edition

Acknowledgments

The city and its back roads are too much for any one person to fully get to know in a lifetime. I had a great deal of help in putting this book together. My friends at the New York City Department of Transportation came up with ideas and constructive criticism. Many thanks to Joel Friedman, Bill Hirsch, Spiros Lambros, Joe Noto, Raman Patel, Mike Primeggia, and Joe Vrana. I thank my colleagues at other agencies, including Mike Francese, Phyllis Hirschberg, Bill Fife, and Paul Carris. This book would not have happened if not for the perseverance of Inez Aimee and the support of Mike D'Ambrose at Shadow Traffic. Shadow's traffic mavens, Bernard Spigner and Fred Bennett, gave me valuable geography lessons. I could always count on my buddies at Hayden-Wegman, Al Meyer and Richard Newhouse, for fact and field checking. Friends Janet Campbell and Mark Weiss were there when I needed them. Robin Schwartz and Larry Levine were my advance team scouting promising shortcuts. A special thanks to my readers who sent in hundreds of shortcuts for my *Daily News* column. Many thanks to my agent, Debra Schneider, for her confidence in this project.

Putting this book together was truly a family affair. My children, David, Adam, and Deena, and my wife, Daria, had to tolerate my searches for perfect shortcuts. For the most part that meant getting lost and arriving late. Thanks for putting up with me.

Shadow Traffic's New York Shortcuts
Book Design and Illustrations: Alida Beck
Art Direction: Fabrizio La Rocca
Cartography: David Lindroth
Cover Design: Fabrizio La Rocca, Alida Beck
Cover Graphic: Jason Küffer
Design Production: Elena Ferrigno, Tigist Getachew, Marco Marinucci
Copy Editor: Denise Nolty

Special Sales

Fodor's Travel Publications are available at special discounts for bulk purchases for sales promotions or premiums. Special editions, including personalized covers, excerpts of existing guides, and corporate imprints, can be created in large quantities for special needs. For more information, contact your local bookseller or write to Special Markets, Fodor's Travel Publications, 201 East 50th Street, New York, NY 10022. Inquiries from Canada should be directed to your local Canadian bookseller or sent to Random House of Canada, Ltd., Marketing Dept., 1265 Aerowood Drive, Mississauga, Ontario L4W 1B9. Inquiries from the United Kingdom should be sent to Fodor's Travel Publications, 20 Vauxhall Bridge Road, London SW1V 2SA.

MANUFACTURED IN THE UNITED STATES OF AMERICA
10 9 8 7 6 5 4 3 2 1

Contents

New York City Area

WESTCHESTER

YONKERS

Saw Mill River Pkwy.

N.Y.S. Thruway

MT. VERNON

New England Thruway

Long Island Sound

PORT WASHINGTON

TENAFLY

Van Cortlandt Park

RIVERDALE

Bronx River Pkwy.

Pelham Bay Park

Hart I.

City I.

KINGS POINT

GREAT NECK

Manhasset Bay

BERGEN

PARAMUS

ENGLEWOOD

Palisades Pkwy.

Spuyten Deyvil

Henry Hudson Bridge

I-87

Fordham University

Bronx Park

New York Botanical Garden

Hutchinson Pkwy.

I-95

Eastchester Bay

Eastchester Bay

Throgs Neck

GREAT NECK ESTATES

NASSAU

NEW JERSEY

ENGLEWOOD CLIFFS

4

FORT LEE

THE BRONX

Bronx Zoo

Crotona Park

Cross-Bronx Expwy.

95

River

Throgs Neck Bridge

Little Neck Bay

LITTLE NECK

I-80

46

CLIFFSIDE PARK

George Washington Bridge

Harlem River Drive

Yankee Stadium

Bruckner Expwy.

HUNTS POINT

East

Whitestone Bridge

Cross Island

BAYSIDE

Pkwy.

17

EAST RUTHERFORD

Meadowlands Sports Complex

I-95

NORTH BERGEN

WEST NEW YORK

Hudson River

Harlem River Pkwy.

Harlem R.

Columbia University

Triboro Bridge

Randall's I.

Rikers I.

COLLEGE POINT

Flushing Bay

La Guardia Airport

678

Northern Blvd.

Clearview Expwy.

FLUSHING

Long Island Expwy.

Grand Central Pkwy.

3

LYNDHURST

SECAUCUS

WEEHAWKEN

N.J. Tpke. West Leg

N.J. Tpke. East Leg

UNION CITY

MANHATTAN

Central Park

FDR Drive

Lincoln Center

Queensboro Bridge

ASTORIA

Grand Central Pkwy.

Northern Blvd.

Roosevelt I.

LONG ISLAND CITY

QUEENS

JACKSON HEIGHTS

Shea Stadium

USTA Nat'l Tennis Center

Flushing Meadow-Corona Park

Grand Central Pkwy.

ST. ALBANS

JAMAICA

SPRINGFIELD GARDENS

17

HUDSON

HOBOKEN

United Nations

34th St.

East River

Queens Midtown Tunnel

GREENPOINT

Queens Blvd.

495

FOREST HILLS

Woodhaven Blvd.

Van Wyck Expwy.

Belt Pkwy.

KEARNY

Lincoln Tunnel

Holland Tunnel

Canal St.

WILLIAMSBURG

Williamsburg Bridge

Brooklyn-Queens Expwy.

MASPETH

Inter Boro Pkwy.

OZONE PARK

SOUTH OZONE PARK

J.F.K. International Airport

9 1

I-280

Manhattan Bridge

Brooklyn Bridge

BROOKLYN HEIGHTS

COBBLE HILL

Atlantic Ave.

Eastern Pkwy.

EAST NEW YORK

Belt Pkwy.

Pulaski Skyway

Battery Park

Ellis I.

Brooklyn-Battery Tunnel

PARK SLOPE

Brooklyn Museum and Botanic Gardens

JERSEY CITY

Liberty State Park

Statue of Liberty

Governors I.

Liberty I.

Prospect Park

Linden Blvd.

CANARSIE

Jamaica Bay Wildlife Refuge

NEWARK

ESSEX

78

Gowanus Expwy.

Prospect Expwy.

Greenwood Cemetery

Flatbush Ave.

Upper Bay

BROOKLYN

Ocean Pkwy.

Marine Park

Floyd Bennett Field

Jacob Riis Park

Newark Bay

BAYONNE

Kill Van Kull

Snug Harbor

The Narrows

BAY RIDGE

Fort Hamilton

Dyker Beach Park and Golf Course

BENSONHURST

Belt Pkwy.

Rockaway Inlet

GATEWAY NATIONAL RECREATION AREA

Newark International Airport

ELIZABETH

UNION

Bayonne Bridge

Alice Austen House

STATEN ISLAND

Verrazano Narrows Bridge

Lower Bay

CONEY ISLAND

New York Aquarium

ATLANTIC OCEAN

Goethals Bridge

Staten Island Expwy.

0   5 miles

0   5 km

N

1

Introduction

I hate traffic. This may sound strange from someone who has made his living out of it, but I detest delays. I prefer the local bodega over the low-priced supermarket any day, just to avoid the long lines. Saturday night at the movies is anathema to me because of the ticket queue. So, from the day I got my driver's license I avoided driving with the hordes. When you follow my shortcuts, you will, too.

Some twenty-five years ago I began my professional traffic career as a New York City taxi driver. This provided the basic training for maneuvering through the city's streets. Though trained in science, I switched majors to transportation engineering in graduate school. I thought I would save the subways, but the Transit Authority wouldn't offer me a job. I ended up as a junior engineer at the old Traffic Department.

Initially I worked developing neighborhood one-way plans but soon I was moved to "Special Projects." John Lindsay was mayor and proposed many innovative and bold schemes to reduce traffic in Midtown. I spent a lot of time on these plans, working with an old-time traffic engineer named Roy Cottam. One day, Roy spoke of his fears that if we closed the streets in the Theater District, the grid system would "lock-up" and all traffic would grind to a halt. Soon we simply juxtaposed the words, and the term gridlock was born.

In 1980, when I was chief engineer in charge of traffic operations during the transit strike, the press heard of our concern about gridlock. The word caught on, and within days I received a phone call from William Safire, the certifier of new words for *The New York Times*. "Gridlock, such a word cannot miss," he wrote in his "On Language" column. I tried to share the credit for the word with Roy, but he didn't want to be blamed for it. So I became the father of the trendiest word of the '90s, earning the moniker "Gridlock" Sam.

The transit strike of 1980 was a tremendous inconvenience for New Yorkers but it's the stuff that makes the careers of traffic engineers. I was "spotted" by City Hall and mercurially went from traffic engineer to traffic commissioner. From 1982 to 1986 I served as the city's traffic chief and from 1986 to 1990 as the chief engineer for the entire transportation department.

During my nineteen-year stint with the city's traffic and transportation agency I studied, planned, and designed roads and street systems in every neighborhood in the city. I knew the front roads backwards and the back roads like the back of my hand. In my own travels I took advantage of this knowledge in my quest to avoid congestion. I collected, in my head, shortcuts for every borough.

When I left city government in 1990 I joined the New York *Daily News* and began writing a column on traffic, offering the next day's traffic forecasts and adding a little spice with traffic tips and shortcuts. The column was a big hit, and soon I was receiving shortcuts from readers. Many cabbies and other veteran drivers vied for the Gridlock Sam T-shirts being offered by the *News* in return for a published tip. All this information would make an indispensible guide for drivers, I realized, and so I began to compile a collection of my favorite tips and shortcuts.

The resulting book is divided into nine chapters. Manhattan, the Bronx, and Queens each gets a chapter; Staten Island is combined with Brooklyn. The BQE gets a chapter of its own because of the heavy volume, constant construction, built-in bottlenecks, and plethora of alternative routes little known to most drivers. There's a chapter for New Jersey commuters with queue-jumping tips for the Hudson River crossings. To reduce anxiety and frustration for travelers catching a plane, I've devoted a seventh chapter to accessing the region's three airports. And since everyone needs to get away from so much traffic, I've added shortcuts to the beaches and mountains.

The traffic system, particularly the traffic signals, is dynamic. It changes constantly and has separate patterns for weekdays and weekends. What may be the perfect shortcut in the morning could prove to be dreadful in the evening. For this reason I have included a final chapter explaining all you need to know about traffic signals.

Midtown Manhattan, the single biggest generator of traffic, has the most confusing rules and restrictions. I'm not sure I should admit this, but I had a hand in setting up most of the rules. You may find some inside information at the end of the Manhattan chapter helpful.

The geographic breakdown of chapters was chosen for convenience. When traveling between boroughs you may need to check more than one map. For example, many of the Queens shortcuts would be useful for Kennedy or La Guardia airports. Commuters heading to Manhattan should review the borough chapters for convenient routes.

Knowing when to use a shortcut is as important as knowing the route. A shortcut using city streets instead of a highway becomes competitive when highway speeds drop below 10–15 mph. When you hear on the radio that there's been an accident on the highway, opt for the shortcut. But, there are reasons for using a shortcut even if the highway appears to be fine. Some people call it reliability; I call it disaster avoidance. I never take the BQE from my house in Brooklyn to catch a plane at La Guardia Airport. The street shortcut takes me 35–40 minutes consistently. The BQE sometimes gets me there in 25 minutes, but it can also take an hour or more. On a highway, if the cars in front of you get into an accident, you're stuck. Local streets, on the other hand, allow for new choices at every intersection.

Happy motoring!

Understanding the Roadways of Central Park

A key to smart driving in Manhattan is to understand the complexities of the roadway system through Central Park. There are three different types of roadways and four different schedules for their closings. The main drives close (with one important exception; *see* summer hours, daytime closings, *below*), as well as the 72nd Street Transpark. The transverse roadways are always open.

A.   Central Park Drive (East Drive and West Drive): This is the main roadway that loops around the park. Entrances and exits are shown below.

B.   Transverse Roadways: The transverse roadways cut across the park, linking Fifth Avenue with Central Park West. Since they pass beneath the park drives, they are always open.

Transverse Roadway	Eastbound		Westbound	
	Enter at Central Park West at	Exit at Fifth Avenue at	Enter at Fifth Avenue at	Exit at Central Park West at
65th Street	65th	65th	66th	66th
79th Street	81st	79th	79th	81st
86th Street	86th	84th	85th	86th
97th Street	96th	96th	97th	97th

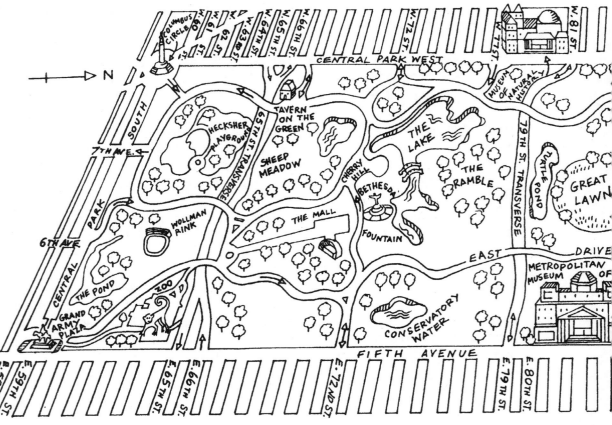

C.   Transpark Roadway: The 72nd Street Transpark is a one-way westbound roadway that links the East Drive with the West Drive. It is a good shortcut from 72nd Street and Fifth Avenue to Seventh Avenue and Central Park South.

Year-round Closings (including summer):

Weekends: 7 PM Friday to 6 AM Monday
Holidays: 7 PM on the night before the holiday until 6 AM on the day after

Summer Hours:

These are in effect from approximately Easter week until the Monday after the New York City Marathon (late October or early November)

Daytime closings: 10 AM to 3 PM. Cars may still enter at Sixth Avenue and Central Park South and go one exit to 72nd Street and Fifth Avenue.
Nighttime closings: 7 PM to 10 PM.

Note: Prospect Park roadway closures follow the same schedule.

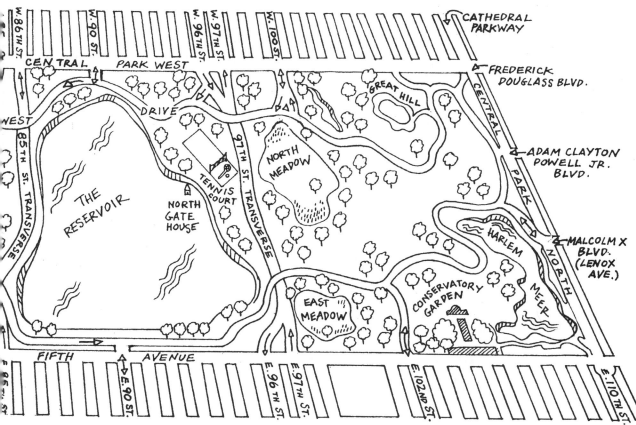

5

From Midtown North to the George Washington Bridge and the Henry Hudson Parkway

Since the collapse of the West Side Highway on December 16, 1973, New Yorkers have been searching for ways to travel north–south through the grid of Manhattan streets. There is no single shortcut that always works, so it's necessary to have a variety of alternate routes from which to choose at the first signs of gridlock.

When Central Park is open to traffic*:

1. Enter Central Park from Eighth Avenue at Columbus Circle (bear right, but don't make a right turn when going around the circle) or from Sixth Avenue at Central Park South.

2. Exit Central Park at 110th Street and Malcolm X Boulevard (Lenox Avenue).

3. After exiting the park, go one block to 111th Street, turn left, then make a quick right. You'll be on St. Nicholas Avenue.

4. At about 115th Street you'll be forced onto Adam Clayton Powell Jr. Boulevard. Go to 117th Street and make a left turn followed by a quick right to return to St. Nicholas Avenue.

5. Continue on St. Nicholas Avenue to 165th Street; turn left.

6. Go down the hill, passing Columbia Presbyterian Hospital on the right. Turn right onto Riverside Drive.

To the George Washington Bridge:

7a. As soon as you turn right onto Riverside Drive you'll see the entrance ramp to the George Washington Bridge on your right.

To the Henry Hudson Parkway northbound:

7b. After turning onto Riverside Drive, keep left and you'll be able to enter the Henry Hudson Parkway after crossing under the George Washington Bridge.

When Central Park is closed to traffic*:

From the East Side: Take any northbound avenue to 111th Street and turn left. Just past Malcolm X Boulevard (Lenox Avenue) turn right onto St. Nicholas Avenue and follow the directions above, starting at number 4.

From the West Side: Take Central Park West straight into Frederick Douglass Boulevard (at Central Park North) and bear left at 121st Street to St. Nicholas Avenue. Follow the directions above, starting at number 5.

*See pages 4–5 for schedule.

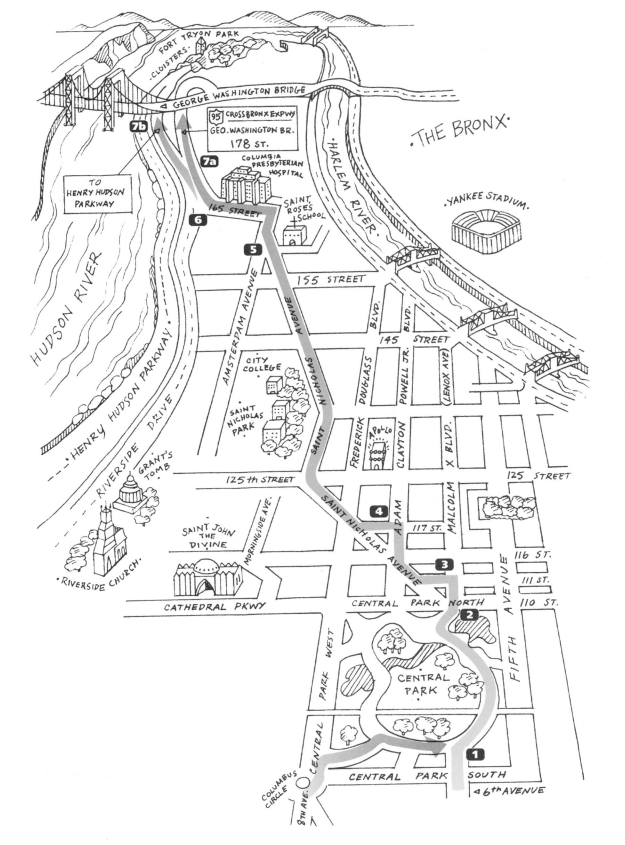

FORT TRYON PARK
CLOISTERS.

GEORGE WASHINGTON BRIDGE

7b

95 CROSS BRONX EXPWY
GEO. WASHINGTON BR.
178 ST.

7a

COLUMBIA
PRESBYTERIAN
HOSPITAL

·THE BRONX·

TO
HENRY HUDSON
PARKWAY

165 STREET

6

SAINT
ROSES
SCHOOL

HARLEM RIVER

·YANKEE STADIUM·

5

155 STREET

HUDSON RIVER

HENRY HUDSON PARKWAY

RIVERSIDE DRIVE

AMSTERDAM AVENUE

CITY
COLLEGE

SAINT
NICHOLAS
PARK

SAINT NICHOLAS AVENUE

145 STREET

FREDERICK DOUGLASS BLVD.

POWELL JR. BLVD.

CLAYTON

MALCOLM X BLVD. (LENOX AVE)

145 STREET

GRANT'S
TOMB

125th STREET

PO-LO

125 STREET

RIVERSIDE CHURCH.

SAINT JOHN
THE
DIVINE

MORNINGSIDE AVE.

SAINT NICHOLAS AVENUE

4

ADAM

117 ST.

116 ST.

111 ST.

110 ST.

3

CATHEDRAL PKWY

CENTRAL PARK NORTH

FIFTH AVENUE

2

PARK WEST

CENTRAL
PARK

1

CENTRAL

COLUMBUS
CIRCLE

8TH AVE.

CENTRAL PARK SOUTH

6TH AVENUE

From Midtown to the Triborough and Willis Avenue Bridges

Between Central Park and 124th Street there are plenty of alternate routes to help you avoid the paralyzing traffic jams that occur northbound from Midtown.

When Central Park is open to traffic*:

1. Enter Central Park at Columbus Circle (bear right, but don't make a right turn, when going around the circle) or from Central Park South at Sixth Avenue. Take Central Park West Drive northbound.

2. Exit at 102nd Street and go one block to Madison Avenue.

3. Turn left onto Madison Avenue to head north.

4. Go to 124th Street and turn right.

To the Triborough Bridge:

5a. Take 124th Street to Second Avenue.

6a. Bear left after crossing Second Avenue and follow signs to the Triborough Bridge.

To the Willis Avenue Bridge:

5b. Take 124th Street to Third Avenue and turn left.

6b. Go one block to 125th Street and turn right. Take 125th Street to First Avenue and turn left to the entrance to the Willis Avenue Bridge.

When Central Park Roadways are closed*:

Take Madison Avenue to 124th Street and turn right. Follow the directions above, starting at number 5a or 5b.

*See pages 4–5 for schedule.

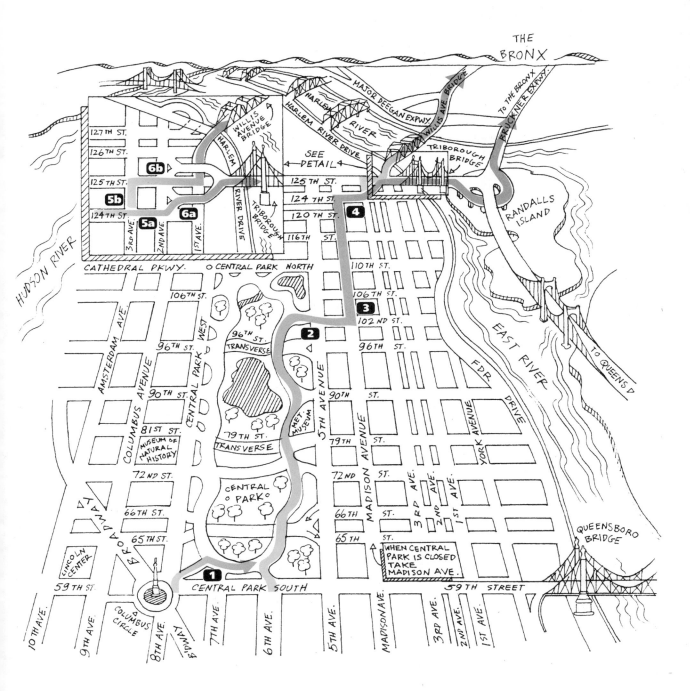

THE BRONX

TO THE BRONX

MAJOR DEEGAN EXPWY.

WILLIS AVE. BRIDGE

BRUCKNER EXPWY.

WILLIS AVENUE BRIDGE

HARLEM RIVER DRIVE

HARLEM RIVER

TRIBOROUGH BRIDGE

SEE DETAIL 4

127TH ST.
126TH ST.
125TH ST.
124TH ST.

6b
5b
5a   **6a**

3RD AVE.   2ND AVE.   1ST AVE.

HARLEM RIVER DRIVE

TRIBOROUGH BRIDGE

125TH ST.
124TH ST.
120TH ST.
116TH ST.

4

RANDALLS ISLAND

HUDSON RIVER

CATHEDRAL PKWY.   0 CENTRAL PARK NORTH

110TH ST.

106TH ST.

106TH ST.

3

102ND ST.

AMSTERDAM AVE.

96TH ST.

96TH ST. TRANSVERSE

96TH

2

5TH AVENUE

96TH   ST.

EAST RIVER

90TH ST.

90TH   ST.

FDR DRIVE

COLUMBUS AVENUE

90TH ST.

81ST ST.

MUSEUM OF NATURAL HISTORY

CENTRAL PARK WEST

79TH ST.

79TH ST. TRANSVERSE

MET. MUSEUM

79TH   ST.

YORK AVENUE

72ND ST.

CENTRAL 0 PARK 0

72ND   ST.

MADISON AVENUE

72ND ST.

3RD AVE.   2ND AVE.   1ST AVE.

66TH ST.

66TH   ST.

TO QUEENS ▷

65TH ST.

65TH   ST.

QUEENSBORO BRIDGE

LINCOLN CENTER

BROADWAY

WHEN CENTRAL PARK IS CLOSED TAKE MADISON AVE.

59TH ST.

1   CENTRAL PARK SOUTH

59TH   STREET

10TH AVE.   9TH AVE.   8TH AVE.   B'DWAY

COLUMBUS CIRCLE

7TH AVE.   6TH AVE.   5TH AVE.   MADISON AVE.   3RD AVE.   2ND AVE.   1ST AVE.

West Midtown to the Battery Tunnel, Holland Tunnel, or Manhattan Bridge

Alternative 1: Through the Meat Market

Ninth Avenue south approaching the Lincoln Tunnel can be a real drag, but once you've reached 36th Street much of the suffering is over.

1. Keep in the left two lanes of Ninth Avenue until you pass the entrances to the Lincoln Tunnel between 41st and 36th streets.

2. At 14th Street turn right; you'll be in the midst of the meat market.

3. Turn left after one block onto Washington Street. Washington Street is one of the few Manhattan streets without traffic signals on every corner, but there are some surprise stop signs at Jane, 11th, 10th, and Leroy streets, so be careful.

To the Battery Tunnel:

4a. Take Washington Street to West Houston Street and turn right (you'll pass underneath a building).

5a. Since West Houston is one-way, move into the left lane and turn left at the next block onto West Street.

6a. Take West Street south past of the World Trade Center; the entrance to the Battery Tunnel will be on the left.

To the Holland Tunnel:

4b. Take Washington Street to Spring Street; turn left.

5b. Take Spring Street a few blocks to Varick Street and turn right.

6b. Move into the right lanes of Varick Street. You'll soon see the entrance to the Holland Tunnel on your right.

To the Manhattan Bridge:

4c. Take Washington Street to Spring Street; turn left.

5c. Take Spring Street to Broadway and turn right.

6c. At Canal Street turn left.

7c. The Manhattan Bridge will be just ahead.

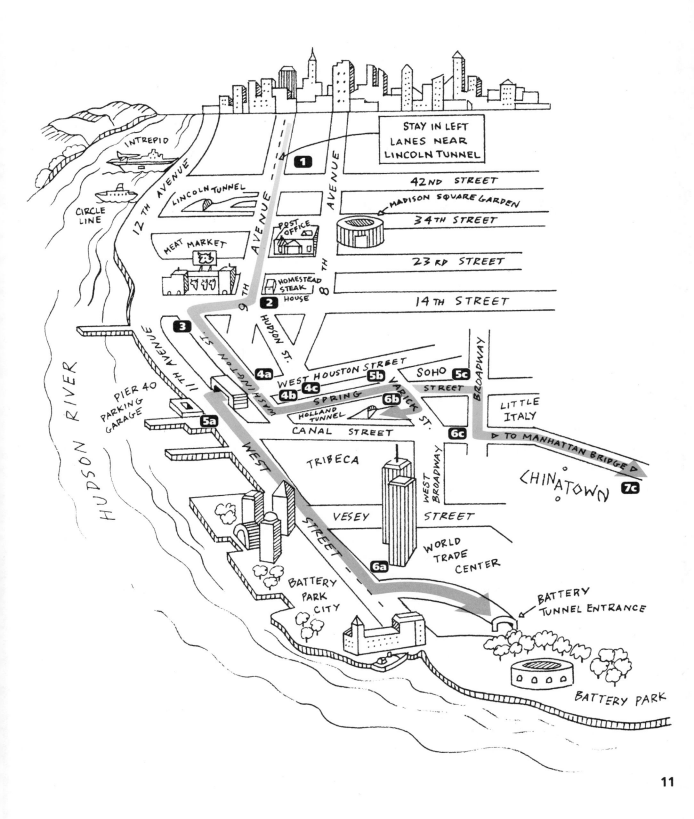

STAY IN LEFT LANES NEAR LINCOLN TUNNEL

INTREPID

CIRCLE LINE

LINCOLN TUNNEL

12TH AVENUE

MEAT MARKET

POST OFFICE

MADISON SQUARE GARDEN

42ND STREET

34TH STREET

23RD STREET

14TH STREET

8TH AVENUE

9TH AVENUE

HOMESTEAD STEAK HOUSE

HUDSON ST.

HUDSON RIVER

11TH AVENUE

PIER 40 PARKING GARAGE

WASHINGTON ST.

WEST HOUSTON STREET

SPRING

VARICK ST.

SOHO STREET

BROADWAY

LITTLE ITALY

HOLLAND TUNNEL

CANAL STREET

TRIBECA

WEST STREET

WEST BROADWAY

VESEY STREET

▷ TO MANHATTAN BRIDGE ▷

CHINATOWN

WORLD TRADE CENTER

BATTERY PARK CITY

BATTERY TUNNEL ENTRANCE

BATTERY PARK

1 **2** **3** **4a** **4b** **4c** **5a** **5b** **5c** **6a** **6b** **6c** **7c**

West Midtown to the Battery Tunnel, Holland Tunnel, or Manhattan Bridge

Alternative 2: Through the West Village

1.   Stay in the left two lanes of Ninth Avenue until you pass the entrance to the Lincoln Tunnel at 36th Street.

2.   When you reach 14th Street, bear left, but don't turn left, onto Hudson Street.

3.   In just a few blocks Hudson Street will end; you should follow the traffic to the left onto Bleecker Street. The first block of Bleecker usually moves well, but you're likely to encounter a backup as you approach Seventh Avenue.

4.   Turn right at Seventh Avenue, which becomes Varick Street south of Houston Street.

To the Battery Tunnel:

5a.   Stay in the two left lanes of Varick Street until you're past the entrance to the Holland Tunnel. Once you cross Canal Street you'll be on West Broadway.

6a.   Take West Broadway to its end at the World Trade Center and turn right onto Vesey Street.

7a.   Turn left onto West Street; the entrance to the Battery Tunnel will be on the left.

To the Holland Tunnel:

5b.   Stay in the right lanes of Varick Street.

6b.   All traffic will feed right into the Holland Tunnel.

To the Manhattan Bridge:

5c.   Stay in the left two lanes of Varick Street until you're past the entrance to the Holland Tunnel.

6c.   Turn left at Canal Street.

7c.   The Manhattan Bridge will be ahead.

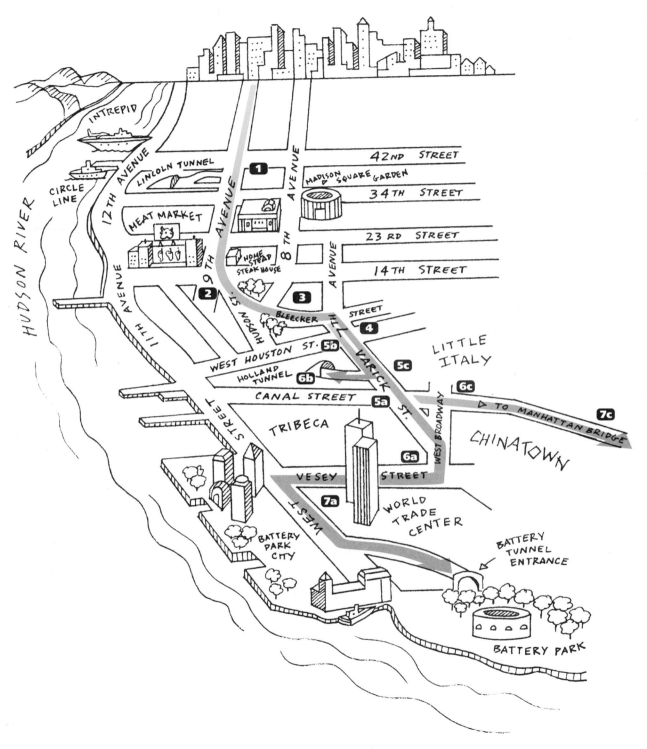

INTREPID

CIRCLE LINE

HUDSON RIVER

12TH AVENUE

LINCOLN TUNNEL

MEAT MARKET

9TH AVENUE

11TH AVENUE

HUDSON ST.

8TH AVENUE

AVENUE

42ND STREET

MADISON SQUARE GARDEN

34TH STREET

23RD STREET

14TH STREET

HOME STEAD STEAK HOUSE

1

2

3

Bleecker **4** Street

WEST HOUSTON ST · **5b**

HOLLAND TUNNEL

6b

CANAL STREET

5a

5c

VARICK ST.

LITTLE ITALY

6c

TO MANHATTAN BRIDGE **7c**

CHINATOWN

WEST BROADWAY

6a

TRIBECA

WEST STREET

VESEY STREET

7a

WORLD TRADE CENTER

BATTERY PARK CITY

BATTERY TUNNEL ENTRANCE

BATTERY PARK

Hudson Street to Midtown: Bypassing the Holland Tunnel Jam

Cab driver extraordinaire Susan Smpadian shared with me her tip for bypassing the Holland Tunnel gridlock when traveling northbound on Hudson Street. From where it originates at Chambers Street, Hudson Street moves well for the first few blocks. This situation changes during the evening rush hour, when thousands of cars head through the tunnel to New Jersey.

1. To avoid this jam, keep to the left on Hudson Street and turn left onto Laight Street. Don't worry if Laight Street looks congested; almost all the drivers are heading straight to West Street.

2. You, however, should turn right onto Washington Street and zip all the way up to Spring Street.

3. Turn right onto Spring Street and go three blocks to Hudson Street.

4. Turn left when you reach Hudson Street. At this point Hudson Street is usually clear and you'll have passed the Holland Tunnel entrance.

5. At Abingdon Square, just past West 11th Street, all northbound traffic will bear right onto Eighth Avenue, heading toward Midtown.

Moving violation for not moving

Believe it or not, you can get a moving violation for not moving! In the mid-1980s Mayor Ed Koch complained about all the limousines parked in front of Manhattan's Regency Hotel while their occupants attended "power breakfasts." Park Avenue had become a parking lot. We responded by issuing lots of parking tickets, but many limo drivers just shrugged it off as the "cost of doing business." Their clients paid for the tickets and the tactic had little effect. We then came up with a plan that could cost the drivers their licenses. We made it a moving violation to not move in a moving lane; this includes double parking in "No Standing" and "No Stopping" zones. The rule is still on the books, though infrequently enforced.

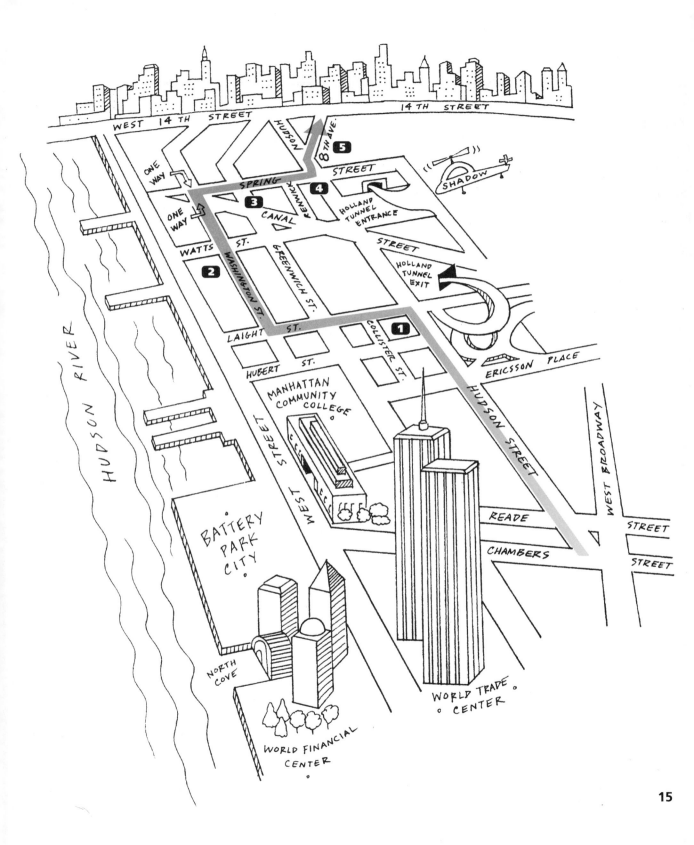

Harlem River Drive South to Midtown via Fifth Avenue or Central Park

The Harlem River Drive southbound usually moves well until you get near the Triborough Bridge. The trick here is to exit the Drive before it merges with the bridge traffic.

1. Take the Harlem River Drive south to Exit 22 (W. 142nd Street, 5 Av). The beauty of this exit is that Manhattan island is so narrow at this point that you'll be on Fifth Avenue southbound just after you exit.

2. Take Fifth Avenue south to 110th Street and Central Park North.

When Central Park is open to traffic*:

3. Turn right onto Central Park North, go one block to Malcolm X Boulevard (Lenox Avenue), and turn left at the entrance to Central Park.

4. You can drive the entire length of the park to the Seventh Avenue and Central Park South exit, but I recommend avoiding the morning rush hour back-up by leaving the park at 72nd Street or 67th Street (take the road leading to the Tavern on the Green).

5. Go west one block to Columbus Avenue and turn left. Columbus becomes Ninth Avenue south of 59th Street.

When Central Park is closed to traffic*:

If you are heading to the West Side: Turn right onto Central Park North and go straight to Cathedral Parkway. Go two blocks to Columbus Avenue and turn left. Columbus Avenue becomes Ninth Avenue south of 59th Street.

If you are heading to the East Side: If your destination is between Park and Fifth avenues, stay on Fifth Avenue. Motorists with destinations east of Park Avenue should turn left at 72nd Street and turn right at the southbound avenue nearest their destination.

See pages 4–5 for schedule.

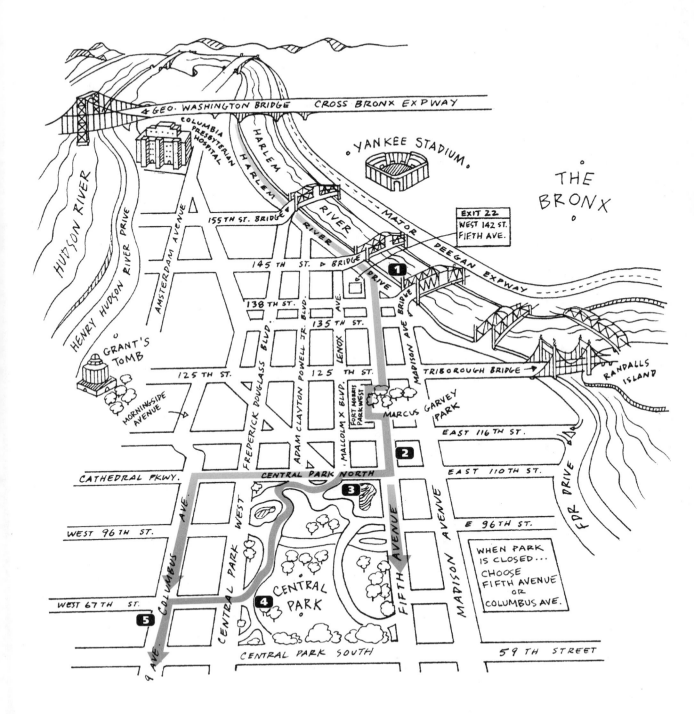

GEO. WASHINGTON BRIDGE   CROSS BRONX EXPWAY

HUDSON RIVER

COLUMBIA PRESBYTERIAN HOSPITAL

HARLEM

HARLEM   RIVER

RIVER   DRIVE

HENRY HUDSON RIVER DRIVE

AMSTERDAM AVENUE

155TH ST. BRIDGE

145TH ST. ▷ BRIDGE

138TH ST.

135TH ST.

FREDERICK DOUGLASS BLVD.

ADAM CLAYTON POWELL JR. BLVD.

LENOX AVE.

MALCOLM X BLVD.

GRANT'S TOMB

MORNINGSIDE AVENUE

125TH ST.

125TH ST.

YANKEE STADIUM

MAJOR DEEGAN EXPWAY

EXIT 22
WEST 142 ST.
FIFTH AVE.

1

THE BRONX

MADISON AVE BRIDGE

MADISON AVE.

TRIBOROUGH BRIDGE ▶

RANDALLS ISLAND

FORT MORRIS PARK WEST

MARCUS GARVEY PARK

EAST 116TH ST.

2

EAST 110TH ST.

FDR DRIVE

CATHEDRAL PKWY.

CENTRAL PARK NORTH

3

AVE.

COLUMBUS AVE.

CENTRAL PARK WEST

WEST 96TH ST.

FIFTH AVENUE

E 96TH ST.

MADISON AVENUE

WHEN PARK
IS CLOSED...
CHOOSE
FIFTH AVENUE
OR
COLUMBUS AVE.

WEST 67TH ST.

5

CENTRAL PARK

4

9 AVE.

CENTRAL PARK SOUTH

59TH STREET

Triborough Bridge to Midtown Through Harlem and Central Park

Most people exiting the Triborough Bridge in Manhattan head south on the FDR Drive. However, during the morning peak period the FDR is often tied up for much of its length from the Queensboro Bridge to the Triborough Bridge. You can avoid this back-up by taking the following shortcut.

1. Keep to the right after passing the Triborough Bridge toll plaza. Exit the bridge onto 126th Street.

2. Take 126th Street westbound (to the left) to Malcolm X Boulevard (Lenox Avenue).

When Central Park is open to traffic*:

3a. Turn left on Malcolm X Boulevard (Lenox Avenue) and follow this for 16 blocks south to Central Park North.

4a. Drive straight ahead to enter the park.

5a. You can drive the entire length of the park to the Seventh Avenue and Central Park South exit, but I recommend avoiding the morning rush hour back-up by leaving the park at 72nd Street or 67th Street (take the road leading to the Tavern on the Green).

6a. Go west one block to Columbus Avenue and turn left. Columbus Avenue becomes Ninth Avenue south of 59th Street.

When Central Park is closed to traffic*:

3b. Take 126th Street west for two more blocks west to Frederick Douglass Boulevard and turn left. In 16 blocks you'll be at the northwest corner of Central Park at Frederick Douglass Circle. Turn right onto Cathedral Parkway, go two blocks to Columbus Avenue, and turn left.

*See pages 4–5 for schedule.

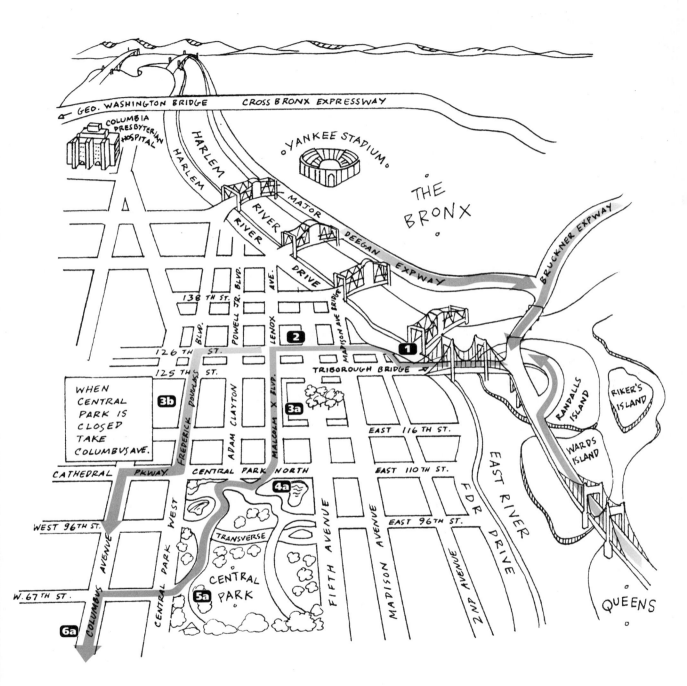

GEO. WASHINGTON BRIDGE

CROSS BRONX EXPRESSWAY

COLUMBIA PRESBYTERIAN HOSPITAL

YANKEE STADIUM

THE BRONX

HARLEM HARLEM RIVER RIVER DRIVE

MAJOR DEEGAN EXPWAY

BRUCKNER EXPWAY

138TH ST.

POWELL JR. BLVD.

LENOX AVE.

MADISON AVE BRIDGE

126TH ST.

125TH ST.

2

1

TRIBOROUGH BRIDGE

RANDALLS ISLAND

RIKER'S ISLAND

FREDERICK DOUGLAS BLVD.

ADAM CLAYTON

MALCOLM X BLVD.

3b

3a

WHEN CENTRAL PARK IS CLOSED TAKE COLUMBUS AVE.

EAST 116TH ST.

WARDS ISLAND

CATHEDRAL PKWY.

CENTRAL PARK NORTH

EAST 110TH ST.

FIFTH AVENUE

EAST RIVER

4a

WEST 96TH ST.

CENTRAL PARK WEST

TRANSVERSE

EAST 96TH ST.

MADISON AVENUE

2ND AVENUE

FDR DRIVE

COLUMBUS AVENUE

CENTRAL PARK

5a

CENTRAL PARK

W. 67TH ST.

QUEENS

6a

FDR Drive at 116th Street South to West Midtown

It's fairly common for the southbound FDR to be jammed from the 60s to 110th Street and beyond.

1. Instead of doing the crawl, abandon the FDR Drive at Exit 16 (E. 116th Street).

When Central Park is open to traffic*:

2a. Take 116th Street west to Malcolm X Boulevard (Lenox Avenue) and turn left.

3a. Take Lenox Avenue six blocks to Central Park North; enter Central Park.

4a. You can drive the entire length of the park to the Seventh Avenue and Central Park South exit, but I recommend avoiding the morning rush hour back-up by leaving the park at 72nd Street or 67th Street (take the road leading to the Tavern on the Green).

5a. Go west one block to Columbus Avenue and turn left. Columbus becomes Ninth Avenue south of 59th Street.

When Central Park is closed to traffic*:

2b. Take 116th Street two blocks past Malcolm X Boulevard (Lenox Avenue) to Frederick Douglass Boulevard and turn left. In just six blocks you'll be at the northwest corner of Central Park at Frederick Douglass Circle.

3b. Turn right onto Cathedral Parkway and go two blocks to Columbus Avenue and turn left. Columbus becomes Ninth Avenue south of 59th Street.

See pages 4–5 for schedule

The block with the most illegal parkers
The block that has the highest average number of illegal parkers is 47th Street between Fifth and Sixth avenues, Diamond and Jewelry Way. Not only are cars parked illegally at the curb, but there are times when it's tough to find space to double-park! If you are heading across tow 47th Street would be a good block to avoid.

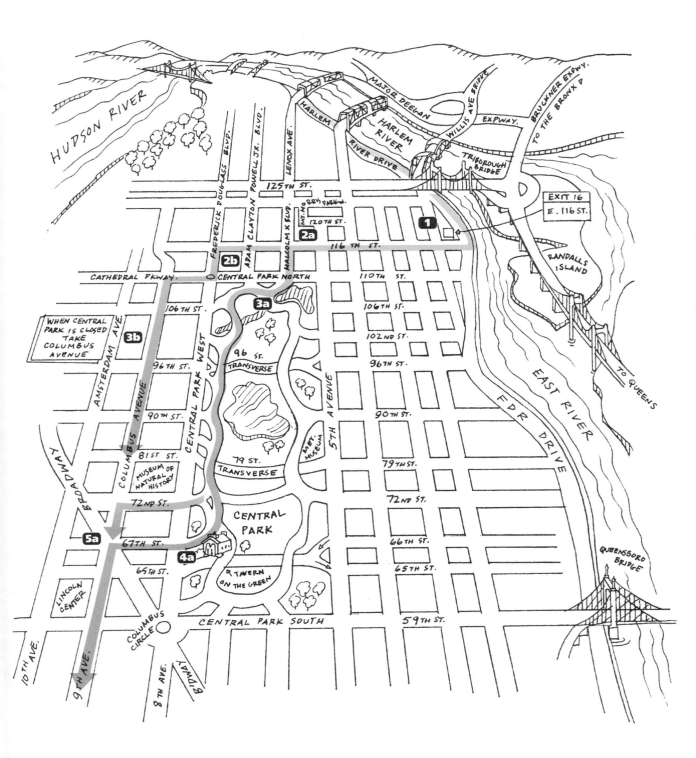

HUDSON RIVER

FREDERICK DOUGLASS BLVD.

ADAM CLAYTON POWELL JR. BLVD.

LENOX AVE.

HARLEM RIVER

MAJOR DEEGAN

WILLIS AVE. BRIDGE

BRUCKNER EXPWY.

TO THE BRONX

HARLEM RIVER DRIVE

TRIBOROUGH BRIDGE

125TH ST.

MT. MORRIS PARK W.

120TH ST.

EXIT 16
E. 116 ST.

MALCOLM X BLVD.

1

2a

116TH ST.

2b

RANDALLS ISLAND

CATHEDRAL PKWY.

CENTRAL PARK NORTH

110TH ST.

3a

106TH ST.

106TH ST.

102ND ST.

WHEN CENTRAL PARK IS CLOSED TAKE COLUMBUS AVENUE

AMSTERDAM AVE.

3b

96TH ST.

96 ST. TRANSVERSE

96TH ST.

EAST RIVER

COLUMBUS AVENUE

90TH ST.

90TH ST.

CENTRAL PARK WEST

5TH AVENUE

FDR DRIVE

81ST ST.

MUSEUM OF NATURAL HISTORY

79 ST. TRANSVERSE

MET. MUSEUM

79TH ST.

BROADWAY

72ND ST.

72ND ST.

5a

67TH ST.

CENTRAL PARK

4a

66TH ST.

65TH ST.

TO QUEENS

QUEENSBORO BRIDGE

65TH ST.

TAVERN ON THE GREEN

LINCOLN CENTER

COLUMBUS CIRCLE

CENTRAL PARK SOUTH

59TH ST.

10TH AVE.

9TH AVE.

8TH AVE.

B'DWAY

Henry Hudson Parkway Southbound to Midtown Manhattan

Exits on the Henry Hudson Parkway southbound, unlike the Harlem River Drive or FDR southbound, occur infrequently; consequently, it's easy to get trapped in traffic with no exit in sight. If you do know from radio reports that the parkway is jammed from 57th Street to past 96th Street, try the following:

From the George Washington Bridge:

1a. Follow the signs to the Henry Hudson Parkway northbound. You will also see signs for Riverside Drive. Take the ramp to Riverside Drive and, once there, turn right. Follow directions below, starting at no.2

From the Henry Hudson Parkway:

1b. Take the Henry Hudson Parkway south to Exit 14–15 (George Washington Bridge, Cross-Bronx Expressway, Riverside Drive). Follow the signs to Riverside Drive and turn right.

2. Continue south on Riverside Drive a little more than three miles to Cathedral Parkway and turn left. Cathedral Parkway intersects with Riverside Drive at about 111th Street; it then runs east to become the equivalent of 110th Street.

3. Take Cathedral Parkway to Central Park West and turn right.

4. Turn left at 100th Street to enter Central Park. Take the Central Park drive to the Seventh Avenue exit.

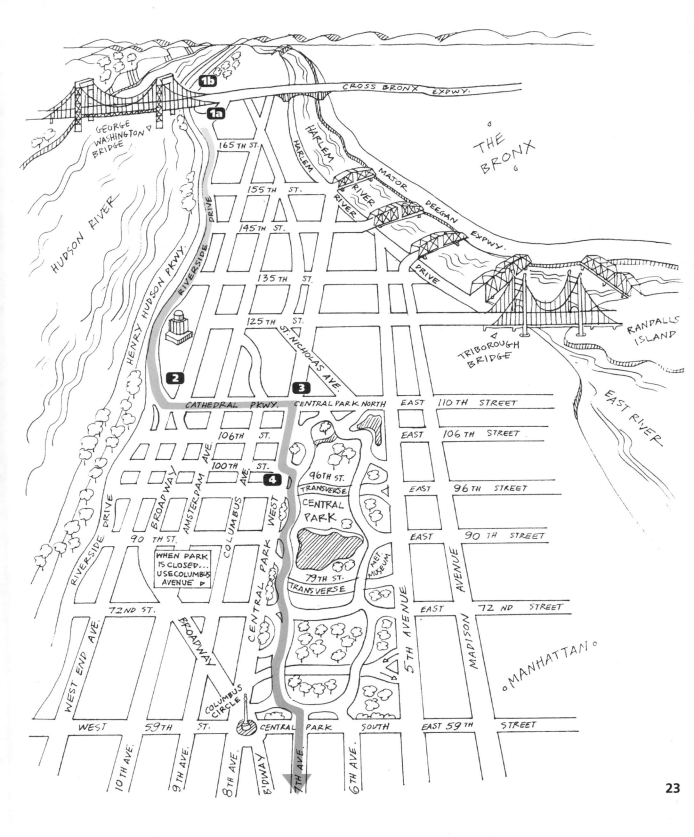

GEORGE WASHINGTON BRIDGE

1b

1a

CROSS BRONX EXPWY.

THE BRONX

HUDSON RIVER

HARLEM RIVER

HARLEM RIVER

MAJOR DEEGAN EXPWY.

165 TH ST.

155 TH ST.

145 TH ST.

135 TH ST.

125 TH ST.

ST. NICHOLAS AVE.

DRIVE

RANDALLS ISLAND

HENRY HUDSON PKWY.

RIVERSIDE DRIVE

2

3

TRIBOROUGH BRIDGE

EAST RIVER

CATHEDRAL PKWY.

CENTRAL PARK NORTH

EAST 110TH STREET

EAST 106 TH STREET

106TH ST.

100TH ST.

4

96TH ST. TRANSVERSE

CENTRAL PARK

EAST 96 TH STREET

BROADWAY

AMSTERDAM AVE.

COLUMBUS AVE.

CENTRAL PARK WEST

EAST 90 TH STREET

MET. MUSEUM

90 TH ST.

WHEN PARK IS CLOSED... USE COLUMBUS AVENUE

79TH ST. TRANSVERSE

RIVERSIDE DRIVE

72ND ST.

EAST 72 ND STREET

WEST END AVE.

BROADWAY

5TH AVENUE

MADISON AVENUE

MANHATTAN

COLUMBUS CIRCLE

WEST 59TH ST.

CENTRAL PARK SOUTH

EAST 59TH STREET

10TH AVE.

9TH AVE.

8TH AVE.

B'DWAY

7TH AVE.

6TH AVE.

Crosstown in the Village

Houston Street (pronounced *house-ton*, not *hyous-ton*), a wide, two-way street, is the most reliable crosstown route in this area. It's also the only street south of 34th Street that connects directly with both the northbound and southbound FDR Drive. But it does have a drawback—it ends at Sixth Avenue. When traveling west, this isn't much of a problem since a smaller, one-way version, West Houston Street, continues all the way to West Street. Traveling east is more difficult, however, since West Houston Street is one-way heading west from Sixth Avenue to West Street. Still, you can go all the way east across the island if you know a few tricks.

If you are coming from the north:

1a. Take Washington Street (the block to the east of West Street) or Seventh Avenue (which becomes Varick Street south of Houston Street) to King Street. King Street is just one block south of West Houston Street. At King Street turn left. Directions continue below at number 2.

If you are coming from the south:

1b. Take Hudson Street to King Street and turn right.

2. Take King Street to Sixth Avenue and turn left . Weave over to the right lane.

3. Make an immediate right on Houston Street. This is the start of Houston Street eastbound.

4. At the very end of Houston Street you'll find the entrance to the southbound FDR Drive on your right and the northbound FDR Drive on your left.

Never on a Wednesday
One of the worst times to travel in west Midtown is Wednesday afternoon. It's matinee day and that means crowds filling the Theater District just before and after the shows. The worst times to travel are between 1 PM and 2 PM and again between 4 PM and 5 PM. Generally avoid the area between Sixth and Eighth avenues from 43rd to 53rd streets. Forty-ninth and 50th streets are bad all the way to Madison Avenue. The worst seasons are from mid-November to the first Wednesday in January, and the weeks around Easter.

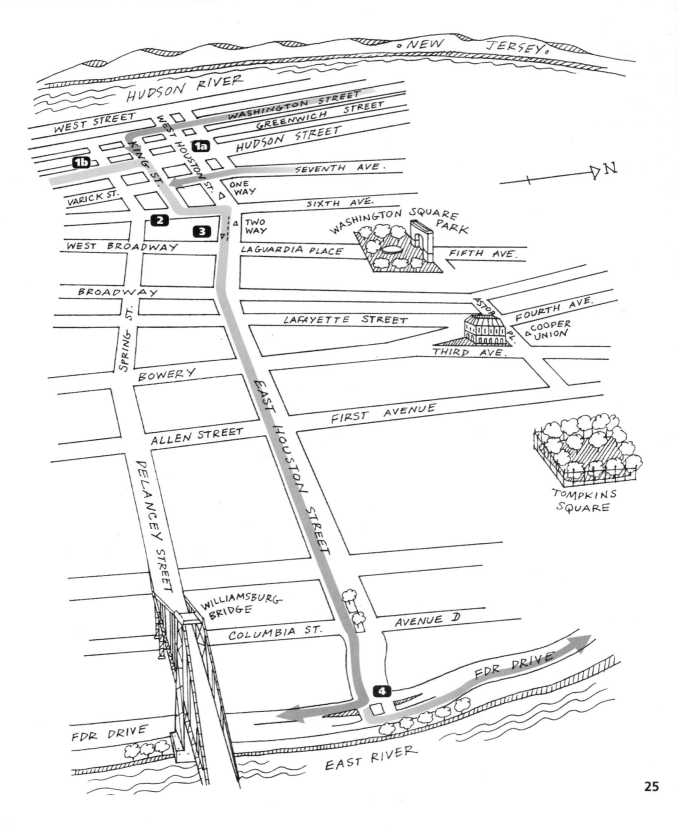

NEW JERSEY

HUDSON RIVER

WEST STREET

WASHINGTON STREET

GREENWICH STREET

WEST STREET

HUDSON STREET

KING ST.

WEST HOUSTON ST.

1a

1b

SEVENTH AVE.

VARICK ST.

ONE WAY

SIXTH AVE.

WASHINGTON SQUARE PARK

2

3

TWO WAY

WEST BROADWAY

LAGUARDIA PLACE

FIFTH AVE.

BROADWAY

SPRING ST.

LAFAYETTE STREET

ASTOR PL.

FOURTH AVE.

COOPER UNION

THIRD AVE.

BOWERY

FIRST AVENUE

EAST HOUSTON STREET

ALLEN STREET

TOMPKINS SQUARE

DELANCEY STREET

WILLIAMSBURG BRIDGE

COLUMBIA ST.

AVENUE D

4

FDR DRIVE

FDR DRIVE

EAST RIVER

N

Crosstown via the Central Park Transverse Roadway at 65th/66th Streets

The simplest and most popular way across Central Park is via the transverse roadway that emerges at 65th/66th streets. That's because, after crossing the park here you end up on the same street as where you started. Eastbound traffic enters at 65th Street and Central Park West and exits at 65th and Fifth Avenue. Similarly, westbound traffic enters at 66th Street and Fifth Avenue and exits at 66th and Central Park West.

Eastbound:

This is an especially good eastbound alternate because with just a couple of turns you can link up with entrances to the FDR going north or south. Also, through a quirk in the street pattern, there are two consecutive eastbound streets.

1. 65th Street starts on the West Side at West End Avenue (an extension of Eleventh Avenue north of 59th Street). West End Avenue is two-way and can be accessed from the north or south.

2. Take 65th Street across Central Park West and enter the Central Park transverse roadway. You will exit at 65th Street and Fifth Avenue.

3. 65th Street can be taken all the way across town to York Avenue, but because it is the "through street" it is often crowded. So, if upon reaching Fifth Avenue you notice that traffic is slow on 65th Street, turn right onto Fifth Avenue and left onto 64th Street. This is a particularly attractive detour during alternate side parking times (weekdays 11 AM to 2 PM, except Wednesdays), when parking is prohibited on one side of 64th Street.

4. Continue east on 64th or 65th street to the end, and turn right on York Avenue.

5. The southbound entrance to the FDR Drive can be reached by turning left at 63rd Street.

6. The northbound entrance to the FDR Drive can be accessed by turning left at 62nd Street.

Westbound:

Exit the FDR Drive at 61st Street and turn right on York Avenue. At 66th Street turn left. Cross Fifth Avenue to enter Central Park's transverse roadway. You'll exit on 66th Street at Central Park West; 66th Street goes as far west as West End Avenue.

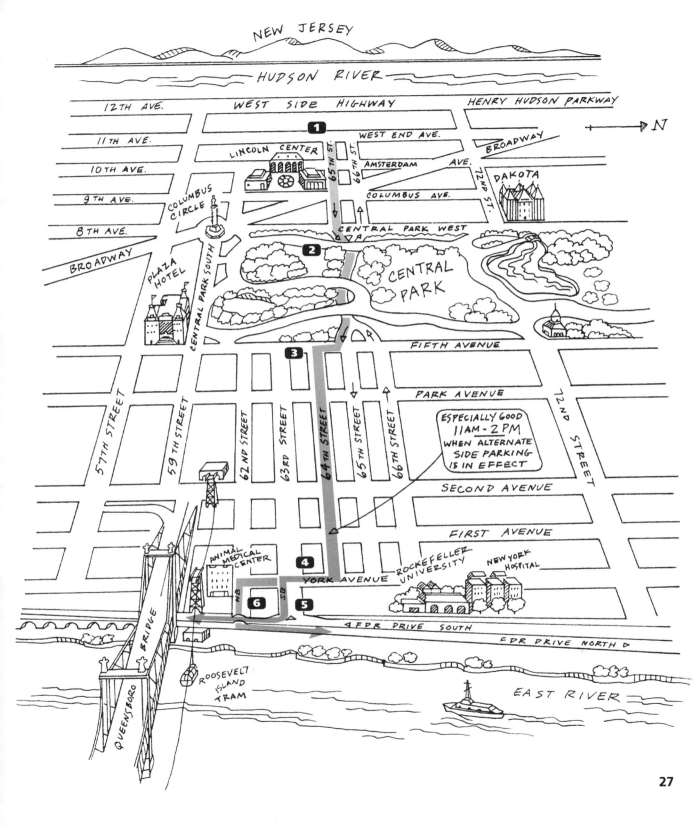

Crosstown at Manhattan's Northern End

Harlem River Drive to the Henry Hudson Parkway and Vice Versa

The island of Manhattan gets very narrow north of 165th Street and south of the Brooklyn Bridge. A good way to avoid much of a torturous crosstown trip is to travel north or south, and then head east or west where the island is narrower.

For example, the island is more than 2 1/2 miles wide at 116th Street, but up at Dyckman Street it's less than a mile wide. Why not head up to the far northern end of Manhattan before attempting to fight crosstown traffic? At that point the Harlem River Drive is just a short distance from the Henry Hudson Parkway via Dyckman Street. The Harlem River Drive begins at Dyckman Street, so you would travel north from the Harlem River Drive to reach the Henry Hudson Parkway and south from the Henry Hudson Parkway to reach the Harlem River Drive. (Dyckman Street is a wide retail strip, so it may be slow going here on heavy shopping days.)

Northbound:

1a. Take the Harlem River Drive to the very end and bear left to Dyckman Street.

2a. Go a few blocks on Dyckman Street to Broadway; bear to the far left onto Riverside Drive.

3a. Keep to the right to access the Henry Hudson Parkway northbound.

Southbound:

1b. Henry Hudson Parkway traffic should exit left just after the Henry Hudson Bridge at Exit 17 (Dyckman Street).

2b. At Seaman Avenue, turn right, then left onto Riverside Drive.

3b. Turn right onto Dyckman Street and continue to the very beginning of the southbound Harlem River Drive.

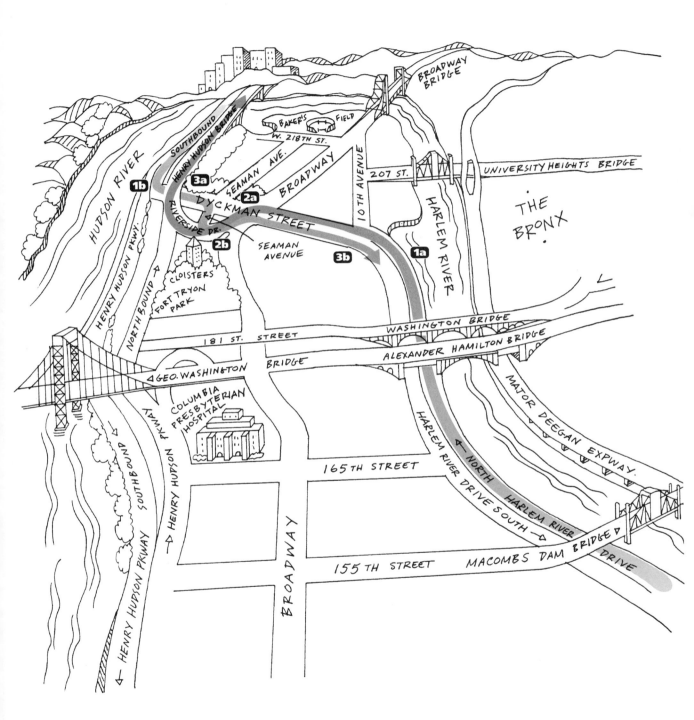

HUDSON RIVER

SOUTHBOUND HENRY HUDSON BRIDGE

BROADWAY BRIDGE

BAKER'S FIELD

W. 218TH ST.

SEAMAN AVE.

BROADWAY

207 ST.

UNIVERSITY HEIGHTS BRIDGE

THE BRONX

1b

3a

2a

DYCKMAN STREET

RIVERSIDE DR.

2b

SEAMAN AVENUE

3b

1a

10TH AVENUE

HARLEM RIVER

HENRY HUDSON PKWY.

NORTHBOUND

CLOISTERS

FORT TRYON PARK

181 ST. STREET

WASHINGTON BRIDGE

ALEXANDER HAMILTON BRIDGE

MATOR DEEGAN EXPWAY.

△ GEO. WASHINGTON BRIDGE

COLUMBIA PRESBYTERIAN HOSPITAL

165TH STREET

HARLEM RIVER DRIVE SOUTH

← NORTH HARLEM RIVER →

SOUTHBOUND

← HENRY HUDSON PKWAY →

BROADWAY

155TH STREET

MACOMBS DAM BRIDGE ▷

DRIVE

← HENRY HUDSON PKWAY →

Crosstown at Manhattan's Southern End

West Street to the Brooklyn Bridge

If you are on what remains of the old West Side Highway (Twelfth Avenue) in Midtown and are heading to the Brooklyn Bridge, you shouldn't go across town until Chambers Street. At 14th Street the island is more than 2.2 miles wide; at Chambers Street it's less than a mile wide.

Take Twelfth Avenue south; it eventually becomes West Street.

To get to the Brooklyn Bridge via Chambers Street:

1a. Just after Stuyvesant High School, which will be on your right (you'll pass beneath the pedestrian bridge to the school), make a left turn onto Chambers Street.

2a. Chambers Street is the only through street here, so it often jams up. Make the first right off Chambers onto Greenwich Street.

3a. Make the next left onto Warren Street and continue three blocks to Broadway.

4a. Turn right onto Broadway.

5a. Stay in the left lane and; at the end of City Hall Park, follow the road around to the left (almost a U-turn). You'll soon see the Park Row ramp to the Brooklyn Bridge on your left.

To reach the Brooklyn Bridge via the Battery Underpass:

1b. Stay on West Street past the World Trade Center.

2b. Keep to the right as you pass the entrance to the Battery Tunnel.

3b. Take the next underpass on your left into the tunnel under Battery Park.

4b. When you emerge from the tunnel bear left onto the highway (the beginning of the FDR Drive). This part of the FDR Drive is almost always moving freely.

5b. Take the next exit to the Brooklyn Bridge.

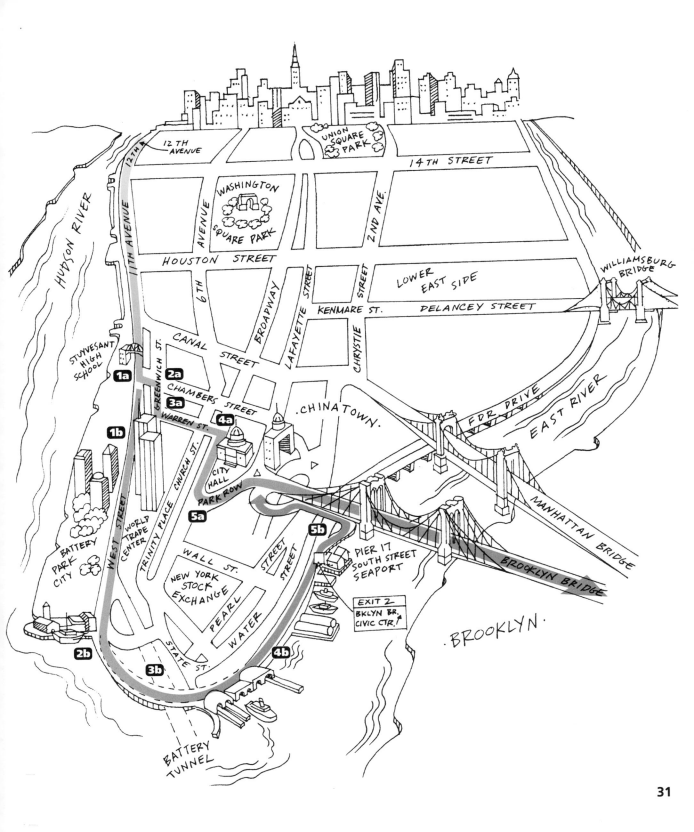

The FDR Drive Southbound to Brooklyn

Alternative 1: Exit at South Street

You can usually count on the southbound FDR Drive approaching the Brooklyn Bridge to be backed up. Instead of sitting and watching three lanes of traffic squeeze into one, try one of these alternatives:

1. Exit the FDR Drive at Exit 3 (South Street, Manhattan Bridge). Go to the stop sign and turn right onto Montgomery Street.

To the Manhattan Bridge via East Broadway:

2a. Follow Montgomery Street to East Broadway and turn left.

3a. Take East Broadway under the Manhattan Bridge. Turn right onto Market Street.

4a. Go one block and follow the traffic left onto Division Street.

5a. Keep to your right and take the right fork. The road will curve around to the right and you'll find yourself on the Bowery.

6a. Bear right to the entrance to the Manhattan Bridge.

To the Manhattan Bridge via Madison Street:

2b. Follow Montgomery Street to Madison Street and turn left.

3b. Follow Madison Street under the Manhattan Bridge. Turn right onto Market Street, go three blocks to the end, and turn left.

4b. Keep to your right and take the right fork at Chatham Square onto the Bowery. The entrance to the Manhattan Bridge is down this road on your right.

To the Brooklyn Bridge via Madison Street:

2c. Follow Montgomery Street to Madison Street and turn left.

3c. Take Madison Street a few blocks past the Manhattan Bridge to St. James Place and turn left. St. James Place becomes Pearl Street.

4c. Follow Pearl Street under the Brooklyn Bridge; you'll see the entrance to the bridge on the right.

The FDR Drive Southbound to Brooklyn

Alternative 2: Exit at Grand Street

There are times when the FDR Drive is so backed up that you should get off before the South Street exit. Savvy drivers listen to radio reports. If there is a problem at the Brooklyn Bridge, here's what to do:

1. Take the FDR Drive to Exit 4 (Grand Street).

2. Turn right at the first intersection onto Grand Street.

To get to the Brooklyn Bridge:

3a. Once on Grand Street, you'll see Madison Street almost immediately on your left. Turn left onto Madison Street.

4a. Follow Madison Street a few blocks past the Manhattan Bridge to St. James Place and turn left. St. James Place becomes Pearl Street.

5a. Follow Pearl Street under the Brooklyn Bridge; you'll see the entrance to the bridge on the right.

To get to the Williamsburg Bridge:

3b. Take Grand Street about 1/2-mile to Clinton Street.

4b. Turn right onto Clinton Street.

5b. The next block is Delancey Street. Turn right (not a sharp right) onto the Williamsburg Bridge.

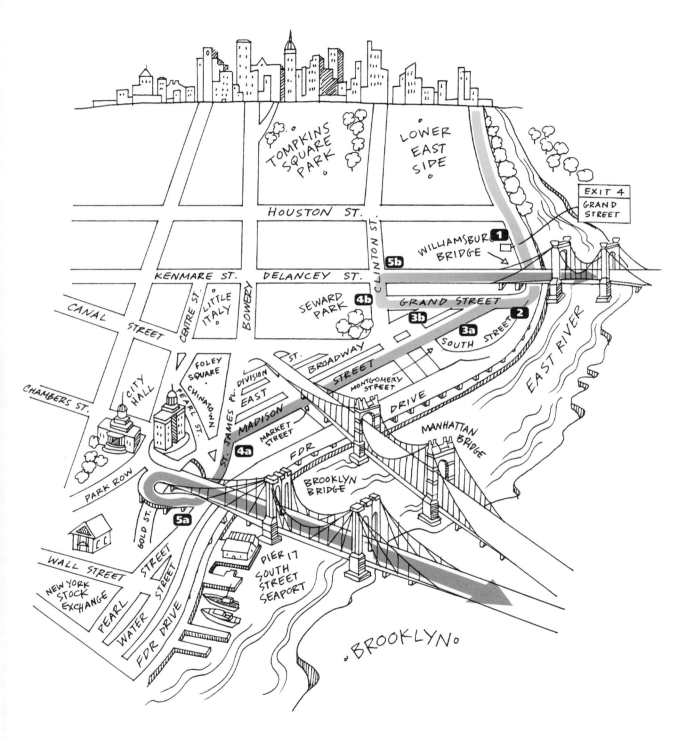

The FDR Drive Southbound to Brooklyn

Alternative 3: Exit at the Battery

There are times when you can't tell if the southbound FDR Drive is backed up until you've passed the South Street exit and are on the viaduct. You want to get to the Brooklyn Bridge but you're still a mile a way and you feel trapped. Don't.

1. The two right lanes will be crawling because both exit to the Brooklyn Bridge. The left lane usually moves the best, so take it past the Brooklyn Bridge exit.

2. The FDR Drive will return to street level and you'll be able to veer right at Exit 1 (Battery Park, SI Ferry) onto the service road.

3. Make the first right onto Broad Street and go one block to Water Street.

4. Turn right onto Water Street and follow this to the Brooklyn Bridge.

5. Just before you pass under the Brooklyn Bridge you'll see the bridge entrance on the left. This route works best on weekends, when the FDR is jammed but the streets of lower Manhattan are empty.

When a street has a center mall, can I turn left through the cross street red signal?
This is one of the least-known traffic rules. Park Avenue has a center mall, and so do parts of Broadway and many other roadways. When you turn left on one of these streets, the signal on the "mall" street will be green, but as you are turning you will face the cross street red signal. Must you stop?

The answer depends on the width of the mall. If the width is equal to or greater than thirty feet, then you must stop. If it is less than thirty feet, and there are no "Stop Here on Red" signs, then you may proceed even though you face a red signal. Since you don't carry a tape measure, follow this rule of thumb: If the mall appears wider than 1 1/2 car lengths, then stop.

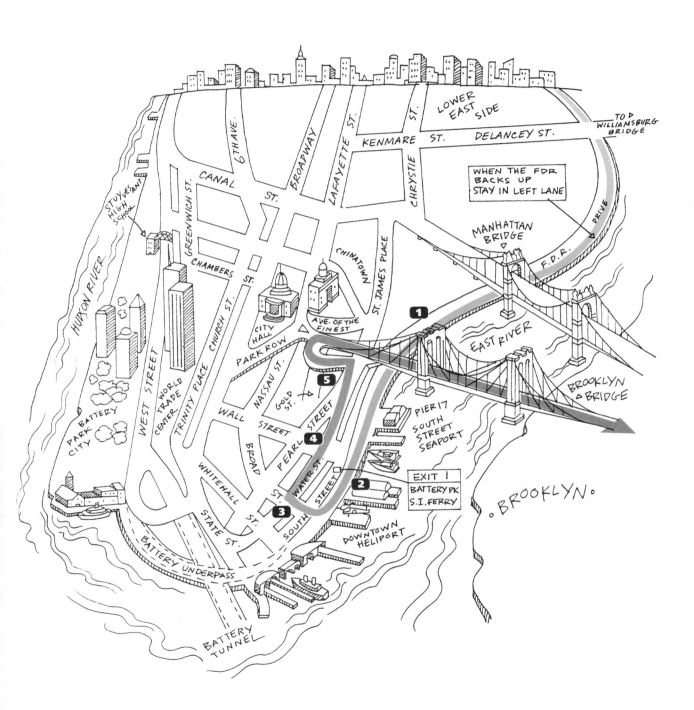

WHEN THE FDR
BACKS UP
STAY IN LEFT LANE

EXIT 1
BATTERY PK
S.I. FERRY

TO ▷
WILLIAMSBURG
BRIDGE

LOWER EAST SIDE

KENMARE ST.

DELANCEY ST.

CHRYSTIE ST.

LAFAYETTE ST.

BROADWAY

CANAL ST.

6TH AVE.

GREENWICH ST.

CHAMBERS ST.

CHURCH ST.

TRINITY PLACE

WEST STREET

WORLD TRADE CENTER

BATTERY PARK CITY

HUDSON RIVER

STUYVESANT HIGH SCHOOL

CITY HALL

PARK ROW

AVE. OF THE FINEST

CHINATOWN

ST. JAMES PLACE

MANHATTAN BRIDGE

F.D.R. DRIVE

EAST RIVER

BROOKLYN BRIDGE

NASSAU ST.

GOLD ST.

PEARL STREET

WATER ST.

SOUTH STREET

WALL STREET

BROAD ST.

WHITEHALL ST.

STATE ST.

BATTERY UNDERPASS

BATTERY TUNNEL

DOWNTOWN HELIPORT

PIER 17
SOUTH STREET SEAPORT

. BROOKLYN.

1

2

3

4

5

The FDR Drive Southbound
to Lower Manhattan

The problem with trying to take the FDR Drive to the Civic Center or Financial District is that you run the risk of getting trapped with thousands of motorists heading to the Brooklyn Bridge. Here's a way of avoiding the Brooklyn Bridge morass:

1. Take the FDR Drive to Exit 4 (Grand Street).

2. Turn right at the first intersection onto Grand Street.

3. Once on Grand Street, you'll almost immediately see Madison Street on your left. Turn left onto Madison Street.

To get to the Financial District:

4a. Follow Madison Street past the Manhattan Bridge for a few blocks to St. James Place and turn left. St. James Place becomes Pearl Street.

5a. Follow Pearl Street under the Brooklyn Bridge and continue south to Wall Street and the Financial District.

To get to the Civic Center area:

4b. Follow Madison Street one block past St. James Place to Pearl Street.

5b. Turn right onto Pearl Street. After two blocks you'll be at Foley Square.

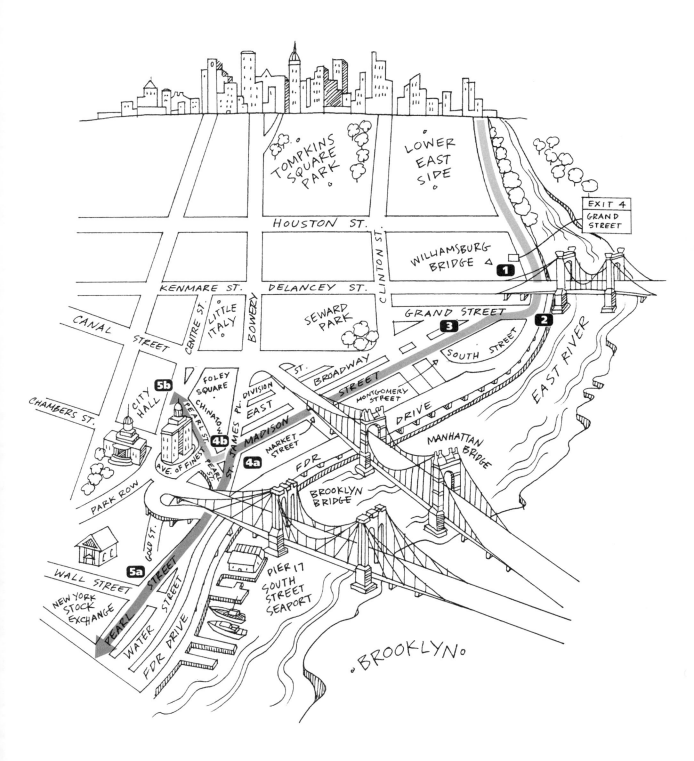

TOMPKINS SQUARE PARK

LOWER EAST SIDE

EXIT 4 GRAND STREET

HOUSTON ST.

WILLIAMSBURG BRIDGE △ **1**

CLINTON ST.

KENMARE ST. DELANCEY ST.

GRAND STREET

3

2

SEWARD PARK

CENTRE ST.

LITTLE ITALY

BOWERY

SOUTH STREET

CANAL STREET

EAST RIVER

FOLEY SQUARE

BROADWAY

ST. MONTGOMERY STREET

CHAMBERS ST.

CITY HALL **5b**

CHINATOWN

DIVISION ST.

EAST

DRIVE

MANHATTAN BRIDGE

PEARL ST.

ST. JAMES PL.

MADISON

4b

MARKET STREET

4a

AVE. OF FINEST

PEARL ST.

FDR

BROOKLYN BRIDGE

PARK ROW

GOLD ST.

PIER 17 SOUTH STREET SEAPORT

WALL STREET

5a

PEARL STREET

WATER STREET

NEW YORK STOCK EXCHANGE

FDR DRIVE

∘BROOKLYN∘

Midtown Manhattan

There is more traffic per square mile in Midtown Manhattan than anywhere else in the United States. There are also more unusual rules and quirks in the traffic system than you'll find elsewhere. Nonetheless, every day some 700,000 motorists attempt to fight their way through this quagmire. Most of them make it, but it's not a pretty sight. This section provides some inside information for surviving Midtown traffic; you'll move along a little quicker, though its not likely you'll ever need your radar detector.

Midtown Speeds

In 1981 I began a semiannual survey to record the speed of traffic on avenues and streets throughout Midtown Manhattan. For a period of three weeks every spring and fall, survey crews armed with stopwatches would record their travel times as they attempted to drive across Midtown. More than 1,000 "travel time runs" are made annually. I've used the results to develop the following list of travel guidelines:

General Midtown Travel Rules

Rule 1: The exterior avenues generally move faster than the interior avenues.
First, Second, Tenth, and Eleventh are usually faster than Lex, Park, Madison, and Fifth.

Rule 2: Two-way cross streets are generally faster than parallel one-way streets.
34th, 42nd, and 57th streets are usually faster than the one-way crosstown streets around them. The one exception is 57th Street westbound, which has consistently been slower than the next westbound street to the north—60th Street/Central Park West.

Rule 3: Forget rules 1 and 2 when passing in front of a bridge or tunnel entrance during the evening peak travel time. Second Avenue is a drag in front of the Queensboro Bridge and in front of the Midtown Tunnel; so is 57th Street at the Queensboro Bridge and 34th Street by the Queens–Midtown Tunnel. Don't even think of using Ninth Avenue near 40th Street by the Lincoln Tunnel.

Rule 4: The worst time to travel across Midtown in either direction is from noon to 3 PM. The trip is actually faster during the rush hour than it is during this three-hour period.

Rule 5: Northbound avenues are slowest from 4 PM to 7 PM, Southbound avenues are slowest from 10 AM to 4 PM. Southbound avenues are okay during the morning rush (everyone is stuck waiting to enter Manhattan at the bridges and tunnels).

The Kings of Gridlock: Traffic Pitfalls to Avoid

Stretches of certain streets and avenues are so slow that they should be avoided at all costs. One of the worst avenue pitfalls, to no one's surprise, is Sixth Avenue approaching Herald Square, where the average speed is 5 miles per hour. The title "King of Gridlock," however, belongs to 37th Street in the heart of the Garment District between Seventh and Eighth avenues, where traffic crawls along at a staggering average of 2.7 miles per hour! From 11 AM to 3 PM car traffic averages in the 1–2 mile per hour range, left in the dust by the average walker, who trots along comfortably at 3–4 miles per hour.

Here are the historic bottom-of-the-barrel street and avenue pitfalls:

The Ten Slowest Street Segments

Rank*	Street	From	To	Average Speed (mph)*
1	37th westbound	Seventh	Eighth	2.7
2	53rd westbound	Park	Madison	3.3
3	34th eastbound	Eighth	Seventh	3.4
4	38th eastbound	Eighth	Seventh	3.2
5	38th eastbound	Seventh	Sixth	3.4
6	53rd westbound	Lexington	Park	3.5
7	37th westbound	Fifth	Sixth	2.8
8	37th westbound	Sixth	Seventh	3.4
9	45th westbound	Lexington	Park	3.3
10	46th eastbound	Seventh	Sixth	3.1

The Ten Slowest Avenue Segments

Rank*	Avenue	From	To	Average Speed (mph)*
1	Sixth	30th	34th	5.0
2	Madison	57th	59th	4.9
3	Madison	50th	57th	5.7
4	Broadway/7th	42nd	34th	5.9
5	Third	57th	59th	5.3
6	Fifth	59th	57th	5.3
7	Madison	30th	34th	5.3
8	Fifth	50th	42nd	6.7
9	Sixth	57th	59th	5.7
10	Park northbound	57th	59th	6.0

*Rank is based on roadway's frequency of appearance among the slowest segments, not on average speed ranking.

Midtown's Quirks

Midtown Manhattan is the most congested business district in the United States. Traffic engineers have been tinkering with its traffic systems for decades in an effort to alleviate the congestion, and as a result we've got some very unusual traffic rules. Knowing these rules can often help save time and avoid costly tickets. Here are the major system "quirks":

Madison Avenue Dual Bus Lanes

More people ride on the buses of Madison Avenue than ride the entire transit system of Salt Lake City, Utah. Some 25,000 people ride the buses every weekday between the hours of 2 PM and 7 PM. To move these masses along quickly, the two right lanes on Madison between 42nd Street and 59th Street have been reserved exclusively for buses from 2 PM to 7 PM. Taxis with passengers may use the lanes from 42nd to 46th streets.

Other motorists must use the three left lanes and may only make right turns at 42nd Street and 62nd Street. If you are on Madison Avenue and need to turn right at, say, 54th Street, you'll have to go to 55th and turn left, then left onto Fifth Avenue, and left again onto 54th Street.
If you are heading east of Madison Avenue between 42nd and 59th streets during these hours, you'll do better by avoiding Madison Avenue altogether and taking Sixth, Park, or any other convenient avenue.

One more point: Parking or even standing is prohibited along the east side of Madison Avenue all day and on the west side from 1 PM to 7 PM.

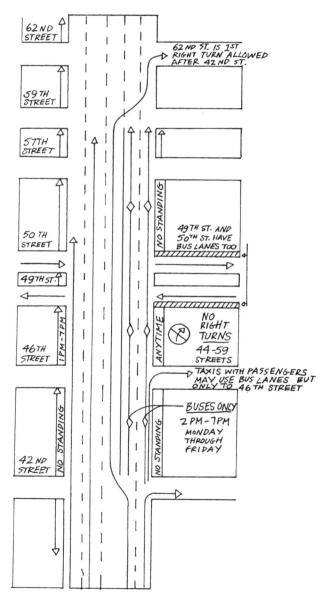

49th/50th Street Transitway

There is only one crosstown bus in Midtown between 42nd and 59th streets, and that's the heavily used M-50 line that crosses the island on 49th Street westbound and 50th Street eastbound. It passes by some of the most exciting and expensive property in the world, including Rockefeller Center, Saks Fifth Avenue, the Palace Hotel, Saint Patrick's Cathedral, and the Waldorf-Astoria Hotel. This route is packed with both pedestrians and vehicles, and at one time had some of the slowest traffic in town. In 1986, to speed crosstown movement for buses and taxis, the city implemented the 49th/50th Street Transitway. Here's how it works:

The transitway is in effect on 49th and 50th streets between Third and Seventh avenues from 8 AM to 6 PM*.

Buses and taxis with passengers are permitted at all times.

Cars and trucks may enter from any avenue but must turn off at the next avenue, except at 50th Street and Madison Avenue where the transitway crosses the Dual Bus Lanes.

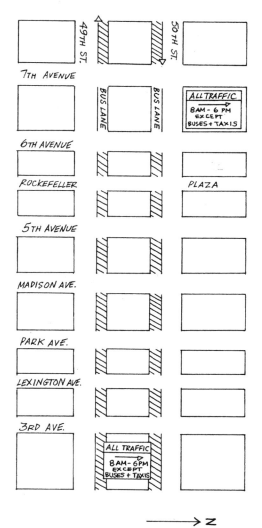

Truck loading is prohibited on 49th Street from 11 AM to 2 PM and on 50th Street from 2 PM to 5 PM.

Trying to get to a 49th or 50th Street destination is like playing chess. Think several moves ahead or you may find yourself going around in circles. Approach the destination from the nearest avenue, not from the cross street.

* Scheduled to be shortened to Lexington Avenue and Seventh Avenue.

Midtown's River Crossings

There are two tunnels and one bridge that bring traffic into Midtown Manhattan. The Queens–Midtown Tunnel links the Long Island Expressway in Queens with Second Avenue in the East 30s. The Queensboro Bridge (also called the 59th Street Bridge) connects Queens Boulevard and Northern Boulevard in Long Island City with Second Avenue between 57th and 63rd Streets in Midtown. The Lincoln Tunnel crosses under the Hudson River, bringing traffic from New Jersey via I-495 to the west side of midtown at Ninth through Eleventh avenues from 30th to 42nd streets.

The bulk of the traffic crosses into Midtown between 7 AM and 10 AM and leaves Midtown between 4 PM and 7 PM. The city, Triborough Bridge and Tunnel Authority, and Port Authority try to match the demands of the traffic by adding inbound lanes in the morning and outbound lanes in the afternoon through lane and roadway reversals. For example, the Queens–Midtown Tunnel normally operates with two lanes inbound and two lanes outbound, but during the morning rush hour one outbound lane is reversed so that three lanes run inbound and just one lane runs outbound.

The best way to take advantage of the reversals is to get to the reversed roadway just after it opens; this way you can be sure that the lane or road will be relatively free of traffic. Here is the approximate schedule for the reversals:

Facility	Inbound Reversal	Outbound Reversal
Queens–Midtown Tunnel	7 AM to 9 AM	4 PM to 5:30 PM
Queensboro Bridge	6 AM to 9:30 AM	3 PM to 7 PM*
Lincoln Tunnel	7 AM to 9 AM	4 PM to 6 PM**

*temporarily suspended for construction
**reversed as conditions warrant

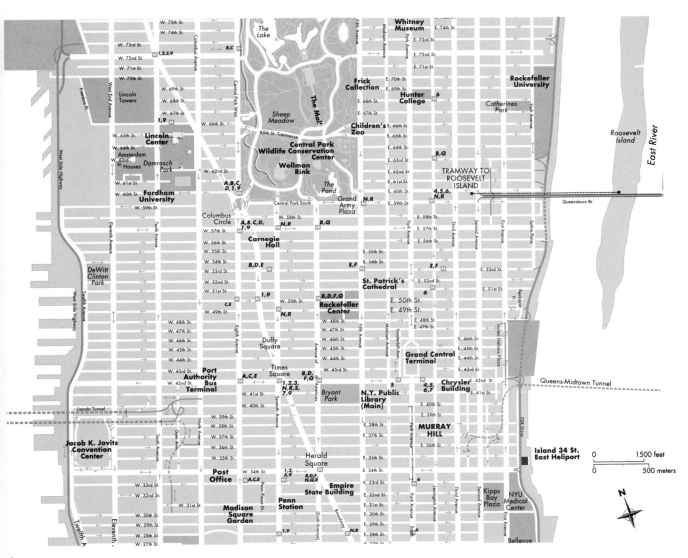

The Lake

W. 75th St.
W. 74th St.
W. 73rd St.
W. 72nd St.
W. 71st St.
W. 70th St.
W. 69th St.
W. 68th St.
W. 67th St. 1,9
W. 66th St.

Lincoln Towers

W. 65th St.
Lincoln Center
W. 64th St.
Amsterdam Houses
W. 63rd St.
Damrosch Park
W. 62nd St.
Fordham University
W. 60th St.
W. 59th St.

West End Avenue
Columbus Avenue
Central Park West

8,C

Sheep Meadow

The Mall

Central Park Wildlife Conservation Center

Wollman Rink

The Pond

Whitney Museum

E. 74th St.
E. 73rd St.
E. 72nd St.
E. 71st St.
Frick Collection
E. 70th St.
E. 69th St.
Hunter College
E. 68th St.
E. 67th St.
Children's Zoo
E. 66th St.
E. 65th St.
E. 64th St.
E. 63rd St.
E. 62nd St.
E. 61st St.
E. 60th St.

Rockefeller University

Catherines Park

Roosevelt Island

East River

6

B,Q

TRAMWAY TO ROOSEVELT ISLAND

4,5,6,
N,R

Queensboro Br.

Fifth Avenue
Madison Avenue
Park Avenue

65th St. Transverse

Columbus Circle

A,B,C, D,1,9

A,B,C,D, 1,9

Central Park South

N,R

B,Q

Grand Army Plaza

N,R

Carnegie Hall

W. 57th St.
W. 56th St.
W. 55th St.
W. 54th St.
W. 53rd St.
W. 52nd St.
W. 51st St.
W. 49th St.

B,D,E

1,9

C,E

Duffy Square

E,F

St. Patrick's Cathedral

E,F

E. 55th St.
E. 54th St.
E. 53rd St.
E. 52nd St.
E. 51st St.
E. 50th St.
E. 49th St.
E. 48th St.
E. 47th St.
E. 46th St.
E. 45th St.
E. 44th St.
E. 43rd St.

6

B,D,F,Q

Rockefeller Center

N,R

W. 48th St.
W. 47th St.
W. 46th St.
W. 45th St.
W. 44th St.
W. 43rd St.
W. 42nd St.

Times Square

A,C,E

B,D, F,Q

1,2, N,R,S, 7,9

Bryant Park

N.Y. Public Library (Main)

Grand Central Terminal

5

4,5, 6,7

Chrysler Building

E. 42nd St.
E. 41st St.

Queens-Midtown Tunnel

Port Authority Bus Terminal

Eighth Avenue
Seventh Avenue
Avenue of the Americas

W. 41st St.
W. 40th St.
W. 39th St.
W. 38th St.
W. 37th St.
W. 36th St.
W. 35th St.

E. 40th St.
E. 39th St.
E. 38th St.
E. 37th St.
E. 36th St.
E. 35th St.

MURRAY HILL

Lincoln Tunnel

Jacob K. Javits Convention Center

Ninth Avenue
Tenth Avenue

Dyer Avenue

Herald Square

Post Office

W. 34th St.
W. 33rd St.
W. 32nd St.
W. 31st St.

1,2, 3,9

B,D,F, N,Q,R

A,C,E

Empire State Building

E. 34th St.
E. 33rd St.
E. 32nd St.
E. 31st St.
E. 30th St.

Island 34 St. East Heliport

0   1500 feet
0   500 meters

NYU Medical Center

Penn Station

Madison Square Garden

Penn Plaza Dr.

Broadway
Sixth Avenue

W. 30th St.
W. 29th St.
W. 28th St.
W. 27th St.

1,9

N,R

E. 28th St.

Kipps Bay Plaza

Bellevue

N

Lexington Avenue
Third Avenue
Second Avenue
First Avenue
FDR Drive

6

Approaching the Reversals

Queens–Midtown Tunnel AM Reversal:

1.   Stay in the left lane of the LIE when approaching the toll plaza.

Queens–Midtown Tunnel PM Reversal:

The south lane of the north tube is reversed from 4 PM to 5:30 PM. You can access this lane from 34th or 35th streets between Second and Third avenues. You can save up to 20 minutes if you get to the portal just after 4 PM.

From First Avenue:

1a.   Turn left onto 34th Street.

2a.   Do not take the first entrance to the tunnel between First and Second avenues.

3a.   The entrance to the tunnel is in the middle of the block, between Second and Third avenues, on the right.

From Second Avenue:

1b.   Turn right onto 34th Street.

2b.   The entrance to the tunnel is in the middle of the block, between Second and Third Avenues, on the right.

From Third Avenue:

1c.   Turn right onto 35th Street.

2c.   The entrance to the tunnel is in the middle of the block, between Second and Third avenues, on the left.

Note: The only drawback to taking this lane is that you will end up in the farthest left lanes of the toll plaza. Consequently, it would be tough for you to reach the exits at the right for Borden Avenue, Jackson Avenue, or the Pulaski Bridge.

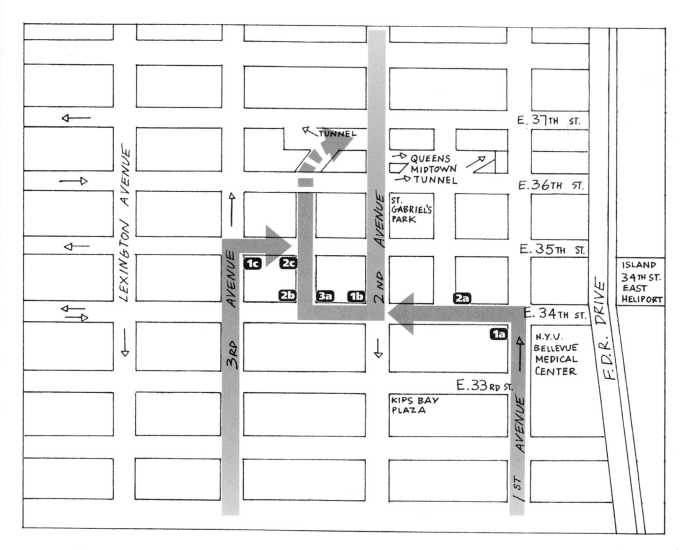

Queens-Midtown Tunnel's manhattan approach to reversed lane, weekdays 4 PM to 5:30 PM

Queensboro Bridge AM Reversal:

The south upper roadway of the Queensboro Bridge is reversed every weekday morning from 6 AM to 10 AM. It connects in Manhattan at 58th and 57th streets between First and Second avenues. There are two ways to reach the roadway:

From Thomson Avenue:

1a. Take Queens Boulevard as far as Van Dam Street. At that point Queens Boulevard bends to the right under the "el."

2a. Go straight instead and you'll find yourself on Thomson Avenue.

3a. Pass by the first entrance to the bridge on the right.

4a. Take the second entrance, onto the ramp leading to the southern upper roadway.

From Queens Plaza:

1b. Take Northern Boulevard or Queens Boulevard to Queens Plaza.

2b. Bear right in the plaza and stay on the service road alongside the bridge.

3b. Go to 21st Street, where you'll see the entrance to the northern upper roadway straight ahead. Don't take it.

4b. Instead, turn left onto 21st Street and pass under the bridge.

5b. Turn left at the southern end of the bridge onto the reversed southern upper roadway.

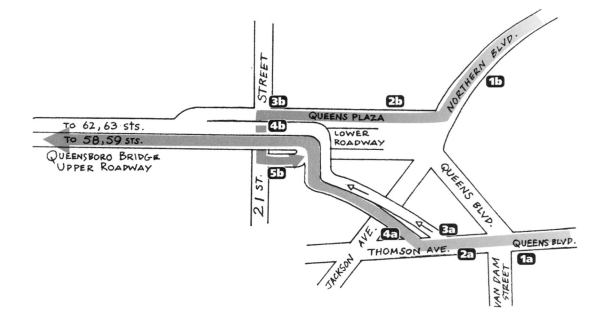

Queensboro Bridge PM Reversal:

The northern upper roadway of the Queensboro Bridge is normally Manhattan-bound. However, once the lower level is completed (scheduled for late 1993) the roadway is scheduled to be reversed from 3 PM to 7 PM every weekday.

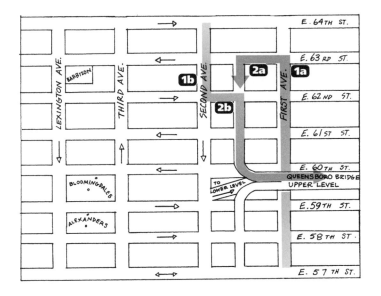

From First Avenue:

1a. Turn left at 63rd Street.

2a. The entrance to the reversed upper roadway will be on your left, midblock between First and Second avenues.

From Second Avenue:

1b. Turn left at 62nd Street.

2b. The entrance to the reversed upper roadway will be on your right, midblock between First and Second avenues.

To get to Queens Boulevard:

1c. Stay in the left lane and take the left fork.

2c. At the traffic light for Thomson Avenue, turn left.

3c. Follow this under the overhead "el" onto Queens Boulevard eastbound.

To get to Northern Boulevard:

1d. Stay in the right lane of the upper roadway.

2d. Take the right fork.

3d. At the traffic light for 21st Street, turn left.

4d. At 38th Avenue, turn right.

5d. Take 38th Avenue to the end at Northern Boulevard; turn left.

Know Your Alpha-Numerics: The Extensions of the Numbered Avenues All Have Names

It's easy to remember that First Avenue is on the East Side and Tenth Avenue is on the West Side and Fifth Avenue is somewhere in the middle. But once you get into the southern or northern sections of Manhattan Island, most of the numbered avenues disappear and are replaced with named roads. On the East Side, avenue names remain essentially unchanged from 23rd Street north to Harlem. West of Fifth Avenue the names change in the Village, at 59th Street/Central Park, and at the northern end of the park at 110th Street. There are no easy acronyms to help you remember these names, so familiarize yourself with these tables.

Lower Manhattan

East Side:

First Avenue	→	Allen Street south of Houston Street
Second Avenue	→	Chrystie Street south of Houston Street
Third Avenue	→	Bowery south of East 4th Street

West Side:

Sixth Avenue	→	Trinity Place/Church Street south of Canal Street
Seventh Avenue	→	Varick Street south of Houston Street
Eighth Avenue	→	Hudson Street south of Bleecker Street
Ninth Avenue	→	Hudson Street south of 14th Street

Midtown and Upper Manhattan

	South of 59th Street	59th to 110th Streets	North of 110th Street
Sixth Avenue	→	Central Park East Drive	→ Malcolm X Boulevard/Lenox Avenue
Seventh Avenue	→	Central Park West Drive	→ Adam Clayton Powell Jr. Boulevard
Eighth Avenue	→	Central Park West	→ Frederick Douglass Boulevard
Ninth Avenue	→	Columbus Avenue	→ Morningside Drive
Tenth Avenue	→	Amsterdam Avenue	→ Amsterdam Avenue
Eleventh Avenue	→	West End Avenue	→ Broadway at 106th Street

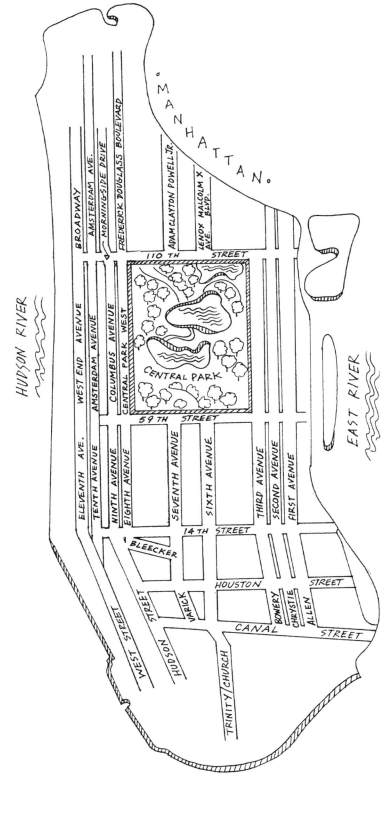

MANHATTAN

Avenue and Street Address Finders
Midtown Avenue Address

Streets	West End Ave	Broadway	Amsterdam Ave	Columbus Ave	Central Park West
	737-700	2554-2520	733-702	740-701	360-350
Streets	699-660	2519-2476	701-656	700-661	336-322
96-94	659-620	2475-2440	655-620	660-621	320-300
94-92	619-578	2439-2401	619-580	620-581	295-279
92-90	577-540	2400-2361	579-540	580-541	275-262
90-88	539-500	2360-2321	539-500	540-501	257-241
88-86	499-460	2320-2281	499-460	500-461	239-212
86-84	459-420	2280-2241	459-420	460-421	211-
84-82	419-380	2240-2201	419-380	420-381	**American Museum of Natural History**
82-80	379-340	2200-2161	379-340	380-341	
80-78	339-300	2160-2121	339-300	340-301	160-145
78-76	299-262	2114-2081	299-261	300-261	135-121
76-74	261-221	2079-2040	260-221	260-221	115-101
74-72	220-176	2030-1999	220-181	220-181	99-80
72-70	175-122	1998-1961	180-140	180-141	79-65
70-68	121-74	1960-1920	139-100	140-101	55-50
68-66	73-44	**Lincoln Center**	99-60	100-61	33-25
66-64	43-20	1880-1841	59-20	60-21	15-
64-62	19-2	**Columbus Circle**	19-1	20-2	**Columbus Circle**

62-60	Eleventh Ave	Broadway	Tenth Ave	Ninth Ave	Eight Ave	Seventh Ave	Sixth Ave
60-58	854-823	1791-1752	889-852	907-864	992-946	921-888	1419-1381
	822-775	1751-1710	851-812	863-824	945-908	887-842	1377-1341
58-56	774-741	1709-1674	811-772	823-782	907-870	841-798	1330-1301
56-54	740-701	1673-1634	770-737	781-742	869-830	797-761	1297-1261
54-52	700-665	1633-1596	735-686	741-702	829-791	760-720	1260-1221
52-50	664-625	1595-1551	685-654	701-662	790-735	719-701	1217-1180
50-48	624-589	1550-1514	653-614	661-622	734-701	**Times Square**	1178-1141
48-46	588-553	1513-1472	613-576	621-582	700-661		1140-1100
46-44	552-503	1471-1440	575-538	**Port Authority**	660-620	598-560	1097-1061
44-42	502-480	1439-1400	537-502		619-570	559-522	1060-1020
42-40	479-431	1399-1352	501-466	501-468	569-520	521-482	1019-981
40-38	430-405	**Macy's**	465-430	467-432	519-480	481-442	
38-36	404-360	1282-1260	429-380	431-412	479-442	**Penn Station**	**Herald Square**
36-34	359-319	1279-1220	379-341	**Post Office**	441-403	399-362	892-855
34-32	318-282	1219-1178	340-314	351-314	402-362	361-322	844-815
32-30	281-242	1177-1135	313-288	313-262	361-321	321-282	814-775
30-28	241-202	1134-1100	287-239	261-230	320-281	281-244	774-733
28-26	201-162	1099-940	238-210	229-198	280-236	243-210	732-696
26-24	161-120	939-902	209-162	197-167	235-198	209-170	695-656
24-22	119-82	901-873	161-130	166-128	197-162	169-134	655-613
22-20	81-54	872-21	129-92	127-92	161-126	133-100	612-574
20-18	53-26	20-1	91-58	91-44	125-80	99-64	573-530

Union Square West

(Map labels: 96TH ST. TRANSVERSE · CENTRAL PARK · 79TH ST. TRANSVERSE · MET MUSEUM)

Crosstown Street Address Finder

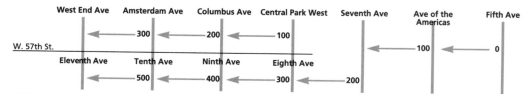

Odd number addresses are on the north side of the street; even numbers are on the south side.

Fifth Ave	Madison Ave	Park Ave	Lexington Ave	Third Ave	Second Ave	First Ave	Streets
1148-1130	1379-1340	1236-1199	1486-1449	1709-1678	1868-1817	1855-1817	**96-94**
1125-1109	1335-1295	1192-1160	1444-1400	1677-1644	1808-1766	1811-1780	**94-92**
1107-1090	1294-1254	1155-1120	1396-1361	1643-1601	1763-1736	1779-1740	**92-90**
1089-1070	1250-1220	1114-1080	1355-1311	1602-1568	1739-1700	1735-1701	**90-88**
1069-1050	1221-1178	1076-1044	1301-1280	1566-1530	1698-1660	1689-1652	**88-86**
1048-1030	1171-1130	1035-1000	1278-1248	1529-1490	1659-1624	1651-1618	**86-84**
1028-1010	1128-1090	993-960	1248-1210	1489-1450	1623-1584	1617-1578	**84-82**
1009-990	1088-1058	959-916	1209-1164	1449-1410	1583-1538	1577-1540	**82-80**
989-970	1046-1012	911-878	1161-1120	1409-1374	1537-1498	1539-1495	**80-78**
969-950	1006-974	877-840	1116-1080	1373-1330	1497-1456	1494-1462	**78-76**
947-930	970-940	830-799	1071-1036	1329-1290	1454-1420	1460-1429	**76-74**
929-910	939-896	791-760	1032-1004	1289-1250	1417-1389	1384-1344	**74-72**
907-895	872-856	755-720	993-962	1249-1210	1363-1328	1343-1306	**72-70**
885-870	850-813	715-680	961-926	1208-1166	1327-1296	1300-1266	**70-68**
860-850	811-772	679-640	922-900	1165-1130	1295-1260	1260-1222	**68-66**
849-830	771-733	639-600	886-841	1129-1084	1259-1222	1221-1168	**66-64**
828-810	727-690	599-560	842-803	1083-1050	1221-1180	1167-1130	**64-62**
807-790	680-654	559-520	802-770	1049-1010	1179-1140	1129-1102	**62-60**
789-755	649-621	519-476	759-722	1009-972	**Queensboro Bridge**		**60-58**
754-720	611-572	475-434	721-677	968-942	1101-1066	1063-1026	**58-56**
719-680	568-532	430-408	665-636	933-894	1062-1028	1021-985	**56-54**
679-656	531-500	399-360	629-596	893-856	1027-984	984-945	**54-52**
655-626	488-452	350-320	593-556	855-818	983-944	944-889	**52-50**
625-600	444-412	300-280	555-518	817-776	943-902	888-860	**50-48**
599-562	400-377	277-240	515-476	775-741	891-862	**U.N.**-827	**48-46**
561-530	375-346	**Metlife Bldg**	475-441	735-702	860-824	**U.N.**-785	**46-44**
529-500	345-316	**Grand Central Terminal**	435-395	701-660	823-793	**U.N.**	**44-42**
499-460	315-284		394-354	659-622	773-748	**Tudor City**	**42-40**
459-424	283-250	99-68	353-314	621-578	747-707	701-666	**40-38**
423-392	249-218	67-40	311-284	577-542	700-666	**Midtwon tun**	**38-36**
391-352	217-188	35-5	283-240	541-508	659-622	626-599	**36-34**
351-320	184-152	4-1	239-196	507-470	621-585	598-556	**34-32**
319-284	150-118	470-444	195-160	469-432	581-543	**Kips Bay**	**32-30**
283-250	117-79	431-404	159-120	431-394	541-500	**N.Y.U. Hosp**	**30-28**
249-213	78-50	403-364	119-81	393-358	499-462	478-446	**28-26**
212-201	37-11	361-323	77-40	355-321	461-422	445-411	**26-24**
200-172	7-1	322-286	39-9	318-282	421-382	410-390	**24-22**
170-154		285-251	8-1	281-244	381-344	389-315	**22-20**
153-109		250-221	78-70	243-206	343-310	314-310	**20-18**
127-85		Union Square East 220-184	Irving Place 69-40	205-166	309-301	309-280	**18-16**
108-69		Union Square East 34-2	Irving Place 30-2	165-126	240-230	279-240	**16-14**

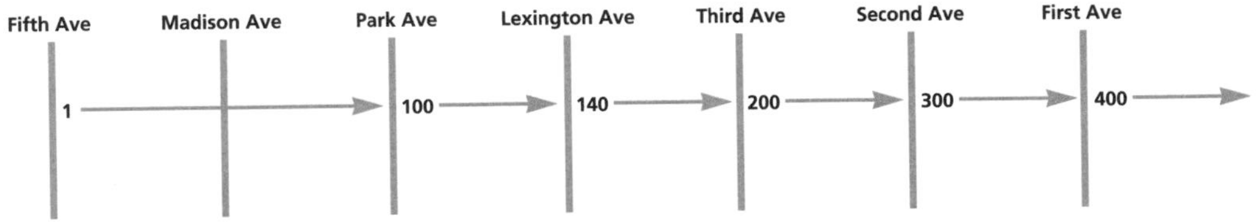

Downtown Street Finder

54

Avoiding Flatbush Avenue Southbound Between Tillary Street and Grand Army Plaza

The traffic situation on Flatbush Avenue has improved in Downtown Brooklyn, but it's still slow through Park Slope and Flatbush. There's a confusing grid of streets to the east of Flatbush Avenue and it's easy to get trapped in congested or dead-end routes. Here's a circuitous but reasonably reliable path from Downtown Brooklyn to Grand Army Plaza or Eastern Parkway.

1. From the Brooklyn Bridge, go to Tillary Street and turn left.

2. Go past Flatbush Avenue and stay to the right of the entrance ramp to the BQE to follow Park Avenue underneath the BQE.

If you're heading to Prospect Park and points south:

3a. Turn right at Vanderbilt Avenue, which runs into Grand Army Plaza.

4a. Go around the circle, staying in the fourth lane from the left (the solid white line should be on your right), and enter Prospect Park. Stay in the third lane from the left to feed onto Flatbush Avenue.

If you want to get to Eastern Parkway and points east:

3b. Go three blocks past Vanderbilt Avenue to Washington Avenue and turn right.

4b. In about two miles you'll hit Eastern Parkway. Turn left at Eastern Parkway to go east.

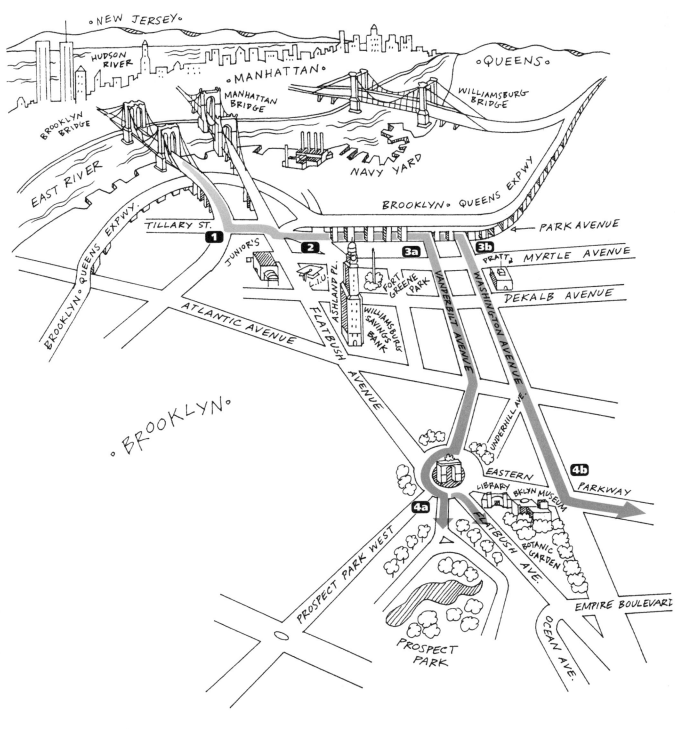

NEW JERSEY

HUDSON RIVER

MANHATTAN

QUEENS

BROOKLYN BRIDGE

MANHATTAN BRIDGE

WILLIAMSBURG BRIDGE

EAST RIVER

NAVY YARD

BROOKLYN·QUEENS EXPWY.

BROOKLYN · QUEENS EXPWY

PARK AVENUE

TILLARY ST.

1

JUNIOR'S

L.I.U.

ASHLAND PL.

FORT GREENE PARK

2

3a

3b

PRATT

MYRTLE AVENUE

DEKALB AVENUE

WILLIAMSBURG SAVINGS BANK

FLATBUSH AVENUE

VANDERBILT AVENUE

WASHINGTON AVENUE

ATLANTIC AVENUE

·BROOKLYN·

UNDERHILL AVE.

EASTERN

4b

PARKWAY

LIBRARY

BKLYN MUSEUM

PROSPECT PARK WEST

4a

FLATBUSH AVE.

BOTANIC GARDEN

EMPIRE BOULEVARD

PROSPECT PARK

OCEAN AVE.

57

Avoiding Flatbush Avenue Northbound through Park Slope/Prospect Heights

Flatbush Avenue northbound was widened and improved north of Atlantic Avenue, but the Park Slope/Prospect Heights segment is still narrow and, usually, painfully slow.

1. On those days that you need a shortcut, turn right off Flatbush Avenue just after Eighth Avenue onto Carlton Avenue. Carlton Avenue intersects with Flatbush Avenue at about a thirty-degree angle.

2. Take Carlton Avenue to its end (one block past where the BQE runs overhead) at Flushing Avenue.

3. Turn left onto Flushing Avenue.

If you are heading to the Manhattan Bridge:

4a. Take Flushing Avenue, which will become Nassau Street. After you pass under the BQE you'll see the entrance to the Manhattan Bridge's upper level.

If the Brooklyn Bridge is your destination:

4b. Take Flushing Avenue to the end of the Brooklyn Navy Yard and turn right onto Navy Street.

5b. Go one block to Sands Street and turn left.

6b. Go under the BQE and under the Manhattan Bridge; you'll soon see the Sands Street entrance to the Brooklyn Bridge on the left.

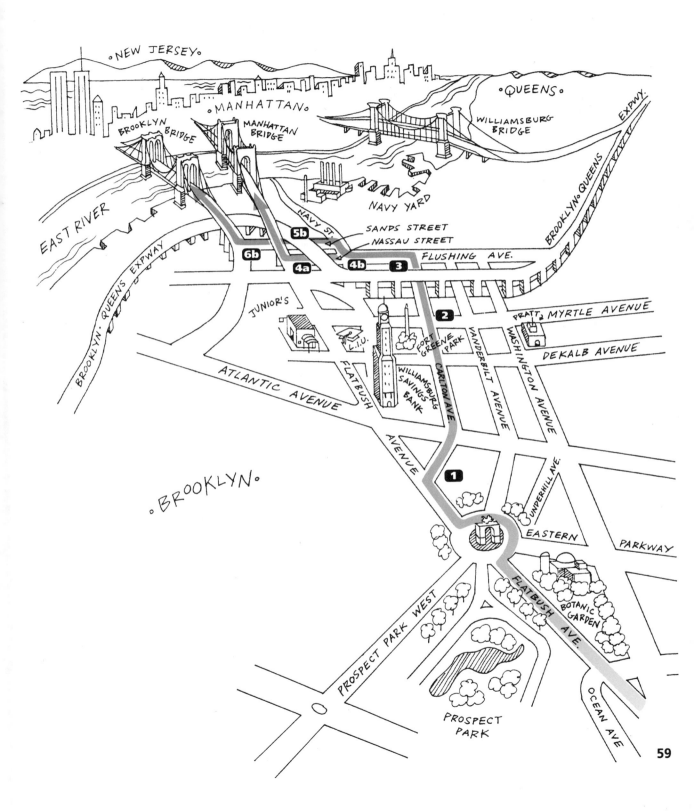

NEW JERSEY

MANHATTAN

QUEENS

BROOKLYN BRIDGE

MANHATTAN BRIDGE

WILLIAMSBURG BRIDGE

BROOKLYN·QUEENS EXPWY.

EAST RIVER

NAVY YARD

NAVY ST.

5b

6b

4a

SANDS STREET

NASSAU STREET

4b

3

FLUSHING AVE.

BROOKLYN·QUEENS EXPWAY

JUNIOR'S

L.I.U.

FORT GREENE PARK

2

PRATT

MYRTLE AVENUE

DEKALB AVENUE

WASHINGTON AVENUE

VANDERBILT AVENUE

CARLTON AVE.

WILLIAMSBURG SAVINGS BANK

FLATBUSH

ATLANTIC AVENUE

AVENUE

·BROOKLYN·

1

UNDERHILL AVE.

EASTERN

PARKWAY

BOTANIC GARDEN

FLATBUSH AVE.

PROSPECT PARK WEST

PROSPECT PARK

OCEAN AVE.

The Williamsburg Bridge to the Westbound BQE

Finding the eastbound BQE from the Williamsburg Bridge is a snap since there is a direct, well-marked ramp. But few people think of taking the Williamsburg Bridge if they are heading west on the BQE to the outbound Gowanus Expressway or southern Brooklyn. This is too bad, since it's actually a pretty reliable route.

1. Get in the farthest right lane of the Williamsburg Bridge to Brooklyn.

2. At the Brooklyn end of the bridge make the sharpest right turn possible.

3. At the first street, Broadway, turn right again. In effect, you will have made a U-turn to the right.

4. Take Broadway to its end and turn left onto Kent Avenue. Continue on Kent Avenue and in less than a mile you will see the elevated BQE.

5. Turn right onto the service road of the BQE (Williamsburg Street West). After one block you'll see the entrance to the westbound BQE on your left.

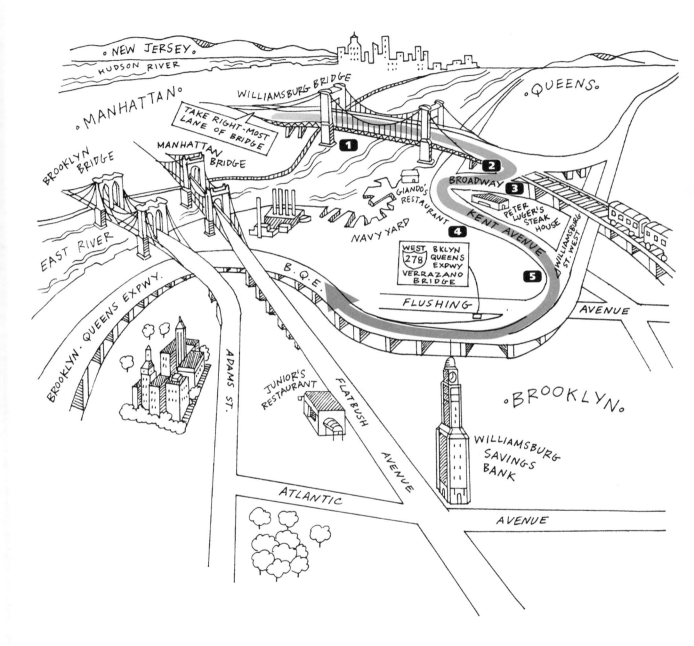

NEW JERSEY

HUDSON RIVER

MANHATTAN

WILLIAMSBURG BRIDGE

QUEENS

TAKE RIGHT-MOST LANE OF BRIDGE

1

BROOKLYN BRIDGE

MANHATTAN BRIDGE

2

BROADWAY

3

GIANDO'S RESTAURANT

PETER LUGER'S STEAK HOUSE

KENT AVENUE

WILLIAMSBURG ST. WEST

EAST RIVER

NAVY YARD

4

WEST 278 BKLYN QUEENS EXPWY VERRAZANO BRIDGE

5

BROOKLYN. QUEENS EXPWY.

B.Q.E.

FLUSHING

AVENUE

ADAMS ST.

JUNIOR'S RESTAURANT

FLATBUSH AVENUE

.BROOKLYN.

WILLIAMSBURG SAVINGS BANK

ATLANTIC

AVENUE

The Manhattan Bridge to the Gowanus Expressway

Most people think they have to take the Brooklyn Bridge to get to the westbound BQE and the outbound Gowanus Expressway. But once you figure out the maze of ramps connecting the Manhattan Bridge to the BQE, you'll find that there is a pretty simple alternative.

1. Stay in the far right lane on the Manhattan Bridge and, at the end of the bridge, turn right onto Tillary Street.

2. Go one block and turn right onto Jay Street.

3. Again, stay in the right lane and turn right under the bridge onto Sands Street. You will see two consecutive entrances to the BQE on the right.

4. The first entrance will connect you with the BQE eastbound (north) toward Queens. The second entrance will connect you with the westbound (south) BQE toward the Gowanus Expressway and the Verrazano–Narrows Bridge.

Can I continue through a red signal if I entered on yellow?
You're approaching an intersection with a traffic light and want to make a left turn. You enter the intersection while the signal is yellow. There is opposing traffic and you have to wait for a gap. Meanwhile the signal turns to red. What do you do?

Make the left turn as soon as you can do so safely. According to New York State Vehicle and Traffic Law Section 1111(b)2., a motorist may enter the intersection on yellow.

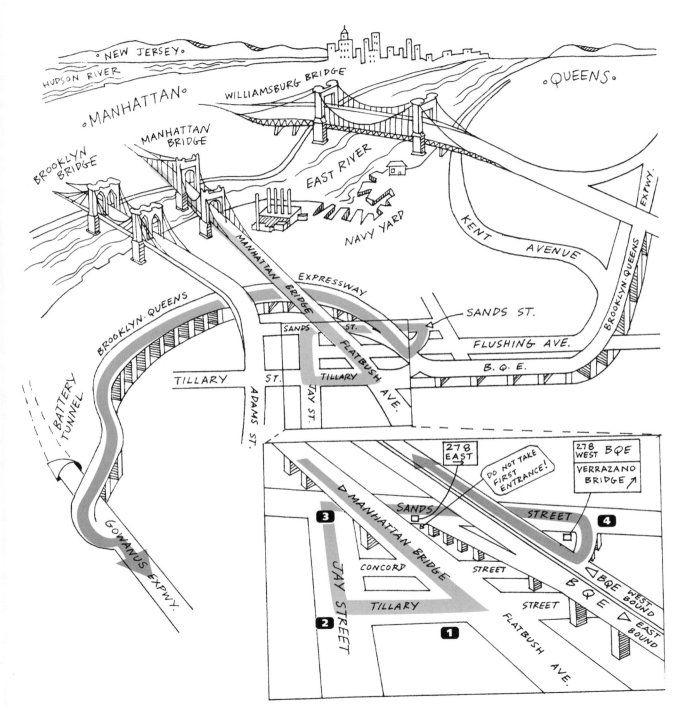

NEW JERSEY

HUDSON RIVER

MANHATTAN

WILLIAMSBURG BRIDGE

QUEENS

MANHATTAN BRIDGE

BROOKLYN BRIDGE

EAST RIVER

NAVY YARD

KENT AVENUE

SANDS ST.

FLUSHING AVE.

B.Q.E.

MANHATTAN BRIDGE EXPRESSWAY

BROOKLYN-QUEENS

SANDS ST.

FLATBUSH AVE.

TILLARY ST.

JAY ST.

TILLARY

ADAMS ST.

BATTERY TUNNEL

BROOKLYN-QUEENS

GOWANUS EXPWY.

278 EAST

DO NOT TAKE FIRST ENTRANCE!

278 WEST BQE

VERRAZANO BRIDGE ↗

SANDS STREET

3

MANHATTAN BRIDGE

4

JAY STREET

CONCORD STREET

TILLARY STREET

B Q E

BQE WEST BOUND

BQE EAST BOUND

2

1

FLATBUSH AVE.

63

Gowanus Expressway Alternative: Southbound via Fort Hamilton Parkway

Ten years of reconstruction. Yes, you read that right; they won't finish rebuilding the Gowanus Expressway until 2003! What's a person to do? Here's what:

1. When the southbound Gowanus is really bad, bear left after the Battery Toll Plaza.

2. Stay in the left two lanes and exit onto the Prospect Expressway.

3. Take the Prospect Expressway less than a mile to the Fort Hamilton Parkway exit. At Fort Hamilton Parkway turn right.

4. Stay on the parkway for three miles until about 78th Street, where you will cross over the Gowanus.

5. Bear left onto the service road and you'll immediately see the entrance to the Gowanus on your left.

Accidents and other tie-ups

When you hear from Shadow Traffic that there's a tie-up on a certain route, it could be bad news, or for astute drivers, good news. Traffic heading into the problem area will be stalled but traffic leaving the area should flow freely. Let's say you hear that there's a jackknifed tractor trailer on the Gowanus Expressway northbound just before the Prospect Expressway. You can be sure two and maybe all three lanes will be closed. Motorists from Flatbush should head toward the Prospect to enter the Gowanus north of the accident. This normally sluggish road should be moving at a reasonable speed.

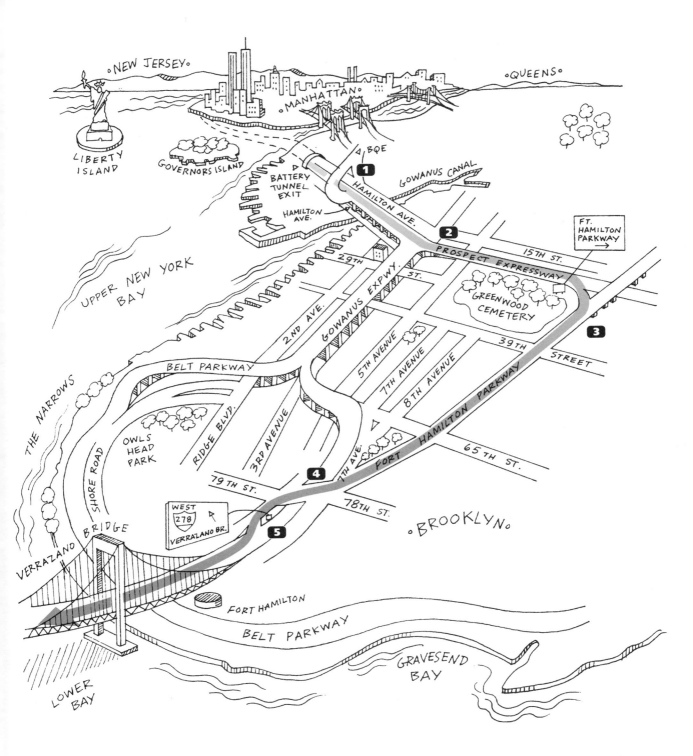

NEW JERSEY

QUEENS

MANHATTAN

LIBERTY ISLAND

GOVERNORS ISLAND

BATTERY TUNNEL EXIT

BQE

1

HAMILTON AVE.

GOWANUS CANAL

HAMILTON AVE.

2

PROSPECT EXPRESSWAY

15TH ST.

FT. HAMILTON PARKWAY

UPPER NEW YORK BAY

29TH ST.

2ND AVE.

GOWANUS EXPWY.

5TH AVENUE

7TH AVENUE

8TH AVENUE

ST.

GREENWOOD CEMETERY

39TH STREET

3

BELT PARKWAY

THE NARROWS

OWLS HEAD PARK

SHORE ROAD

RIDGE BLVD.

3RD AVENUE

7TH AVE.

FORT HAMILTON PARKWAY

65TH ST.

79TH ST.

4

78TH ST.

BROOKLYN

WEST 278 VERRAZANO BR.

5

VERRAZANO BRIDGE

FORT HAMILTON

BELT PARKWAY

GRAVESEND BAY

LOWER BAY

Bypassing the Inbound Gowanus Expressway from the Verrazano–Narrows Bridge

The Verrazano–Narrows Bridge may be the only way to get into Brooklyn, but once you are in the county of Kings you've got plenty of alternatives. Third and Fourth avenues can be used as detours, but on those dog days when the Gowanus and Third and Fourth avenues are all at a standstill, try this alternative:

1. Exit the Gowanus at Fort Hamilton Parkway.

2. Stay on the service road of the Gowanus Expressway (Seventh Avenue) past McKinley Park on your right. Bear right onto Eighth Avenue.

3. Take Eighth Avenue about 1 1/2 miles into Brooklyn's version of Chinatown. At the end of Eighth Avenue turn left onto 39th Street.

4. Go three blocks to Fifth Avenue and turn right.

5. Take Fifth Avenue a little more than a mile to 15th Street and turn left. In just three blocks 15th Street runs into Hamilton Avenue just before the Hamilton Avenue Bridge.

6. Follow Hamilton Avenue to the Battery Tunnel on your left or the eastbound BQE on your right.

Can I turn left into a shopping center across a double yellow line?
You may not cross a double painted yellow line for any reason other than to turn left into a driveway— unless such a turn is prohibited by signs.

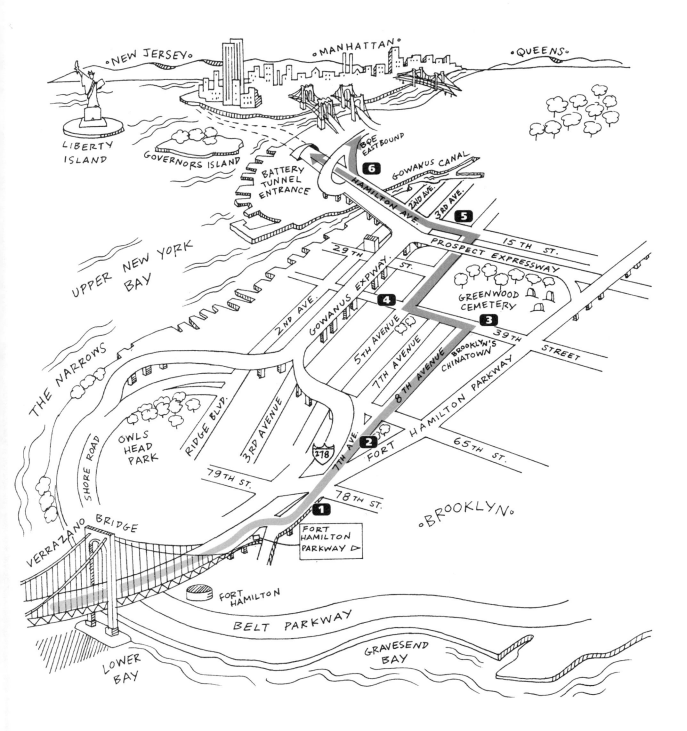

NEW JERSEY

MANHATTAN

QUEENS

LIBERTY ISLAND

GOVERNORS ISLAND

BATTERY TUNNEL ENTRANCE

BQE Eastbound

6

GOWANUS CANAL

HAMILTON AVE.

2ND AVE.

3RD AVE.

5

15TH ST.

PROSPECT EXPRESSWAY

UPPER NEW YORK BAY

29TH

2ND AVE.

GOWANUS EXPWAY.

ST.

5TH AVENUE

4

7TH AVENUE

8TH AVENUE

BROOKLYN'S CHINATOWN

GREENWOOD CEMETERY

3

39TH

STREET

THE NARROWS

SHORE ROAD

OWLS HEAD PARK

RIDGE BLVD.

3RD AVENUE

278

7TH AVE.

2

FORT HAMILTON PARKWAY

65TH ST.

79TH ST.

78TH ST.

1

FORT HAMILTON PARKWAY ▷

BROOKLYN

VERRAZANO BRIDGE

FORT HAMILTON

BELT PARKWAY

GRAVESEND BAY

LOWER BAY

Bypassing the Inbound Gowanus Expressway When Coming from the Belt Parkway

The name "Gowanus" was derived from the Canarsie Indian word "Go-nowhere"— rather appropriate in light of this roadway's often sluggish traffic conditions. Here's one way to avoid the "Go-nowhere" and really get somewhere.

1. Take the Belt Parkway to Exit 1 (65–67 Sts.).

2. Once on the service road, bear left at the first fork. Follow the road as it curves to the right and bear right at the second fork.

3. At the traffic signal (Ridge Boulevard), turn left.

4. Cross under the Belt Parkway onto Second Avenue.

5. Take Second Avenue for just under two miles to 29th Street and turn right. (Be careful around 41st Street, where the road surface is rough and there are active railroad tracks.)

6. Take 29th Street one block to Third Avenue and turn left.

7. Pass 17th Street and follow the traffic to the left onto Hamilton Avenue.

8. Hamilton Avenue leads directly to the Battery Tunnel (enter on the left) or the BQE eastbound (enter on the right).

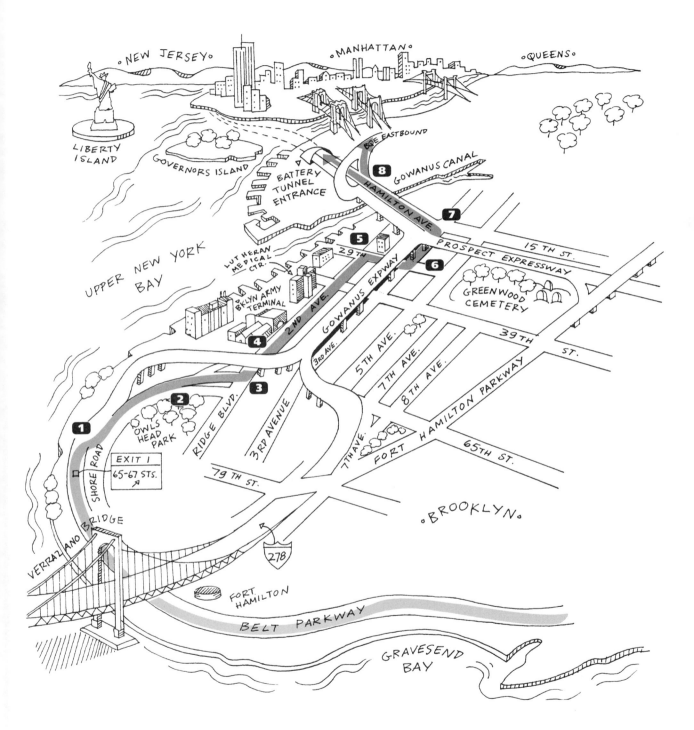

NEW JERSEY

MANHATTAN

QUEENS

LIBERTY ISLAND

GOVERNORS ISLAND

BATTERY TUNNEL ENTRANCE

BQE EASTBOUND

GOWANUS CANAL

8

HAMILTON AVE.

7

UPPER NEW YORK BAY

LUTHERAN MEDICAL CTR.

5

29TH

PROSPECT EXPRESSWAY

15TH ST.

BKLYN ARMY TERMINAL

4

2ND AVE.

GOWANUS EXPWY

6

GREENWOOD CEMETERY

3RD AVE.

5TH AVE.

7TH AVE.

8TH AVE.

39TH ST.

2

OWLS HEAD PARK

RIDGE BLVD.

3

3RD AVENUE

7TH AVE.

FORT HAMILTON PARKWAY

65TH ST.

1

SHORE ROAD

EXIT 1
65-67 STS.

79TH ST.

BROOKLYN

VERRAZANO BRIDGE

278

FORT HAMILTON

BELT PARKWAY

GRAVESEND BAY

69

Coney Island Avenue to the Battery/BQE: Avoiding the Prospect Expressway

Coney Island Avenue runs parallel to Ocean Parkway and the southern end of the Prospect Expressway. With construction on the Prospect and Gowanus expressways, try this steady and reliable (albeit not swift) alternative.

1. Take Coney Island Avenue straight to Park Circle. Go halfway around the circle to Prospect Park Southwest. Prospect Park should be on your right.

2. Continue for about a mile and you'll come upon another circle, called Bartel Pritchard Square. Again, go halfway around onto 15th Street.

3. Take 15th Street seven blocks to Second Avenue—you'll see Hamilton Avenue ahead.

4. Follow Hamilton Avenue below the elevated Gowanus. Keep right if you want the eastbound BQE; left for the Battery Tunnel.

Sign colors mean something.
There are federal and state Manuals of Uniform Traffic Control Devices. Every state complies with them and, for the most part, every city does too. One major "rule" is that regulatory signs (that is, those signs that moving summonses can be written against) must have white backgrounds and black lettering. Other colors should be used for advisory or warning signs. If a summons is written against a color combination other than black and white, the summons may be challenged. Of course, intersection signs for stopping, "Do-not-enter", and yielding have their own distinctive color combinations.

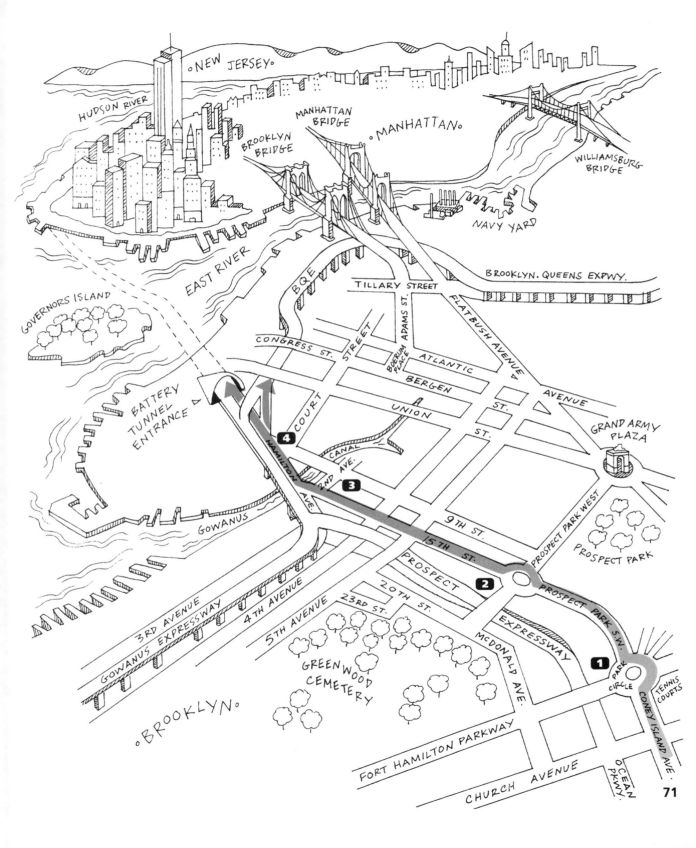

NEW JERSEY

HUDSON RIVER

MANHATTAN BRIDGE

BROOKLYN BRIDGE

MANHATTAN

WILLIAMSBURG BRIDGE

NAVY YARD

EAST RIVER

GOVERNORS ISLAND

BROOKLYN. QUEENS EXPWY.

BQE

TILLARY STREET

CONGRESS ST.

STREET

BOERUM ADAMS ST.

PLACE

ATLANTIC

AVENUE

FLATBUSH AVENUE

COURT

BERGEN

ST.

UNION

ST.

GRAND ARMY PLAZA

BATTERY TUNNEL ENTRANCE

HAMILTON AVE.

CANAL

2ND AVE.

4

3

9TH ST.

PROSPECT PARK WEST

PROSPECT PARK

GOWANUS

15TH ST.

PROSPECT

2

PROSPECT PARK S.W.

3RD AVENUE

GOWANUS EXPRESSWAY

4TH AVENUE

5TH AVENUE

23RD ST.

20TH ST.

GREENWOOD CEMETERY

EXPRESSWAY

McDONALD AVE.

PARK CIRCLE

1

CONEY ISLAND AVE.

TENNIS COURTS

BROOKLYN.

FORT HAMILTON PARKWAY

OCEAN PKWY.

CHURCH AVENUE

In Lieu of a Cross-Brooklyn Expressway: Linden Boulevard to Caton Avenue to Fort Hamilton Parkway

Once upon a time a man named Robert Moses planned a network of highways meant to crisscross Brooklyn and solve the area's traffic problems. The people of Brooklyn, still reeling from the expansion of the Gowanus and seeing the Cross-Bronx Expressway destroy the neighborhoods of that borough to the north, blocked any new highway development. Consequently, Brooklyn is poor in highways but rich in neighborhoods. Other than the BQE, there is no direct path across the borough. Here's the closest thing to a Cross-Brooklyn route:

1. If you're already on the westbound Belt Parkway in Queens and heading toward Brooklyn, hop off at Exit 17W (North Conduit Avenue).

2. Keep to your left and you'll soon be on the ramp to Linden Boulevard. Linden Boulevard crosses Kings Highway, Nostrand Avenue, Flatbush Avenue, and all major north–south routes in Brooklyn.

3. Just past Bedford Avenue, bear right (don't turn right) onto Caton Avenue.

4. In just over a mile, Caton Avenue becomes Fort Hamilton Parkway at McDonald Avenue.

5. Take Fort Hamilton Parkway just over two miles. At approximately 78th Street, bear right and cross over the expressway.

6. Once you cross the expressway, bear left and you'll see the entrance to the outbound I-278 to the Verrazano–Narrows Bridge.

Note: This route is reversible. After exiting the Verrazano–Narrows Bridge, hop off I-278 at Fort Hamilton Parkway, which will run into Caton Avenue. Caton becomes Linden Boulevard at Bedford Avenue. Linden runs into South Conduit Avenue, which you can take to the Belt, Kennedy Airport, or the Van Wyck Expressway.

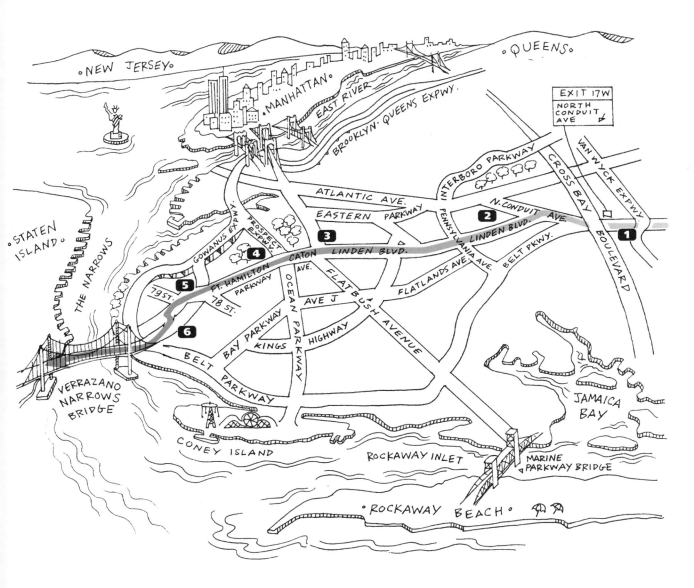

NEW JERSEY

MANHATTAN

QUEENS

STATEN ISLAND

THE NARROWS

EAST RIVER

BROOKLYN·QUEENS EXPWY.

EXIT 17W
NORTH
CONDUIT
AVE.

INTERBORO PARKWAY

CROSS BAY

VAN WYCK EXPWY.

ATLANTIC AVE.

EASTERN PARKWAY

2 N. CONDUIT AVE.

1

BOULEVARD

GOWANUS EXPWY.

PROSPECT EXPWY.

3

LINDEN BLVD.

PENNSYLVANIA AVE.

LINDEN BLVD.

BELT PKWY.

4

CATON

5

FT. HAMILTON PARKWAY

AVE.

FLATLANDS AVE.

79 ST.

78 ST.

PARKWAY

OCEAN PARKWAY

AVE J

FLATBUSH AVENUE

6

BAY PARKWAY

KINGS HIGHWAY

VERRAZANO NARROWS BRIDGE

BELT PARKWAY

CONEY ISLAND

ROCKAWAY INLET

JAMAICA BAY

MARINE PARKWAY BRIDGE

·ROCKAWAY BEACH·

73

Flatbush Avenue to the Interboro (or, Passing by the Birthplace of Gridlock Sam)

The Interboro Parkway remains one of the best-kept secrets in New York City's highway system. It's the least crowded of the three Brooklyn–Queens highway links (BQE, Belt, and Interboro).

It's no problem to find the Interboro in Queens, where it's well-connected to the Grand Central Parkway and Van Wyck Expressway. But finding it in Brooklyn can be tricky. Here's how to do it:

1. Let's say you're in Flatbush. Take Kings Highway to its very end (East 98th Street) and cross under the "el." You'll find yourself on Tapscott Street (the birthplace of Gridlock Sam).

2. Bear right onto Howard Avenue.

3. Go a few blocks to Pitkin Avenue*, turn right, and then make an immediate left onto Legion Street, followed by an immediate right onto East New York Avenue.

4. Continue for about 1/2 mile, through a tunnel. Upon exiting the tunnel (you'll now be on Jamaica Avenue), stay in the left lane.

5. After just a few blocks you'll see the entrance to the Interboro Parkway.

* The Pitkin Avenue sign has been missing for years, but you'll be able to spot this intersection by the sign on its far side, reading, East New York Avenue. Turn right at the near side of the intersection.

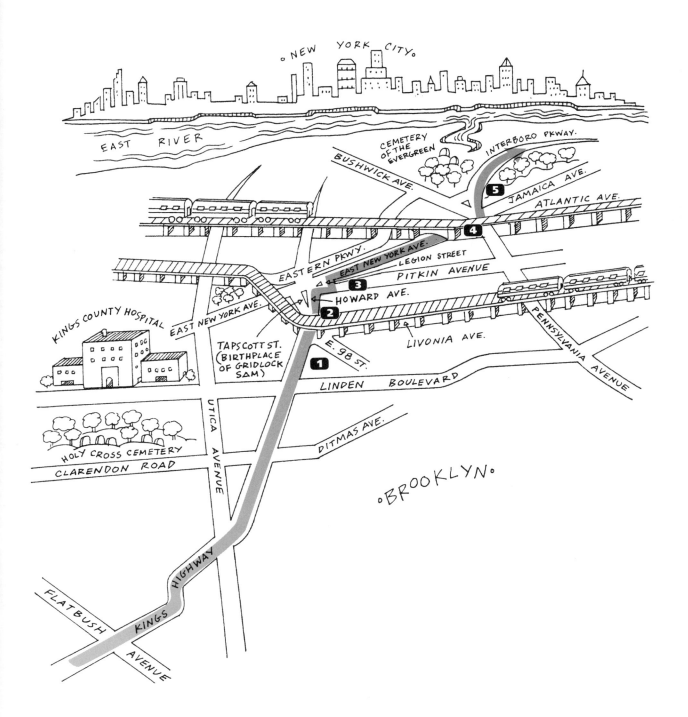

° NEW YORK CITY °

EAST RIVER

CEMETERY OF THE EVERGREEN

INTERBORO PKWAY.

BUSHWICK AVE.

JAMAICA AVE.

ATLANTIC AVE.

5

4

EASTERN PKWY.

EAST NEW YORK AVE.

LEGION STREET

PITKIN AVENUE

3

HOWARD AVE.

2

KINGS COUNTY HOSPITAL

EAST NEW YORK AVE.

LIVONIA AVE.

PENNSYLVANIA AVENUE

TAPSCOTT ST. (BIRTHPLACE OF GRIDLOCK SAM)

E. 98 ST.

1

LINDEN BOULEVARD

HOLY CROSS CEMETERY

UTICA AVENUE

DITMAS AVE.

CLARENDON ROAD

° BROOKLYN °

KINGS HIGHWAY

FLATBUSH AVENUE

Getting to Brooklyn from the Queens–Midtown Tunnel

Most people assume that if they are heading to Brooklyn from Manhattan, they must first go to lower Manhattan and then use one of the Manhattan–Brooklyn crossings. However, the drive to lower Manhattan can be torturously slow, and the lower East River crossings are no bargain, either. So why not exit Manhattan as soon as you can, via the Queens–Midtown Tunnel?

1.   Take the right lane of the Queens–Midtown Tunnel and use the farthest right toll booth (no.14).

2.   Make a sharp right at the sign marked, "Borden Ave, Jackson Ave, Pulaski Br." This will put you on Borden Avenue.

3.   Go one block and turn right into what looks like a parking lot, but is really Vernon Boulevard. Make another right at the end of the parking area onto Jackson Avenue.

4.   Go two blocks; just past 11th Street you'll see the entrance to the Pulaski Bridge on your right. The Pulaski Bridge will take you into McGuinness Boulevard in Brooklyn's Greenpoint section.

5.   Follow McGuinness Boulevard to Greenpoint Avenue and turn right. Be careful on McGuinness Boulevard—it's a speed trap. Stick to the 25 mph speed limit.

6.   Go a few blocks to Franklin Street and turn left. Franklin Street becomes Kent Avenue.

7.   Take Kent Avenue to the BQE service road, Williamsburg Street West. Follow this alongside the BQE as it runs overhead; the entrance is on the left after 1 1/2 blocks.

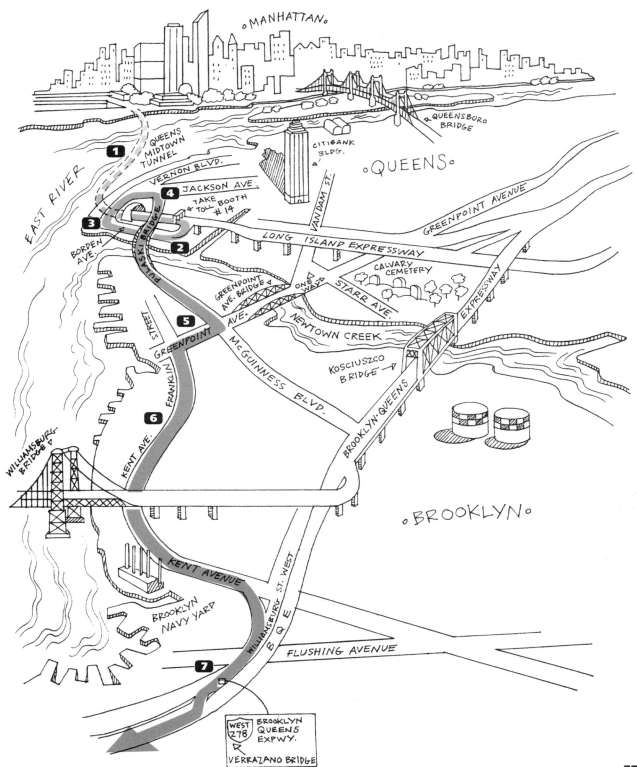

MANHATTAN

EAST RIVER

QUEENS MIDTOWN TUNNEL

1

VERNON BLVD.

JACKSON AVE. **4**

TAKE TOLL BOOTH # 14

3

BORDEN AVE.

PULASKI BRIDGE

2

QUEENSBORO BRIDGE

CITIBANK BLDG.

QUEENS

VANDAM ST.

GREENPOINT AVENUE

LONG ISLAND EXPRESSWAY

GREENPOINT AVE. BRIDGE

AVE.

ONE WAY

STARR AVE.

CALVARY CEMETERY

5

STREET

GREENPOINT

McGUINNESS BLVD.

NEWTOWN CREEK

KOSCIUSZCO BRIDGE →

BROOKLYN-QUEENS EXPRESSWAY

6

FRANKLIN

KENT AVE.

WILLIAMSBURG BRIDGE ▽

BROOKLYN

KENT AVENUE

BROOKLYN NAVY YARD

WILLIAMSBURG ST. WEST

B Q E

FLUSHING AVENUE

7

WEST 278 — BROOKLYN QUEENS EXPWY.

↙ VERRAZANO BRIDGE

The Outerbridge Crossing to the Verrazano–Narrows Bridge: Avoiding the West Shore Expressway

The West Shore Expressway is one of the few area highways built to interstate standards (i.e., wide lanes, shoulders on both sides). It is usually the fastest way to get to the Staten Island Expressway, but since it is only two lanes wide in each direction, an accident can bring the entire expressway to a standstill. You won't have to stand for it if you use the following alternate.

1. After exiting the Outerbridge Crossing in Staten Island, keep left onto the Richmond Parkway (only cars are allowed on the parkway).

2. Take the Richmond Parkway to the last exit (Richmond Avenue north, Arthur Kill Road).

3. Proceed to the second traffic signal and turn left onto Richmond Avenue.

4. Take Richmond Avenue to Victory Boulevard; bear right at the fork just before Victory, and then turn right.

5. Just before you reach the Staten Island Expressway (running overhead), follow the signs for "Staten Island Expressway, Verrazano–Narrows Bridge," and turn right onto the service road (South Gannon Avenue).

6. The entrance to the eastbound Staten Island Expressway will be on your left.

Note: This is reversible. Exit the Staten Island Expressway westbound at Richmond Avenue and take Richmond south about half a mile past the Staten Island Mall. Turn right onto Drumgoole Road, which is the service road for Richmond Parkway. Enter the parkway on your left, and follow it to the Outerbridge Crossing.

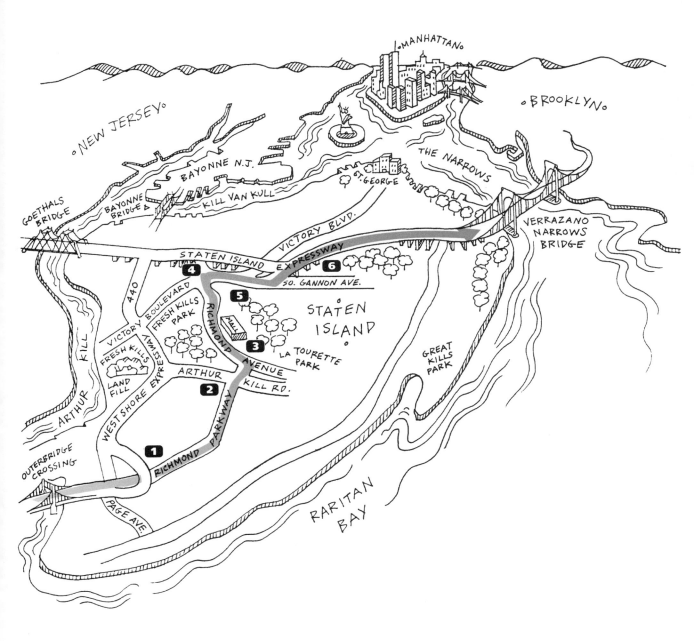

MANHATTAN

BROOKLYN

NEW JERSEY

THE NARROWS

BAYONNE N.J.

ST. GEORGE

GOETHALS BRIDGE

BAYONNE BRIDGE

KILL VAN KULL

VICTORY BLVD.

VERRAZANO NARROWS BRIDGE

STATEN ISLAND EXPRESSWAY

4

6

SO. GANNON AVE.

ARTHUR KILL

440

VICTORY BOULEVARD

FRESH KILLS PARK

5

STATEN ISLAND

RICHMOND AVENUE

MALL

3

LA TOURETTE PARK

GREAT KILLS PARK

FRESH KILLS LAND FILL

ARTHUR KILL RD.

2

WEST SHORE EXPRESSWAY

1

RICHMOND PARKWAY

OUTERBRIDGE CROSSING

PAGE AVE.

RARITAN BAY

Bypassing the Staten Island Expressway

The Staten Island Expressway is usually sluggish eastbound during the morning peak period because of the glare from the sun and the incline at Bradley Avenue. In the evening the westbound traffic is slow until the Todt Hill Road area. The following shortcuts should get you past the worst of it.

Eastbound:

1a. Exit the Staten Island Expressway at Victory Boulevard; turn left when you reach Victory Boulevard.

2a. Go under the Staten Island Expressway and continue almost three miles to Clove Road (*not* Little Clove Road) and turn right.

3a. After passing over the Staten Island Expressway turn left onto the service road.

4a. Continue on the service road (do not make the first left). You will soon see the entrance to the expressway on your left.

Westbound:

1b. After exiting the Verrazano–Narrows Bridge toll plaza, bear right but don't exit until the Hylan Boulevard exit. You will be on Narrows Road North.

2b. Take Narrows Road North about 1 1/2 miles. Just past the Clove Road intersection, take the entrance ramp on the left to the Staten Island Expressway westbound.

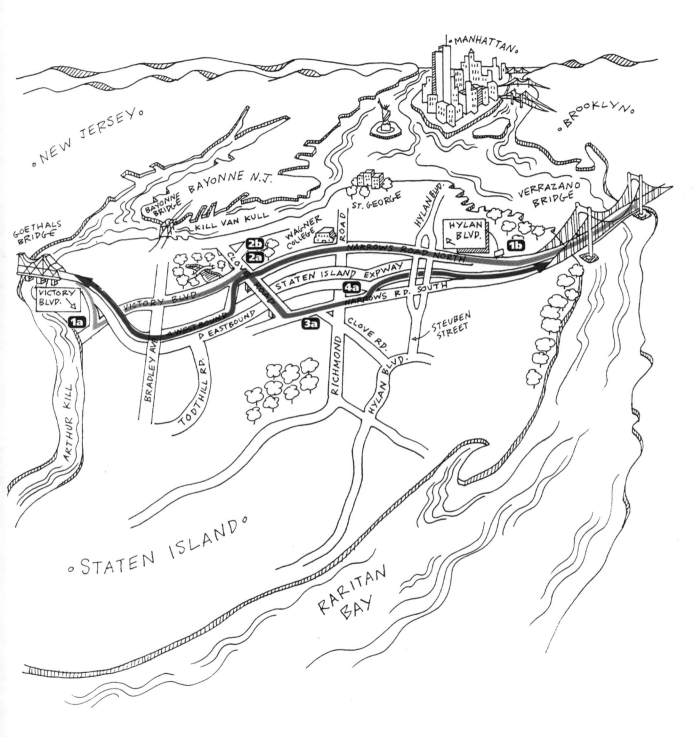

MANHATTAN

BROOKLYN

NEW JERSEY

BAYONNE N.J.

BAYONNE BRIDGE

KILL VAN KULL

VERRAZANO BRIDGE

GOETHALS BRIDGE

ST. GEORGE

HYLAN BLVD.

WAGNER COLLEGE

HYLAN R BLVD.

2b

2a

1b

NARROWS ROAD NORTH

VICTORY BLVD.

1a

CLOVE ROAD

STATEN ISLAND EXPWAY

4a

NARROWS RD. SOUTH

VICTORY BLVD.

WESTBOUND

EASTBOUND

3a

CLOVE RD.

STEUBEN STREET

ARTHUR KILL

BRADLEY AVE.

TOODTHILL RD.

RICHMOND

HYLAN BLVD.

STATEN ISLAND

RARITAN BAY

Getting to Manhattan from Queens

Queens motorists generally use one of four river crossings to get to Manhattan: the Triborough Bridge, Queensboro Bridge, and Queens–Midtown Tunnel in Queens, and the Williamsburg Bridge in Brooklyn. The Queensboro is by far the most popular river crossing, because it has a central location and no toll.

The best strategy for reaching Manhattan from Queens involves choosing a river crossing at the last possible moment. Remain flexible by heading toward 21st Street in Long Island City. All three Queens–Manhattan crossings can be reached easily from 21st Street; with a little maneuvering, the Williamsburg Bridge is accessible too.

There are numerous ways to get to 21st Street, but let's deal with a worst-case scenario: You are just blocks from the Queensboro Bridge when you learn that the lower roadway inbound has a multi-car accident. Instead of heading into the jam, stay on the service road (keep right) of Queens Plaza and go past the outer roadway of the Queensboro Bridge, as if you were going to take the upper roadway. In a few blocks you will come to 21st Street, running perpendicular to Queens Plaza. You now have four (or five, if it's between 6 and 10 AM) choices:

A. Queensboro Bridge upper roadway: Proceed across 21st Street to the north upper level to Manhattan. You will end up on 62nd or 63rd Street between First and Second avenues.

B. Queensboro Bridge reversed upper roadway: Turn left onto 21st Street, pass under the bridge, and make another left. You will be on the reversed upper roadway heading to 58th or 57th Street between First and Second avenues. This ramp is open weekdays from 6 to 10 AM.

C. Triborough Bridge: Turn right at 21st Street, go to 24th Avenue, and turn right again. At 29th Street turn right and go one block to the entrance to the Triborough Bridge.

D. Queens–Midtown Tunnel: Turn left onto 21st Street and take it to its very end. You will see signs leading to the tunnel.

E. Williamsburg Bridge: Turn left onto 21st Street and turn right at Jackson Avenue. Go over the Pulaski Bridge, take McGuinness Boulevard to Norman Avenue, and turn right. Norman becomes Wythe Avenue, which you take to South Third Street. Turn left at South Third Street. Turn right onto Roebling Street and turn right onto the bridge.

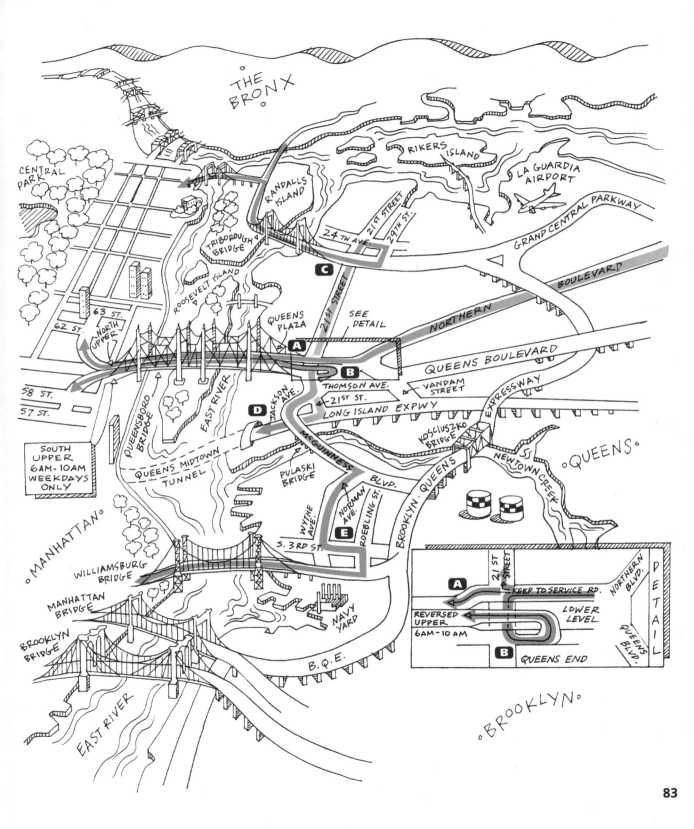

THE BRONX

CENTRAL PARK

RANDALLS ISLAND

RIKERS ISLAND

LA GUARDIA AIRPORT

GRAND CENTRAL PARKWAY

TRIBOROUGH BRIDGE

24TH AVE

21ST STREET

29TH ST.

C

63 ST.

62 ST.

NORTH UPPER

QUEENS PLAZA

21ST STREET

SEE DETAIL

NORTHERN BOULEVARD

A

QUEENS BOULEVARD

58 ST.

57 ST.

QUEENSBORO BRIDGE

ROOSEVELT ISLAND

EAST RIVER

JACKSON AVE.

B

THOMSON AVE.

VANDAM STREET

EXPRESSWAY

D

21ST ST.

LONG ISLAND EXPWY

KOSCIUSZKO BRIDGE

NEWTOWN CREEK

°QUEENS°

SOUTH UPPER 6AM-10AM WEEKDAYS ONLY

QUEENS MIDTOWN TUNNEL

McGUINNESS BLVD.

PULASKI BRIDGE

BROOKLYN-QUEENS

°MANHATTAN°

WYTHE AVE.

NORMAN AVE.

E

ROEBLING ST.

WILLIAMSBURG BRIDGE

S. 3RD ST.

MANHATTAN BRIDGE

NAVY YARD

BROOKLYN BRIDGE

B.Q.E.

EAST RIVER

DETAIL

21 ST STREET

A

KEEP TO SERVICE RD.

NORTHERN BLVD.

LOWER LEVEL

REVERSED UPPER 6AM-10AM

QUEENS BLVD.

B

QUEENS END

°BROOKLYN°

83

Bypassing Northern Boulevard in Jackson Heights

Alternative 1: Via 34th Avenue

Northern Boulevard moves reasonably well east of Flushing Meadow Park, but you could get bogged down in Jackson Heights. The good news is that there are a couple of good parallel routes—you just need to know how to find them.

1.　Take Northern Boulevard eastbound. Move into the right lane and after 54th Street, just before the "el," bear right onto Broadway.

2.　Turn left onto 60th Street.

3.　Go one short block to 34th Avenue and turn right.

To get back to Northern Boulevard:

4a.　Turn left at 111th Street.

5a.　Go one block and turn right onto Northern Boulevard.

To get to the Grand Central Parkway:

4b.　Take 34th Avenue to the end at 114th Street; you will run right into the Grand Central Parkway eastbound.

Note: This is easily reversed for travel westbound, but remember that the signals on 34th Avenue are centrally controlled by computer and are timed to favor inbound (westbound) traffic from 7 to 10 AM and outbound (eastbound) traffic from 4 to 7 PM.

*Northern Boulevard is under construction between 114th and 126th Street, until late 1993. Until then, take 34th Avenue to 108th Street, and turn left. Turn right at Astoria Boulevard, and follow the signs to Northern Boulevard.

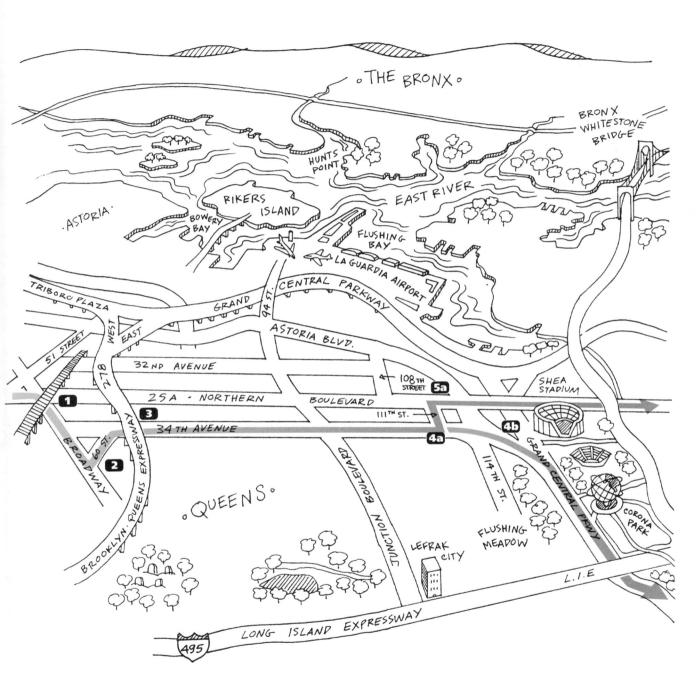

THE BRONX

BRONX WHITESTONE BRIDGE

HUNTS POINT

EAST RIVER

ASTORIA

RIKERS ISLAND

BOWERY BAY

FLUSHING BAY

LA GUARDIA AIRPORT

TRIBORO PLAZA

GRAND CENTRAL PARKWAY

94 ST.

ASTORIA BLVD.

51 STREET

WEST

EAST

278

60 ST.

32ND AVENUE

25A - NORTHERN BOULEVARD

108TH STREET

5a

SHEA STADIUM

111TH ST.

34TH AVENUE

4a

4b

BROADWAY

1

3

2

BROOKLYN QUEENS EXPRESSWAY

JUNCTION BOULEVARD

114TH ST.

GRAND CENTRAL PKWY

CORONA PARK

QUEENS

FLUSHING MEADOW

LEFRAK CITY

L.I.E

LONG ISLAND EXPRESSWAY

495

85

Bypassing Northern Boulevard in Jackson Heights

Alternative 2: Via 32nd Avenue

Another good parallel route exists via 32nd Avenue, one block to the north of Northern Boulevard. Alternative 1 on the previous page works nicely if you follow rush hour patterns—inbound in the morning, outbound in the afternoon. This is because the traffic signals on 34th Avenue are centrally controlled by computer and favor the peak direction of flow. The signals on 32nd Avenue are not centrally controlled, and so don't favor either direction. Consequently, if you are "reverse commuting," you will be better off on 32nd Avenue.

1. Take Northern Boulevard to 51st Street and turn left.

2. Go about 1 1/2 blocks and turn right onto 32nd Avenue.

3. Take 32nd Avenue to its end at 108th Street and turn left.

4. Go one block and turn right onto Astoria Boulevard. You will immediately see signs to the Grand Central Parkway and Northern Boulevard.

Note: To travel in the westbound direction, take Northern Boulevard to 108th Street and turn right. Go one block to 32nd Avenue, turn left, and reverse the above directions.

Tickets with time on the meter
You can receive a parking ticket at a meter even if you fed it and there is "time" on the meter! Alongside parking meters are signs with a time limit (i.e., 1-hour parking, 2-hour parking, 30-minute parking, etc.). Let's say you park at a 1-hour meter and come back when 55 minutes are up and put another quarter in to stay another hour. A traffic agent may come by after the first hour is up and give you a ticket for "meter feeding." You may still have more than 50 minutes left on the meter but you will get a ticket for violating the sign.

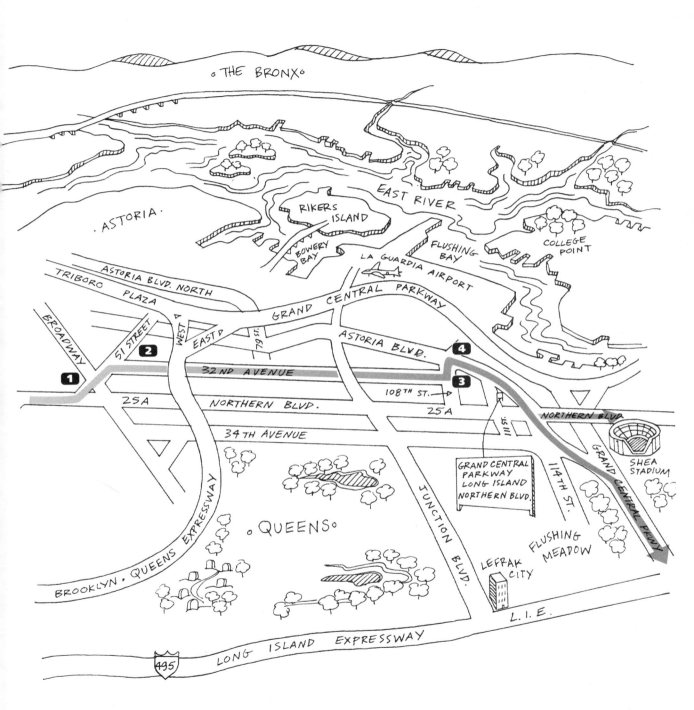

THE BRONX

ASTORIA

EAST RIVER

RIKERS ISLAND

BOWERY BAY

FLUSHING BAY

LA GUARDIA AIRPORT

COLLEGE POINT

TRIBORO PLAZA

ASTORIA BLVD. NORTH

BROADWAY

51 STREET

WEST

EAST

79 ST.

GRAND CENTRAL PARKWAY

ASTORIA BLVD.

2

1

4

3

32 ND AVENUE

108 TH ST.

25A

NORTHERN BLVD.

25A

34TH AVENUE

BROOKLYN · QUEENS EXPRESSWAY

JUNCTION BLVD.

111 ST.

GRAND CENTRAL PARKWAY LONG ISLAND NORTHERN BLVD.

NORTHERN BLVD.

GRAND CENTRAL PKWY

SHEA STADIUM

QUEENS

114TH ST.

FLUSHING MEADOW

LEFRAK CITY

L.I.E.

495

LONG ISLAND EXPRESSWAY

Bypassing the Grand Central Parkway near La Guardia Airport en Route to the Triborough Bridge

The Grand Central Parkway is often sluggish in the morning in the vicinity of the Brooklyn–Queens Expressway and La Guardia Airport. Astoria Boulevard, on the other hand, is centrally controlled by computer so that the morning traffic light pattern favors traffic in the direction of the Triborough Bridge. Astoria Boulevard is also useful during peak airport days, when traffic is at a standstill on the GCP.

1. Bear left and exit the westbound GCP at Exit 9B (Northern Boulevard West, 25A).

2. Follow the ramp onto Northern Boulevard westbound.

3. Go a few blocks to 108th Street and turn right.

4. At Astoria Boulevard turn left.

5. At 80th Street, follow Astoria Boulevard to the right and cross over the Grand Central Parkway to Astoria Boulevard North.

6. Continue on Astoria Boulevard North under the elevated train tracks at 31st Street. The entrance to the Triborough Bridge is on your left.

Note: This can be reversed by taking the first exit off the Triborough Bridge onto Hoyt Avenue. Pass under the elevated train tracks at 31st Street and follow Astoria Boulevard South to its very end at 112th Street (about four miles). There you will see signs for the GCP to Long Island, Northern Boulevard, and I-678 (the Van Wyck Expressway).

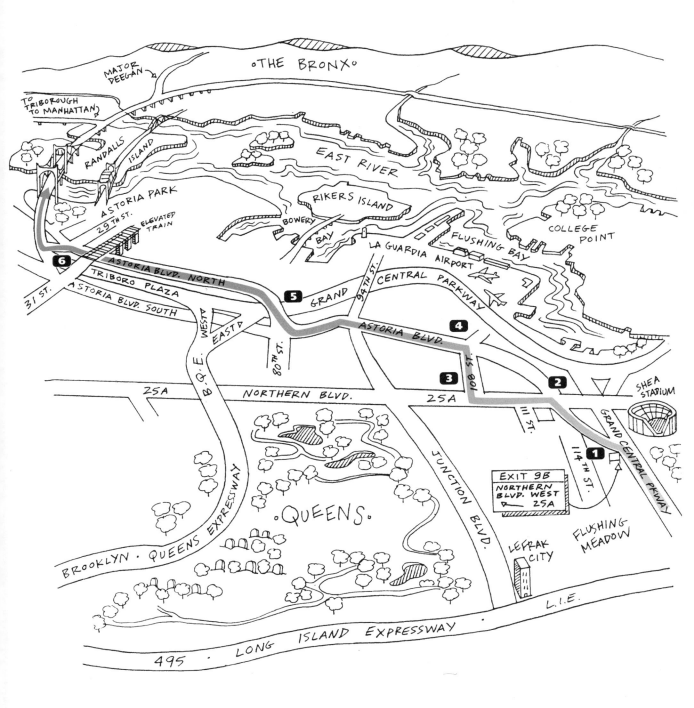

The BQE to the Bronx–Whitestone Bridge: Bypassing the Grand Central Parkway

Usually, the fastest way to get to the Bronx–Whitestone Bridge from the eastbound (due north) BQE is to take the east leg of the BQE to the eastbound Grand Central Parkway, and connect with the Whitestone Expressway and the bridge. However, since the GCP by La Guardia Airport is often sluggish, here's an easy-to-follow alternative:

1. Take the right fork of the BQE to Exit 39 (GCP east, La Guardia Airport, Astoria Blvd East).

2. Just before the GCP entrance, take the exit on your right (Marine Air Terminal, Astoria Blvd East).

3. Take Astoria Boulevard east for about two miles. At about 111th Street, bear left to the entrance to the Whitestone Expressway.

4. The Whitestone Expressway leads right onto the Bronx–Whitestone Bridge.

Note: This is especially good from 4 to 7 PM, when the traffic signals on Astoria Boulevard favor eastbound traffic.

Statute of limitations for parking tickets
The statute of limitations for a parking ticket is eight years after the summons has been entered into judgment. Since it takes months for a summons to be entered into judgment, any ticket that you receive could remain "live" into the next century.

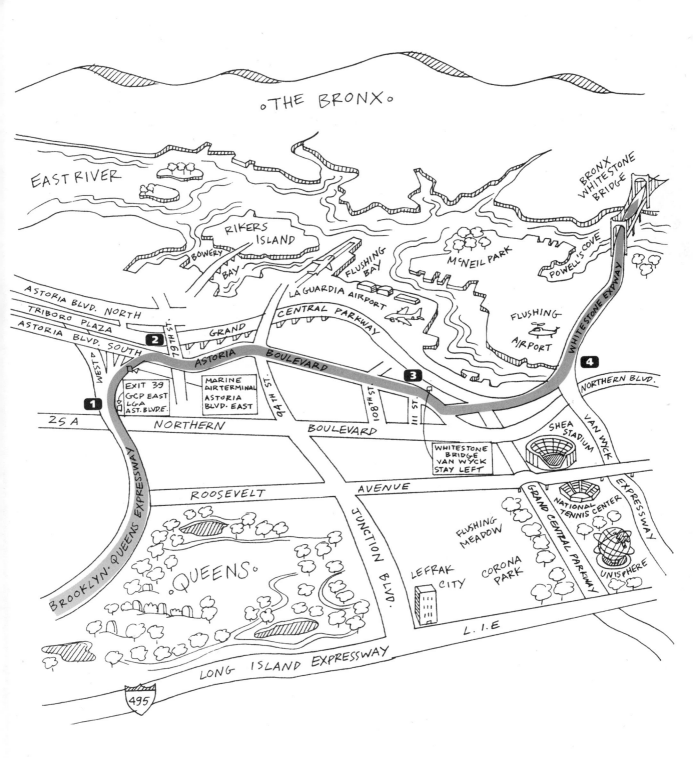

THE BRONX

EAST RIVER

RIKERS ISLAND

BOWERY BAY

FLUSHING BAY

LA GUARDIA AIRPORT

McNEIL PARK

POWELL'S COVE

BRONX WHITESTONE BRIDGE

FLUSHING AIRPORT

WHITESTONE EXPRESSWAY

ASTORIA BLVD. NORTH

TRIBORO PLAZA

ASTORIA BLVD. SOUTH

2

79TH ST.

GRAND

CENTRAL PARKWAY

ASTORIA   BOULEVARD

3

4

NORTHERN BLVD.

WEST ST.

EXIT 39
GCP EAST
LGA
AST. BLVD. E.

MARINE
AIR TERMINAL
ASTORIA
BLVD. EAST

94TH ST.

108TH ST.

111 ST.

1

25 A

NORTHERN   BOULEVARD

WHITESTONE
BRIDGE
VAN WYCK
STAY LEFT

SHEA STADIUM

VAN WYCK

ROOSEVELT   AVENUE

JUNCTION BLVD.

NATIONAL
TENNIS CENTER

GRAND CENTRAL PARKWAY

EXPRESSWAY

FLUSHING MEADOW

LEFRAK CITY

CORONA PARK

UNISPHERE

BROOKLYN · QUEENS EXPRESSWAY

·QUEENS·

L.I.E

LONG   ISLAND   EXPRESSWAY

495

The Belt Parkway Eastbound to the Van Wyck Expressway: Avoiding the Kew Gardens Knot

One of the most dreaded routes in New York City is the Belt Parkway to the Van Wyck Expressway northbound. Not only does it jam up on the Belt approaching Kennedy Airport, but once you reach the Van Wyck it is often bumper-to-bumper until the Grand Central Parkway. Here's one way to loosen the knot.

1. Take the Belt Parkway to Exit 17N (Cross Bay Boulevard North).

2. At Cross Bay Boulevard turn left. Cross Bay Boulevard becomes Woodhaven Boulevard at Rockaway Boulevard/Liberty Avenue.

3. Continue straight on Woodhaven Boulevard a few blocks past Forest Park and make a left turn at Myrtle Avenue.

4. Go straight on Myrtle Avenue for less than 1/2 mile, past the entrance for the westbound Interboro Parkway to Brooklyn. Take the next left instead, at the entrance marked "Interboro Parkway, Eastern LI."

5. The eastbound parkway leads straight to the Van Wyck Expressway northbound, or the Grand Central Parkway eastbound.

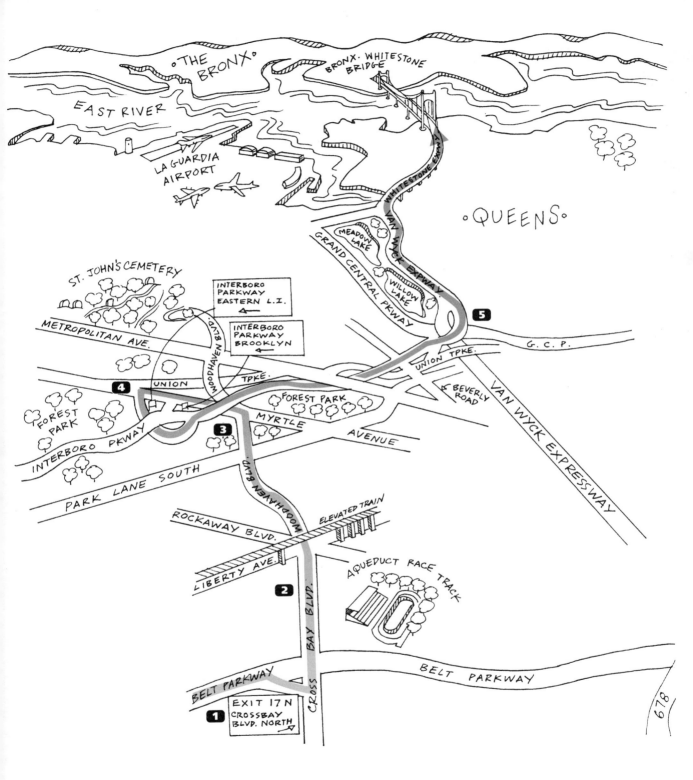

THE BRONX

BRONX · WHITESTONE BRIDGE

EAST RIVER

LA GUARDIA AIRPORT

WHITESTONE EXPWY.

VAN WYCK EXPWAY

·QUEENS·

MEADOW LAKE

WILLOW LAKE

GRAND CENTRAL PKWY.

ST. JOHN'S CEMETERY

INTERBORO PARKWAY EASTERN L.I.

INTERBORO PARKWAY BROOKLYN

METROPOLITAN AVE.

WOODHAVEN BLVD.

UNION   TPKE.

UNION TPKE.

G.C.P.

BEVERLY ROAD

5

4

FOREST PARK

FOREST PARK

MYRTLE

INTERBORO PKWAY

PARK LANE SOUTH

AVENUE

VAN WYCK EXPRESSWAY

3

WOODHAVEN BLVD.

ROCKAWAY BLVD.

ELEVATED TRAIN

LIBERTY AVE.

AQUEDUCT RACE TRACK

2

CROSS BAY BLVD.

BELT PARKWAY

BELT PARKWAY

678

1 EXIT 17 N CROSSBAY BLVD. NORTH

Whitestone Expressway to the Belt Parkway Bypass: Avoiding the Worst of the Van Wyck Expressway

If you're on the southbound Whitestone Expressway and you've got to get to the westbound Belt Parkway, you'd better either take along rations or opt for the following alternative, which I got from cabby-turned-bus-driver Neal Linden of Brooklyn.

1. Take the Whitestone into the Van Wyck southbound, but exit at Exit 8 (Union Turnpike West). Bear left and follow the signs to Union Turnpike.

2. Go west on Union Turnpike for a little less than two miles. Turn left at Woodhaven Boulevard, which becomes Cross Bay Boulevard south of Liberty Avenue.

3. Just past South Conduit Avenue, you will see the entrance to the Belt Parkway westbound and Verrazano–Narrows Bridge on your right.

Note: If you want to bypass the Belt Parkway to central Brooklyn, take Cross Bay Boulevard and turn right at Redding Street, which is just after the eastern leg of Linden Boulevard on the left and Gold Road on the right. You will see the ramp to Linden Boulevard on the left.

Most frequent technical defect on a parking summons
Parking summonses must be filled out correctly to be valid. Most people check the time, location, and violation on their parking summonses to see if they were filled incorrectly. Few people realize that for a summons to be valid, the complete car registration date must be filled out. That means that if your registration expiration date is December 23, 1994, and the officer simply notes December 1994, the summons should be dismissed. Registration defects lead the pack of technical dismissals.

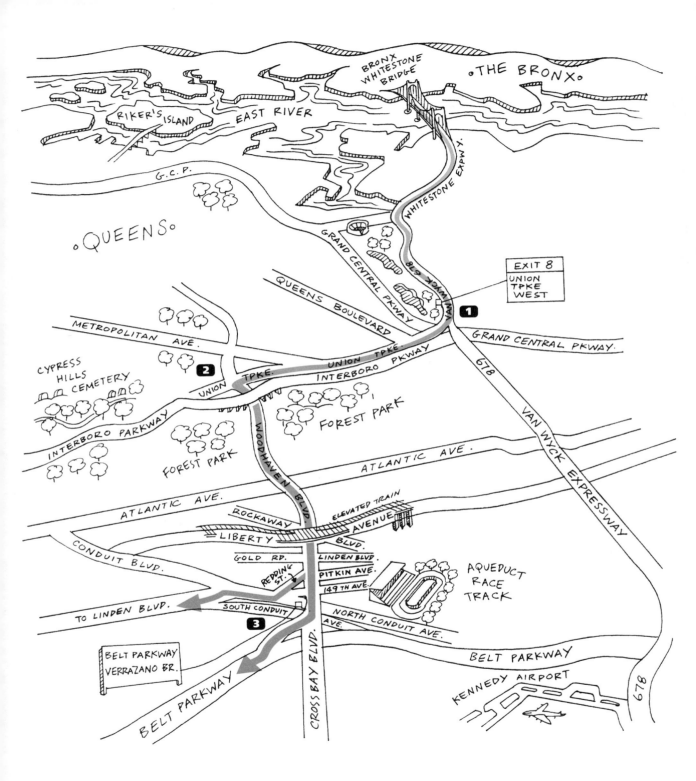

Bypassing the Long Island Expressway Westbound Between the Clearview and Van Wyck Expressways

One of New York City's top traffic engineers, Joel Friedman, shared with me his secret for getting past the daily congestion on the LIE. Freidman's Bypass avoids the molasses-like traffic jam that invariably occurs between the Clearview Expressway and Van Wyck Expressway. It also offers a nice option to Northern Boulevard.

1.   Take the LIE to Exit 28 (Oceania St., Francis Lewis Boulevard).

2.   Follow the service road for about 3/4 of a mile to 198th Street, which is one block past Francis Lewis Boulevard. Make a right turn onto 198th Street.

3.   Go one block to 58th Avenue and turn left. Follow 58th Avenue across Utopia Parkway, where it becomes Booth Memorial Avenue.

4.   Continue for a little more than two miles on Booth Memorial Avenue, which ends at College Point Boulevard.

If you want to get back on the LIE:

5a.   Turn left onto College Point Boulevard and continue about 1/3 of a mile to the westbound LIE.

If you want to get to Northern Boulevard:

5b.   Follow signs to the northbound Van Wyck Expressway, which you can take to Exit 13 (Northern Boulevard).

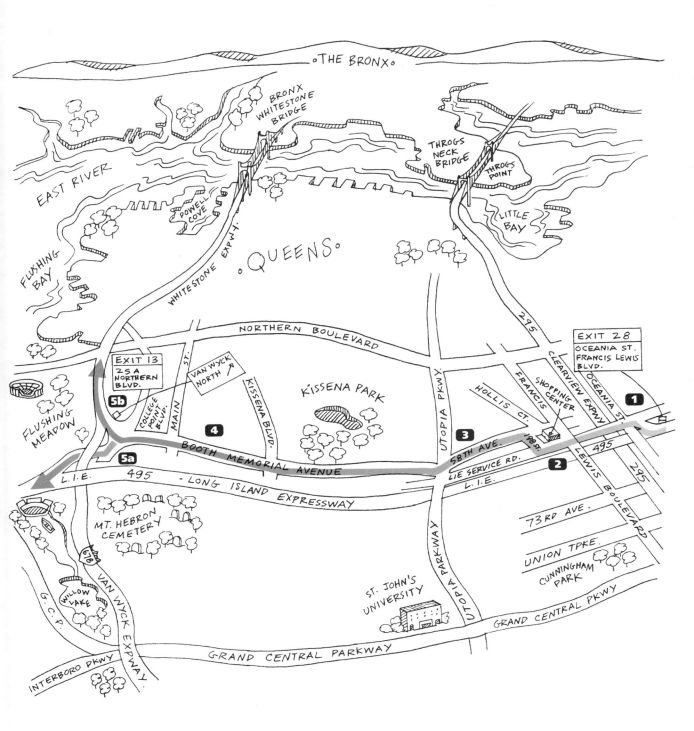

THE BRONX

BRONX WHITESTONE BRIDGE

THROGS NECK BRIDGE

THROGS POINT

EAST RIVER

POWELL COVE

LITTLE BAY

FLUSHING BAY

QUEENS

WHITESTONE EXPW'Y.

295

NORTHERN BOULEVARD

EXIT 28
OCEANIA ST.
FRANCIS LEWIS
BLVD.

EXIT 13
25 A
NORTHERN
BLVD.

VAN WYCK NORTH

KISSENA PARK

CLEARVIEW EXP'WY.

OCEANIA ST.

5b

COLLEGE POINT BLVD.

MAIN ST.

KISSENA BLVD.

UTOPIA PKWY.

HOLLIS CT.

FRANCIS

SHOPPING CENTER

1

4

3

FLUSHING MEADOW

5a

BOOTH MEMORIAL AVENUE

58TH AVE.

198 ST.

LEWIS BOULEVARD

495

L.I.E.   495   - LONG ISLAND EXPRESSWAY

LIE SERVICE RD.

L.I.E.

2

295

73RD AVE.

MT. HEBRON CEMETERY

678

UNION TPKE.

CUNNINGHAM PARK

VAN WYCK EXPWY.

WILLOW LAKE

G.C.P.

UTOPIA PARKWAY

ST. JOHN'S UNIVERSITY

GRAND CENTRAL PKWY.

INTERBORO PKWY.

GRAND CENTRAL PARKWAY

97

Westbound Grand Central Parkway to the Van Wyck Expressway to Kennedy Airport: You Can't Get There From Here

This has got to be one of the most significant missing links in our highway system. If you're on the GCP heading toward Manhattan and you want to go south on the Van Wyck to Kennedy Airport or to the Belt Parkway into Brooklyn, you'll find that it can't be done. What were those highway planners thinking when they designed this system? Here are three of the best alternatives:

Alternative 1: Via Main Street

1a. Take the Grand Central Parkway to Exit 17 (168th Street).

2a. Take the service road about 1 1/4 miles to Main Street and turn left.

3a. Bear left on Main Street. Continue for about 1/2 mile, passing under Queens Boulevard and the Van Wyck. You'll then see the entrance to the southbound Van Wyck on your left.

Alternative 2: Via Jewel Avenue (under construction until early '94)

1b. Take the Grand Central Parkway to Exit 11 (Harry Van Arsdale Boulevard eastbound, 69th Rd, Jewel Av) .

2b. At the fork, bear right onto Jewel Avenue.

3b. At the first traffic signal, make a right onto the entrance ramp to the southbound Van Wyck Expressway.

Alternative 3: Via the eastbound GCP

1c. Take the Grand Central Parkway to Exit 11 (Harry Van Arsdale Boulevard eastbound, 69th Rd, Jewel Av).

2c. At the first fork, bear left to 69th Road.

3c. At the next fork, bear right to "69 Rd West, Harry Van Arsdale Jr. Ave." Follow the loop road around to the right and cross over the GCP.

4c. Move into the left lane. Make a left turn onto the GCP service road, and at 72nd Road, enter the GCP eastbound ramp on the left.

5c. Stay in the right lanes of the GCP. Follow the signs to the Van Wyck, Kennedy Airport.

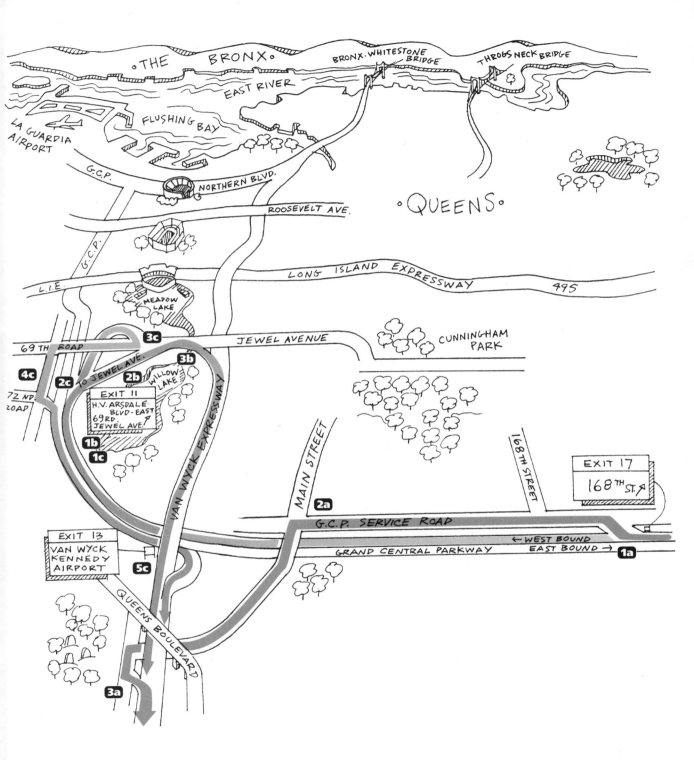

THE BRONX

EAST RIVER

BRONX WHITESTONE BRIDGE

THROGS NECK BRIDGE

LA GUARDIA AIRPORT

FLUSHING BAY

G.C.P.

NORTHERN BLVD.

QUEENS

ROOSEVELT AVE.

G.C.P.

LONG ISLAND EXPRESSWAY 495

L.I.E.

MEADOW LAKE

69TH ROAD

JEWEL AVENUE

CUNNINGHAM PARK

3c

TO JEWEL AVE.

3b

4c

2c

2b

WILLOW LAKE

72ND ROAD

EXIT 11
H.V. ARSDALE
BLVD.-EAST
69 RD.
JEWEL AVE.

1b

1c

VAN WYCK EXPRESSWAY

MAIN STREET

168TH STREET

EXIT 17
168TH ST.↗

2a

G.C.P. SERVICE ROAD

EXIT 13
VAN WYCK
KENNEDY
AIRPORT

5c

←WEST BOUND
EAST BOUND →

GRAND CENTRAL PARKWAY

1a

QUEENS BOULEVARD

3a

From Brooklyn to Queens: Getting to the Kosciuszko Bridge Eastbound

Alternative 1: Via Meeker Avenue

The Kosciuszko Bridge (pronounced Kosh-Koosh-Ko by the Polish community and Koss-Key-Oss-Ko by most New Yorkers) is affectionately called the "Koz" by traffic professionals. The bridge, which passes over Newtown Creek to connect Brooklyn with Queens, is a slippery, concrete-filled, steel-grated bridge. During wet weather accidents abound, and even during dry weather poor traction contributes to a very high accident rate. There is often a long line of cars waiting to cross the Koz, which you can bypass using the following route.

This is an alternative for those who like to keep the highway in sight. It is a very clear and straightforward detour, but it is also one of the better-known detours and doesn't get you past the "Koz." It is a meek detour not only because it uses Meeker Avenue but because it is not terribly daring.

1. Hop off the BQE at Exit 32 (Metropolitan Av, Williamsburg Bridge).

2. From the exit ramp continue under the BQE. You will be on Meeker Avenue.

3. Follow Meeker Avenue until you see the entrance to the BQE on your left, at the Brooklyn end of the Kosciuszko Bridge.

Why is the northbound BQE referred to as eastbound?
The BQE runs from the Verrazano–Narrows Bridge at its southern end (those in the know call it the Gowanus Expressway south of the Battery Tunnel) to the Grand Central Parkway at its northern end. Essentially, it runs north–south through Brooklyn and Queens, but since it's part of the interstate highway system, it is marked according to federal rules. A three-digit number indicates a "spur" off an interstate with the same last two digits. In this case, I-278, the BQE, is a spur off I-78, which runs east–west through New Jersey. If the roadway runs east–west, then the last digit is even. The feds are very rigid about these rules, so even if part of an even-numbered interstate system runs north–south, it will always be marked east–west. On the BQE, just remember the acronym NEWS—north is east and west is south.

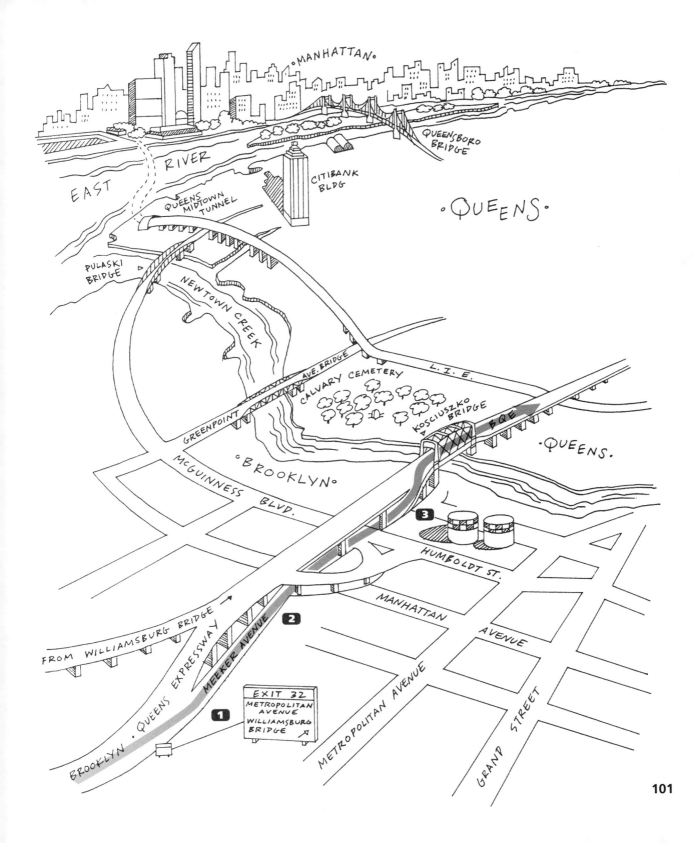

MANHATTAN

QUEENSBORO BRIDGE

EAST RIVER

QUEENS MIDTOWN TUNNEL

CITIBANK BLDG

°QUEENS°

PULASKI BRIDGE

NEWTOWN CREEK

AVE. BRIDGE

CALVARY CEMETERY

L.I.E.

KOSCIUSZKO BRIDGE

BQE

GREENPOINT

°BROOKLYN°

°QUEENS°

McGUINNESS BLVD.

3

HUMBOLDT ST.

MANHATTAN

AVENUE

FROM WILLIAMSBURG BRIDGE →

BROOKLYN · QUEENS EXPRESSWAY

MEEKER AVENUE

2

1

EXIT 32
METROPOLITAN AVENUE
WILLIAMSBURG BRIDGE ↗

METROPOLITAN AVENUE

GRAND STREET

From Brooklyn to Queens:
Avoiding the Kosciuszko Bridge

Alternative 2: Via Greenpoint Avenue

When the BQE is crawling and it's clear that the problem is way up at the Kosciuszko Bridge (which happens probably half the time), it's time for a super alternate route.

1. Hop off the BQE at Exit 30 (Flushing Avenue), go 1 1/2 blocks to Kent Avenue, and turn left. You'll notice that nearly everyone then makes an immediate right to continue alongside the BQE; ignore them.

2. Continue straight under the BQE on Kent Avenue, a wide, fast-moving street. Follow Kent under the Williamsburg Bridge.

3. About a mile past the Williamsburg Bridge, the road bends to the left and becomes Franklin Street.

4. Go another few blocks to Greenpoint Avenue and turn right. In 3/4 of a mile you'll cross the Greenpoint Avenue Bridge.

5. At the Queens end of the bridge, bear right to ride alongside First Calvary Cemetery.

6. At the end of the cemetery, a sign on the right reads, "I-495 L.I. Expwy, west (arrow pointing ahead,) east (arrow pointing to the right)." Turn right onto Borden Avenue, the Long Island Expressway's service road.

7. Follow the overhead signs marked "Bklyn Qns Expwy, La Guardia Airport." Once back on the BQE, you'll be north of both the Koz and the LIE.

The worst stretches of the BQE
All of the BQE is pretty slow, but there are two stretches that are almost always crawling: the Kosciuszko Bridge and the "trench," a stretch of road that dips below street level in downtown Brooklyn.

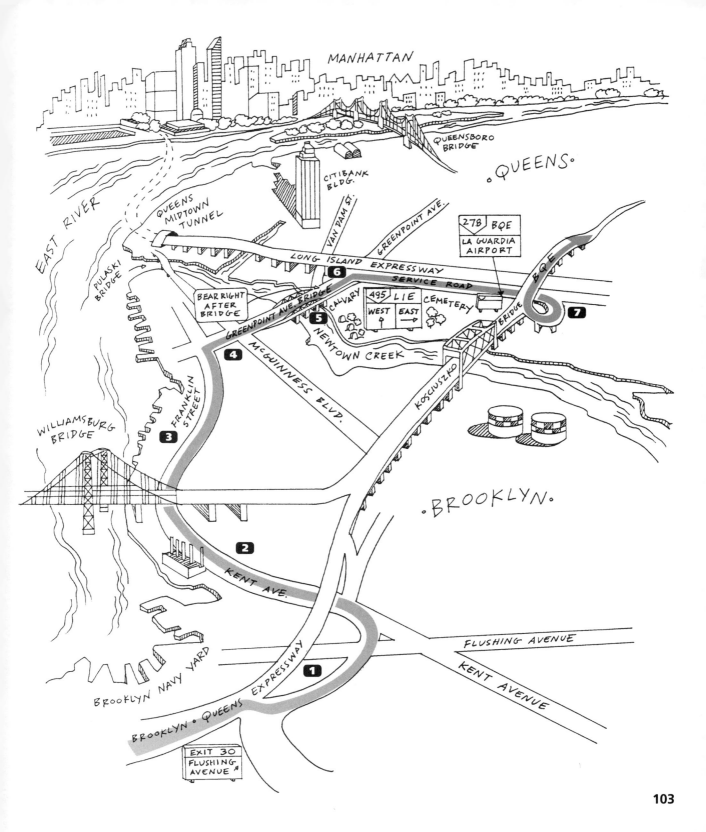

MANHATTAN

QUEENS

EAST RIVER

QUEENSBORO BRIDGE

CITIBANK BLDG.

QUEENS MIDTOWN TUNNEL

VAN DAM ST.

GREENPOINT AVE.

278 BQE
LA GUARDIA AIRPORT

LONG ISLAND EXPRESSWAY

SERVICE ROAD

PULASKI BRIDGE

BEAR RIGHT AFTER BRIDGE

GREENPOINT AVE BRIDGE

CALVARY

495 LIE
WEST | EAST

CEMETERY

BQE

6

5

7

4

McGUINNESS BLVD.

NEWTOWN CREEK

KOSCIUSZKO BRIDGE

FRANKLIN STREET

3

WILLIAMSBURG BRIDGE

BROOKLYN.

2

KENT AVE.

BROOKLYN NAVY YARD

FLUSHING AVENUE

KENT AVENUE

1

BROOKLYN · QUEENS EXPRESSWAY

EXIT 30
FLUSHING AVENUE

From Brooklyn to Queens: Avoiding the Kosciuszko Bridge Eastbound

Alternative 3: The Williamsburg Bridge to the LIE

The route leading from the Williamsburg Bridge to the Queensbound BQE is a nightmare on a Friday afternoon. In fact, it's a nightmare whenever there's a problem at the Kosciuszko Bridge (which is just about daily). I can't guarantee that this shortcut will be a daydream, but at least it will keep you moving.

1. When leaving Manhattan, take the outer roadway of the Williamsburg Bridge and make a sharp right when you reach Brooklyn.

2. Make another right at the first intersection onto Broadway.

3. Bear right just past Driggs Avenue and make the next right onto Bedford Avenue.

4. Take Bedford Avenue for less than a mile and you'll pass through McCarren Park. At the end of the park there will be a fork in the road. The right fork will take you to McGuinness Boulevard via Nassau Avenue, but I prefer the left fork, which goes just one block and ends at Manhattan Avenue. Turn left onto Manhattan Avenue; it's a bit slow, but it is a nice shopping street in the Greenpoint area.

5. Go a few blocks on Manhattan Avenue to Greenpoint Avenue and turn right.

6. Take Greenpoint Avenue over the Greenpoint Avenue Bridge and bear right.

7. Once you pass Calvary Cemetery on the right, turn right onto Borden Avenue, the service road for the LIE eastbound. At that point you'll see signs for the LIE eastbound and the BQE eastbound.

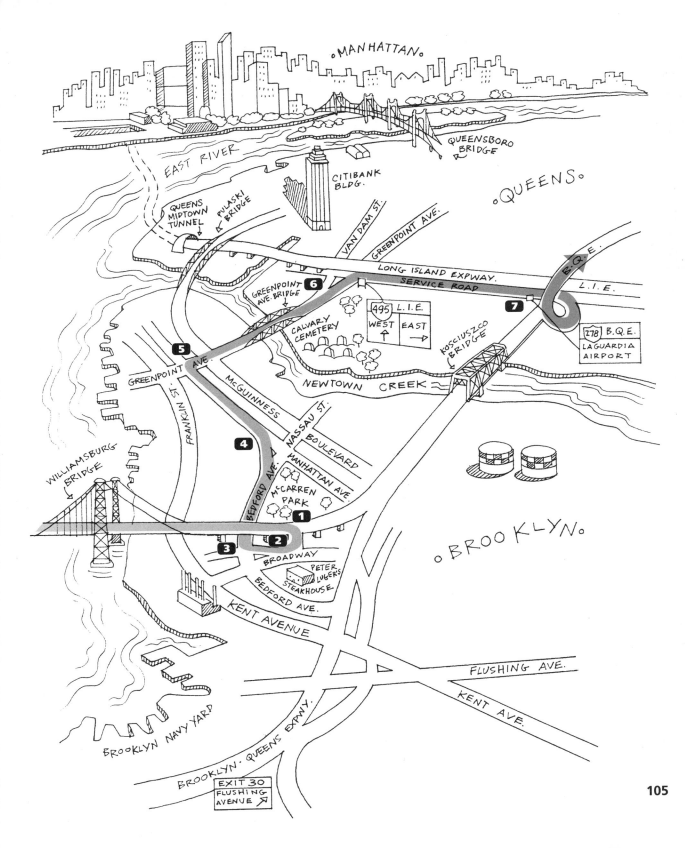

From Queens to Brooklyn:
Avoiding the Kosciuszko Bridge

Westbound traffic on the BQE is often slow all the way from the LIE to the Williamsburg Bridge. Consequently, it's best to exit the BQE before this point, and only return farther south (west).

1. After you pass the Roosevelt Avenue exit on the BQE, move into the right lane and prepare to exit at the LIE westbound.

2. Take Exit 35 (LI Expwy, Greenpoint Av, Midtown Tun), but don't get on the LIE. Instead, keep to the right on the service road and at the fork take the ramp marked "Greenpoint Avenue."

3. At Greenpoint Avenue turn left under the expressway.

4. Take Greenpoint Avenue to the "Do not enter" sign at Starr Avenue, and turn right.

5. Make an immediate left onto Van Dam Street; you'll be facing the Greenpoint Avenue Bridge.

6. Cross the bridge and continue on Greenpoint Avenue for about 3/4 of a mile to Franklin Street.

7. At Franklin Street, turn left; in just a few blocks Franklin becomes Kent Avenue.

8. In about a mile you'll pass under the Williamsburg Bridge. Continue for another 1/2-mile alongside the Brooklyn Navy Yard to the elevated BQE.

9. Turn right just before the BQE onto the service road, Williamsburg Street West, and go one block. The entrance ramp to the westbound BQE will be on your left.

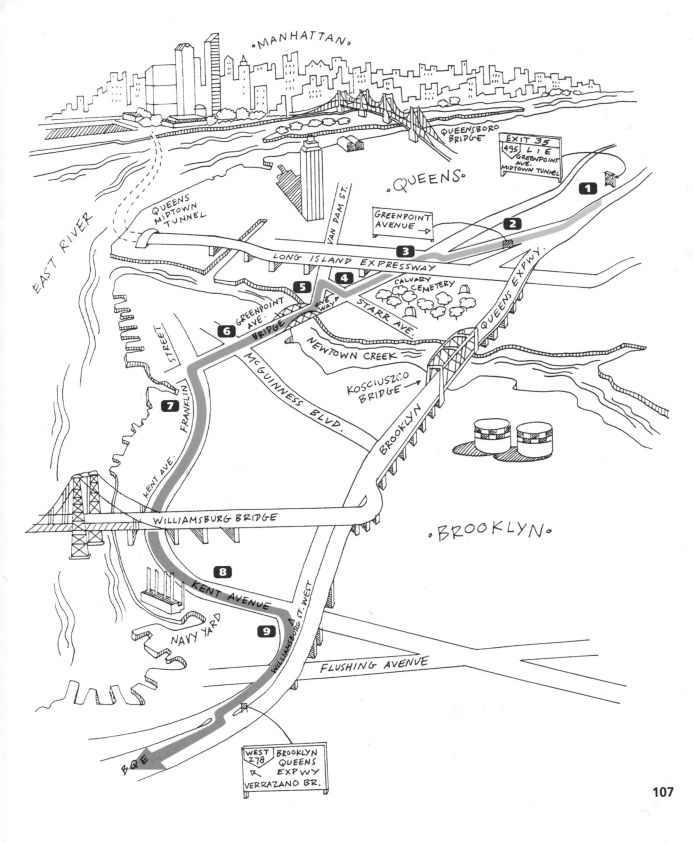

Avoiding the BQE "Trench" Westbound

Alternative 1:
Flatbush Avenue to the Prospect Expressway
via Fourth Avenue

The label "trench" really fits: The section of the BQE from Atlantic Avenue to Rapelye Street is well below ground level and speeds are well below walking speeds. There is often a traffic jam along this section for 18–20 hours a day. The state spent $45 million just a few years ago to widen the westbound roadway, but that did little good since construction on the Gowanus further narrowed the roadway downstream. In general, the BQE should be avoided in both directions from the Battery Tunnel to the Brooklyn Bridge.

To circumvent the westbound BQE, it's best to visualize the BQE into the Gowanus as the letter "L." The westbound (southbound) portion of the BQE is the vertical part of the "L" and the Gowanus from the Battery Tunnel to the Prospect Expressway is the horizontal portion. The trick is to find alternate ways to connect the top of the "L" with the right end of the horizontal portion.

1. Take BQE Exit 29 (Tillary Street, Manhattan Bridge, Brooklyn Civic Ctr). Move into one of the two left-most lanes once you're on Tillary Street.

2. Go two blocks to Flatbush Avenue and turn left. Lots of people avoid Flatbush Avenue because of its reputation as a sluggish street, but in Downtown Brooklyn it has been rebuilt and moves reasonably well.

3. Continue south on Flatbush Avenue past the Brooklyn Academy of Music on the left. At the Williamsburg Savings Bank (the tallest building in Brooklyn, on the left) make a right turn onto Fourth Avenue. Take Fourth Avenue a little more than a mile, passing under the Prospect Expressway.

4. Make a left turn onto 17th Street. Within 100 feet you'll see the ramp to the Prospect Expressway on your left.

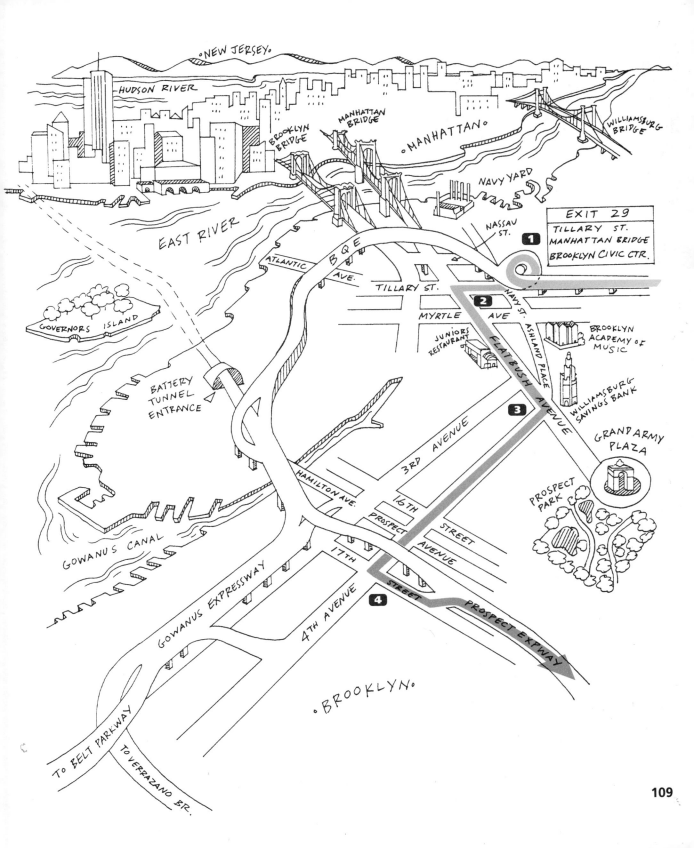

NEW JERSEY

HUDSON RIVER

MANHATTAN BRIDGE

WILLIAMSBURG BRIDGE

BROOKLYN BRIDGE

MANHATTAN

NAVY YARD

EAST RIVER

ATLANTIC AVE.

B Q E

NASSAU ST.

1

EXIT 29
TILLARY ST.
MANHATTAN BRIDGE
BROOKLYN CIVIC CTR.

TILLARY ST.

2

NAVY ST.

MYRTLE AVE

ASHLAND PLACE

BROOKLYN ACADEMY OF MUSIC

JUNIORS RESTAURANT

GOVERNORS ISLAND

BATTERY TUNNEL ENTRANCE

FLATBUSH AVENUE

WILLIAMSBURG SAVINGS BANK

3

3RD AVENUE

GRAND ARMY PLAZA

HAMILTON AVE.

16TH STREET

PROSPECT AVENUE

PROSPECT PARK

GOWANUS CANAL

17TH STREET

4

4TH AVENUE

GOWANUS EXPRESSWAY

PROSPECT EXPWAY

BROOKLYN

TO BELT PARKWAY

TO VERRAZANO BR.

109

Avoiding the BQE "Trench" Westbound

Alternative 2:
Flatbush Avenue to the Gowanus via Third Avenue

Third Avenue, unlike Fourth Avenue, appears to be a minor street where it intersects Flatbush Avenue. But, like Fourth, its traffic signals are centrally controlled by computer and offers better connections to the Belt Parkway and Gowanus Expressway.

1. Hop off the BQE at Exit 29 (Tillary Street, Manhattan Bridge, Brooklyn Civic Ctr). Move into one of the two left-most lanes once you're on Tillary Street.

2. Go two blocks to Flatbush Avenue and turn left. Take Flatbush Avenue about a mile.

3. Just before the Williamsburg Savings Bank Building, veer to the right onto Third Avenue and follow this for about 1 1/2 miles.

4. Just past 16th Street, and just before passing under the elevated Prospect Expressway, you'll see a narrow ramp on your right marked "Brooklyn Queens Expressway, Verrazano Bridge." Take that ramp and you'll find yourself in the left lane of the outbound Gowanus.

Alternative 3: Third Avenue to Bay Ridge

The ramp to the outbound Gowanus is in pretty poor condition and is occasionally closed for repairs. If this is the case, don't fret; the Third Avenue alternative is nearly as good.

3a. Just before the Williamsburg Savings Bank Building on Flatbush Avenue, veer off to the right onto Third Avenue. Continue on Third Avenue past 16th Street and you'll be riding directly below the Gowanus Expressway.

4a. In a little more than two miles, at approximately 60th Street, the road splits: The right lanes lead to Third Avenue, the center lanes to the outbound Gowanus and the Verrazano–Narrows Bridge, and the left lane to Fourth Avenue, which will take you to the Belt Parkway eastbound.

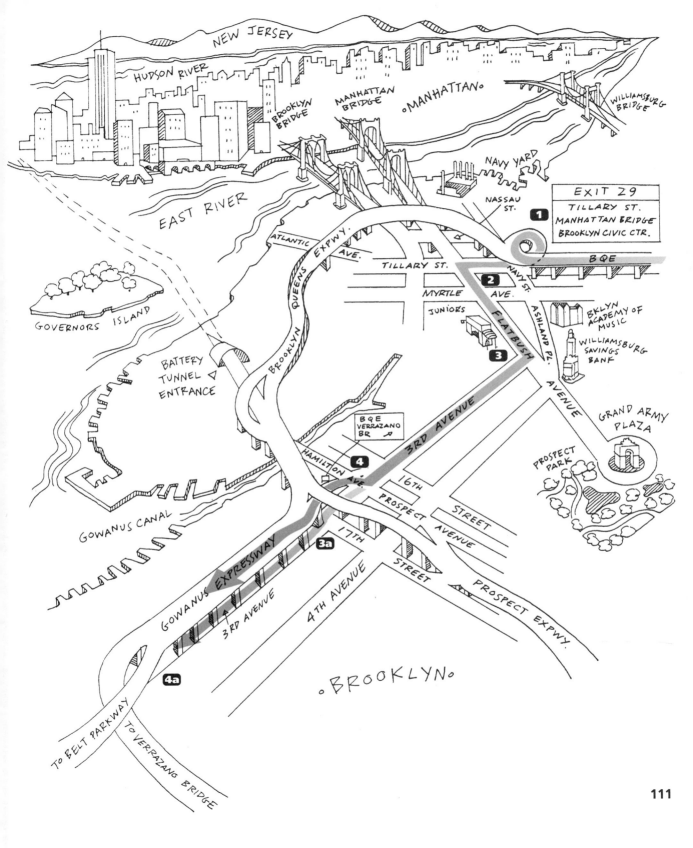

NEW JERSEY

HUDSON RIVER

BROOKLYN BRIDGE

MANHATTAN BRIDGE

MANHATTAN

WILLIAMSBURG BRIDGE

NAVY YARD

EAST RIVER

NASSAU ST.

EXIT 29
TILLARY ST.
MANHATTAN BRIDGE
BROOKLYN CIVIC CTR.

1

BQE

ATLANTIC AVE.

TILLARY ST.

2

NAVY ST.

MYRTLE AVE.

ASHLAND PL.

BKLYN ACADEMY OF MUSIC

JUNIORS

BROOKLYN QUEENS EXPWY.

3

FLATBUSH AVE.

WILLIAMSBURG SAVINGS BANK

GOVERNORS ISLAND

BATTERY TUNNEL ENTRANCE

BQE VERRAZANO BR.

3RD AVENUE

AVENUE

GRAND ARMY PLAZA

4

HAMILTON AVE.

16TH STREET

PROSPECT PARK

GOWANUS CANAL

3a

17TH STREET

PROSPECT AVENUE

GOWANUS EXPRESSWAY

3RD AVENUE

4TH AVENUE

STREET

PROSPECT EXPWY.

4a

BROOKLYN

TO BELT PARKWAY

TO VERRAZANO BRIDGE

Avoiding The BQE "Trench" Westbound

Alternative 4: Staying under the Highway

Many people don't like to lose sight of the highway they are detouring from for fear that they will get lost. Here's an alternate that keeps the BQE and Gowanus in full view.

1. Take the westbound BQE to Exit 28 (Cadman Plaza West, Brooklyn Bridge).

2. Turn right at the end of the exit ramp onto Old Fulton Street. Follow this for two blocks and, just before reaching the water, turn left onto Furman Street, beneath the BQE in Brooklyn Heights.

3. Take Furman Street to its end; make a left and then an immediate right onto Columbia Street.

4. Just before Columbia Street ends, turn right onto Woodhull Street.

5. Cross over the Battery Tunnel Plaza and turn left onto Hamilton Avenue. At this point you can get on the Gowanus by making an unusual left turn through an opening in a fence just past the toll booths. DO NOT take the ramp on the left signed "BQE eastbound, Atlantic Avenue"; go to the left of that ramp.

Note: Sometimes a TBTA patrol car blocks the entrance to the Gowanus, so you'll be forced to stay on Hamilton Avenue. Here's what to do:

If you're heading to the Prospect Expressway:

5a. Take Hamilton Avenue 4/10 of a mile past the Hamilton Avenue Bridge to 17th Street and turn left. (This route is poorly marked. After the Hamilton Avenue Bridge keep to the left lane. Just past the sign on your right for "Strober Brothers" and just before "Bruno's Truck Sales," turn left under the highway onto 17th Street.) In 1 1/2 blocks you'll see the entrance to the Prospect Expressway on your left.

If you're heading to the Verrazano–Narrows Bridge or Belt Parkway:

5b. Stay on Hamilton Avenue to Third Avenue. At approximately 60th Street, the road divides: The right lanes lead to Third Avenue, the center lanes to the outbound Gowanus and the Verrazano–Narrows Bridge, and the left lane to Fourth Avenue, which will take you to the Belt Parkway eastbound.

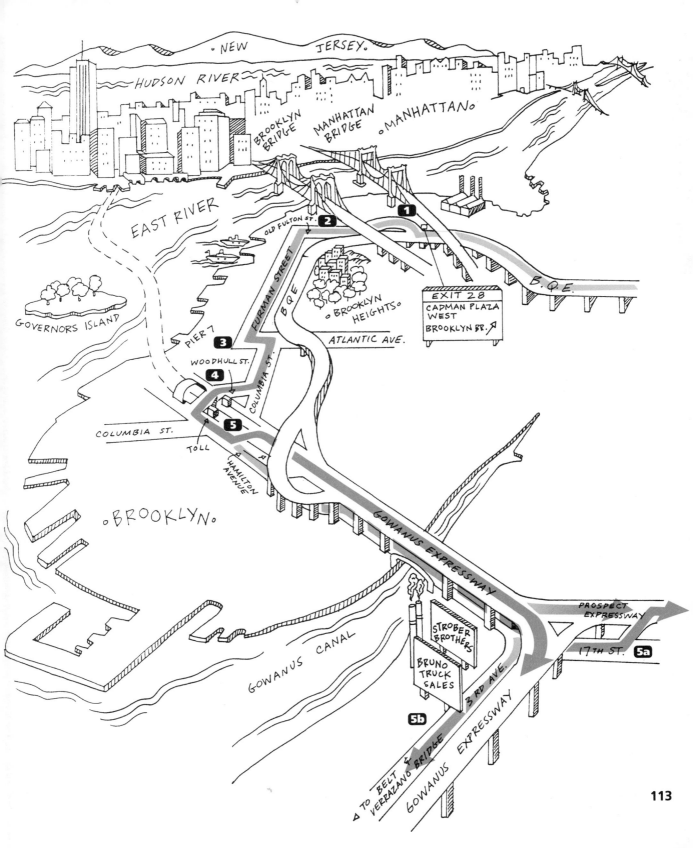

NEW JERSEY

HUDSON RIVER

BROOKLYN BRIDGE

MANHATTAN BRIDGE

MANHATTAN

EAST RIVER

OLD FULTON ST.

FURMAN STREET

B.Q.E.

B Q E

BROOKLYN HEIGHTS

ATLANTIC AVE.

EXIT 28
CADMAN PLAZA
WEST
BROOKLYN BR.

GOVERNORS ISLAND

PIER 7

WOODHULL ST.

COLUMBIA ST.

COLUMBIA ST.

TOLL

HAMILTON AVENUE

BROOKLYN

GOWANUS EXPRESSWAY

GOWANUS CANAL

STROBER BROTHERS

BRUNO TRUCK SALES

PROSPECT EXPRESSWAY

17TH ST.

3 RD AVE.

TO BELT &
VERRAZANO BRIDGE

GOWANUS EXPRESSWAY

1 **2** **3** **4** **5** **5a** **5b**

Avoiding the BQE "Trench" Westbound

Alternative 5:
BQE to Ocean Parkway via Vanderbilt Avenue

The expressways are so unpredictable that I generally try to avoid them altogether. Here's one of my favorite alternatives, though I recommend that only more adventurous drivers try it.

1. Leave the BQE westbound at Exit 30 (Flushing Avenue). Stay on the service road as it curves around to the right. You'll be on Park Avenue just below the expressway.

2. After a few blocks, move to the left lane and turn left onto Vanderbilt Avenue. Vanderbilt Avenue ends in 1 1/4 miles at the circle at Grand Army Plaza.

3. At the Grand Army Plaza circle stay in the fourth lane from the left on the seven-lane roadway. Keep the solid white line on the pavement just to your right; it will lead you into Prospect Park.

4. Take the Park Drive 1 1/2 miles to the Ocean Parkway/Coney Island Avenue exit.

5. On exiting the park, take the ramp to Ocean Parkway. This ramp will bring you to the southern end of the Prospect Expressway at the intersection of Ocean Parkway and Church Avenue.

Note: Prospect Park is closed to cars on weekends year-round and during off-peak weekday hours in the spring, summer, and early fall (see Central Park, pages 4–5, for closing times). At these times, use the following alternate:

When passing through Grand Army Plaza, bear right (but not far right) and take Prospect Park West along the right side of the park. Follow this for 1 3/4 miles, just past 14th Street, to the traffic circle at Bartel Pritchard Square. Follow the circle 3/4 of the way around (the equivalent of a left turn) the circle, and you will still be on the right side of the park on Prospect Park Southwest. In another mile you'll come to another circle, Park Circle, where you'll see a wide ramp on the right. Follow the signs to Ocean Parkway.

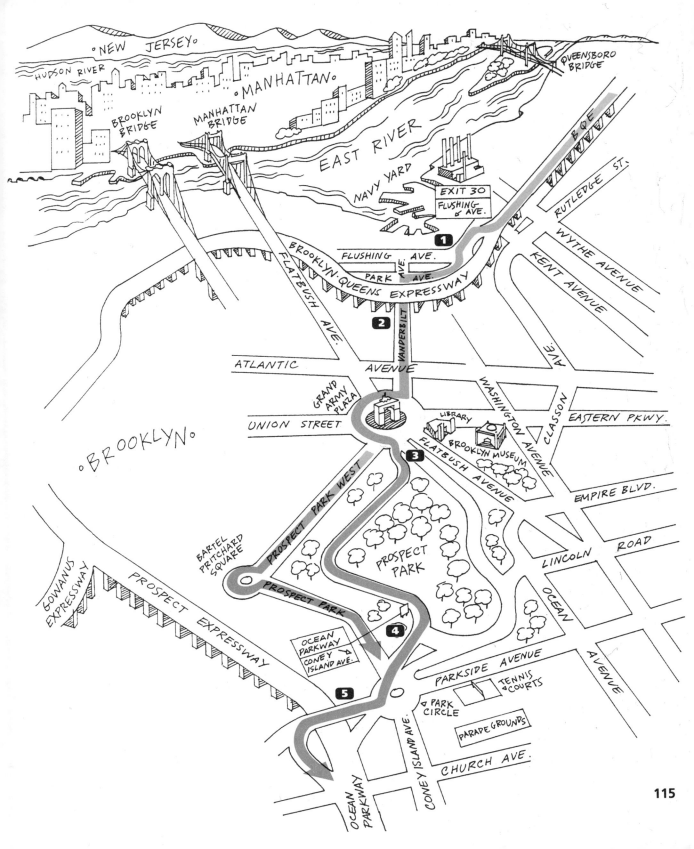

Avoiding the BQE "Trench" Eastbound

Alternative 1:
Hicks Street to Atlantic Avenue to Boerum Place

Much of the eastbound (northbound) traffic on the Gowanus Expressway that enters the BQE north of the Battery Tunnel is headed to Manhattan via the Brooklyn or Manhattan bridges. Consequently, our eastbound strategies focus on getting to the bridges.

1.   Stay in the far right lane of the Gowanus Expressway and exit at Hamilton Avenue, about 4/10 mile after you pass the Prospect Expressway exit.

2.   Move over to the right lane on Hamilton Avenue and turn right onto Hicks Street, which runs at street level alongside the BQE's "trench."

3.   Take Hicks Street to Atlantic Avenue and turn right.

4.   After a few blocks, turn left onto Boerum Place (you'll see the Brooklyn House of Detention on the far left side of the intersection). Boerum is a very wide, two-way street that becomes Adams Street at its intersection with Fulton Street.

If you're heading to the Brooklyn Bridge:

5a.   Continue on Adams Street to the Brooklyn Bridge.

If you're heading to the Manhattan Bridge:

5b.   Take the Adams Street service road and turn right onto Tillary Street. Bear left after turning onto Tillary Street, then turn left onto Flatbush Avenue. This is the approach road to the Manhattan Bridge.

If you're heading to the BQE eastbound toward Queens:

5c.   From the service road of Adams Street turn right onto Tillary Street. Cross Flatbush Avenue, then bear left; the ramp to the eastbound BQE will be on the left.

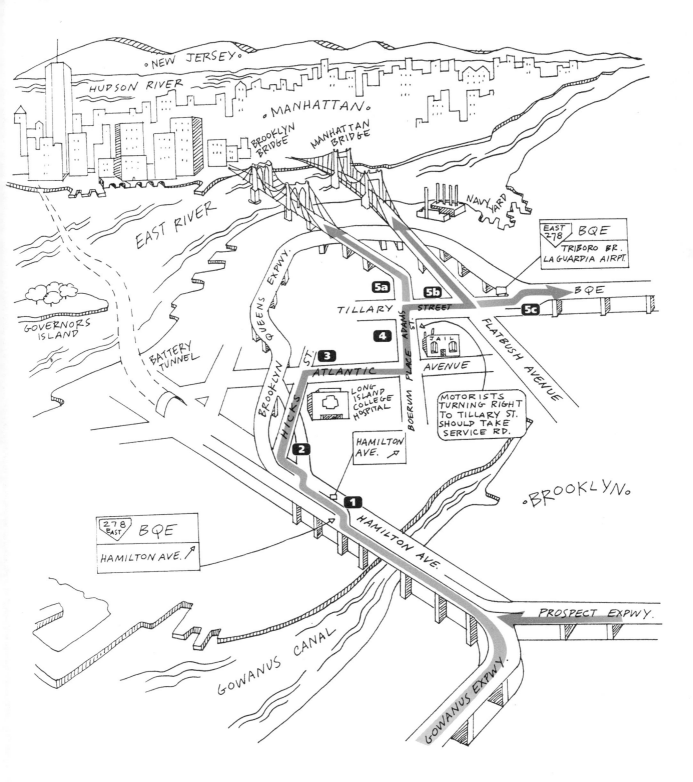

NEW JERSEY

HUDSON RIVER

MANHATTAN

BROOKLYN BRIDGE

MANHATTAN BRIDGE

NAVY YARD

EAST RIVER

GOVERNORS ISLAND

BATTERY TUNNEL

QUEENS EXPWY.

BROOKLYN ST.

HICKS

TILLARY STREET

ATLANTIC

BOERUM PLACE

ADAMS ST.

JAIL

AVENUE

FLATBUSH AVENUE

EAST 278 BQE

TRIBORO BR.
LA GUARDIA AIRPT.

5a

5b

5c

BQE

4

3

LONG ISLAND COLLEGE HOSPITAL

MOTORISTS TURNING RIGHT TO TILLARY ST. SHOULD TAKE SERVICE RD.

BROOKLYN

HAMILTON AVE. →

2

1

HAMILTON AVE.

278 EAST BQE

HAMILTON AVE. ↗

PROSPECT EXPWY.

GOWANUS CANAL

GOWANUS EXPWY.

Avoiding the BQE "Trench" Eastbound

Alternative 2: Via Fourth Avenue

Fourth Avenue is one of the faster moving avenues in Brooklyn. During the morning rush hours the traffic signals favor northbound traffic toward Flatbush Avenue. In the evening the signals favor traffic heading outbound toward Bay Ridge. At other times the signal pattern is simultaneous, and you can usually cover 12–15 blocks without stopping.

If you're on the Gowanus Expressway:

1a. Hop off at 38th Street and turn left onto Fourth Avenue.
(Directions continue at no. 2, below.)

If you're on the Prospect Expressway:

1b. Exit at Fourth Avenue and turn right.

2. Take Fourth Avenue to Flatbush Avenue and turn left. Flatbush was recently improved, and usually moves well through downtown Brooklyn.

3. Take Flatbush Avenue to Tillary Street, where you'll have three choices.

4a. Turn left on Tillary Street, then right on Adams Street to the Brooklyn Bridge.

4b. Continue on Flatbush Avenue to the Manhattan Bridge.

4c. Turn right on Tillary Street to the eastbound BQE.

Note: When it's obvious that Flatbush Avenue is jammed, and you're headed to Manhattan, continue past Flatbush and make an immediate left onto Ashland Place. Ashland runs northbound, essentially parallel to Flatbush Avenue, and becomes Navy Street past Myrtle Avenue. You can reach the upper level of the Manhattan Bridge by taking Navy Street to Nassau Street and turning left. The Brooklyn Bridge can be reached by going past Nassau Street and turning left onto Sands Street.

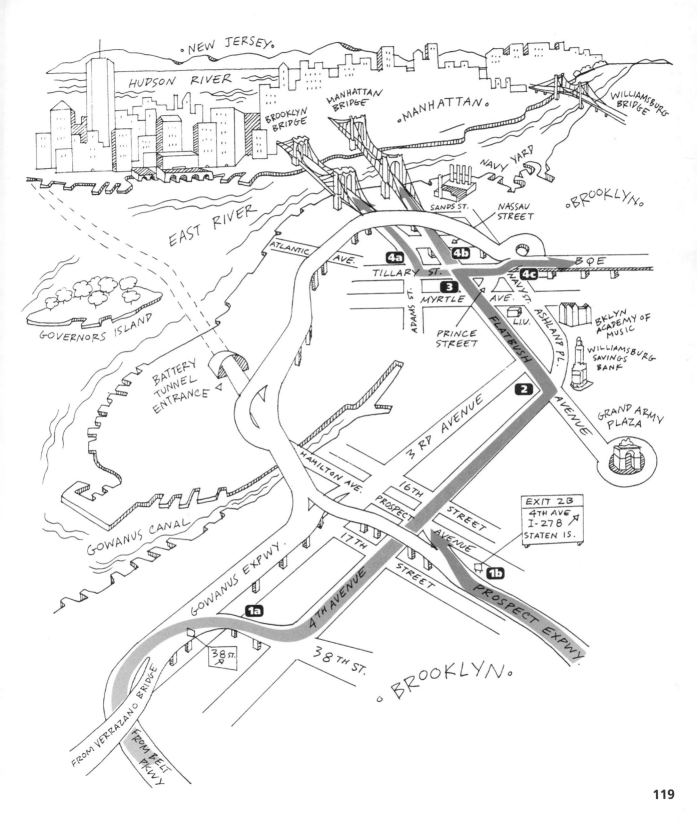

NEW JERSEY

HUDSON RIVER

MANHATTAN BRIDGE

MANHATTAN

WILLIAMSBURG BRIDGE

BROOKLYN BRIDGE

NAVY YARD

BROOKLYN

EAST RIVER

SANDS ST.

NASSAU STREET

ATLANTIC AVE.

4a

4b

4c

B Q E

TILLARY ST.

3

MYRTLE AVE.

ADAMS ST.

NAVY ST.

ASHLAND PL.

BKLYN ACADEMY OF MUSIC

GOVERNORS ISLAND

PRINCE STREET

L.I.U.

WILLIAMSBURG SAVINGS BANK

BATTERY TUNNEL ENTRANCE

FLATBUSH AVENUE

2

GRAND ARMY PLAZA

3 RD AVENUE

HAMILTON AVE.

16TH STREET

PROSPECT

EXIT 2B
4TH AVE
I-278
STATEN IS.

GOWANUS CANAL

17TH STREET

AVENUE

GOWANUS EXPWY.

4TH AVENUE

1b

1a

PROSPECT EXPWY.

38 ST.

38 TH ST.

BROOKLYN

FROM VERRAZANO BRIDGE

FROM BELT PKWY

Avoiding the BQE "Trench" Eastbound

Alternative 3:
Prospect Expressway to Classon Avenue to the BQE

Here's one of my favorites, but only the most adventurous drivers should attempt it. The route leads through local streets, so you won't set any speed records, but it's very reliable; I always use it if I'm catching a plane at La Guardia Airport.

1. Take the Prospect Expressway northbound to the Prospect Park exit.

2. Go half-way around the circle and enter Prospect Park. (If the park is closed, take Parkside Avenue to Ocean Avenue and turn left.)

3. Stay in the right lane and go one exit to Lincoln Road.

4. At the end of the exit ramp, turn left onto Ocean Avenue. The road will bend to the right, and at Flatbush Avenue will change names to become Empire Boulevard.

5. Most traffic will turn left onto Flatbush Avenue, but you should go one more block and turn left onto Washington Avenue. The Brooklyn Botanic Gardens will be on your left.

6. You'll see Clara Barton High School, and Classon Avenue veering off at an angle to the right. Turn onto Classon, a one-way street.

7. Take Classon Avenue for about two miles to the BQE, where you'll be forced to the right.

8. After 1 1/2 blocks, turn left onto Kent Avenue.

9. Make an immediate right onto the BQE service road. Go one block and cross the intersection with Wythe Avenue. The entrance to the BQE will be on the left.

If the BQE is jammed:

You'll have had plenty of opportunity to see how the traffic on the BQE is doing, since the roadway is elevated and clearly visible from the end of Classon Avenue. If it's jammed, don't worry. Just continue on Kent Avenue to Greenpoint Avenue, turn right, and in a few blocks go over the Greenpoint Avenue Bridge. After crossing the bridge, stay to the right; just past Calvary Cemetery turn right onto the LIE service road and watch for signs for the BQE/La Guardia Airport (see pages 102–103).

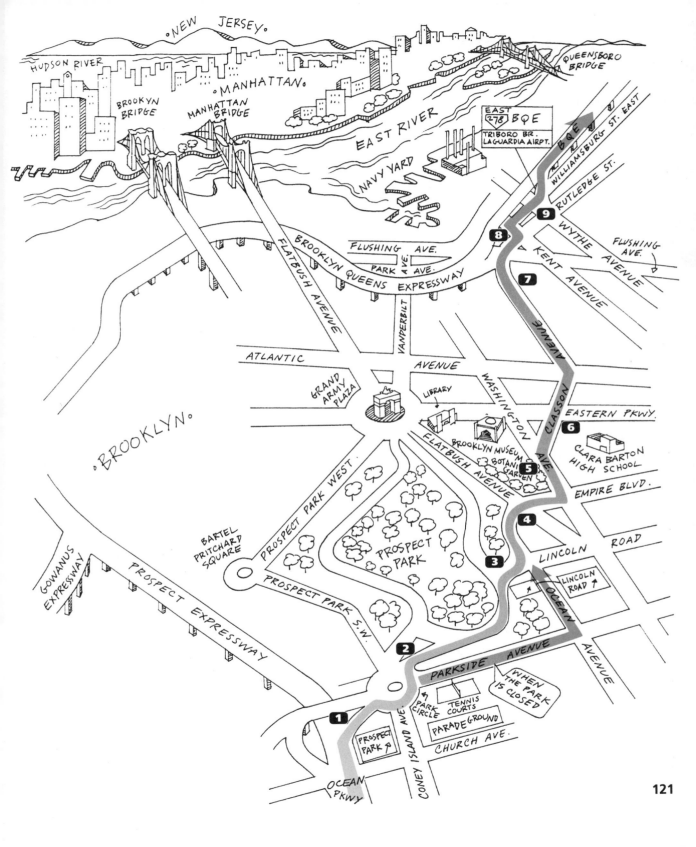

Bypassing the Bruckner Drawbridge

Alternative 1:
The Bronx River Parkway to the Bruckner Expressway

When traveling through the center of the Bronx it is helpful to take advantage of the highway to nowhere, the General Sheridan Expressway. Started by Robert Moses but never completed, the Sheridan interchanges nicely with the Bruckner Expressway to the south, but ends abruptly in the north at the obscure intersection of 177th Street and Devoe Avenue. If used wisely it can serve as a pretty good shortcut, since it is always moving freely.

1. From the southbound Bronx River Parkway take Exit 5 (E.177 St, to I-895 south, Sheridan Expressway).

2. Move into the left lane on 177th Street. After a couple of blocks you'll see a ramp ahead marked "Sheridan Expressway, Triborough Bridge, Cross-Bronx Expressway."

3. Stay to your left on the ramp to join the southbound Sheridan Expressway.

4. In less than a mile, the Sheridan will end and you'll find yourself in the left lane of the Bruckner Expressway, past the drawbridge.

To get to the Triborough Bridge:

5a. Bear left on the Bruckner Expressway and follow signs for the Triborough Bridge.

To get to the Major Deegan Expressway:

5b. Bear right on the Bruckner Expressway and follow signs marked "I-87 North, Thruway Upstate." This will lead you onto the Major Deegan Expressway.

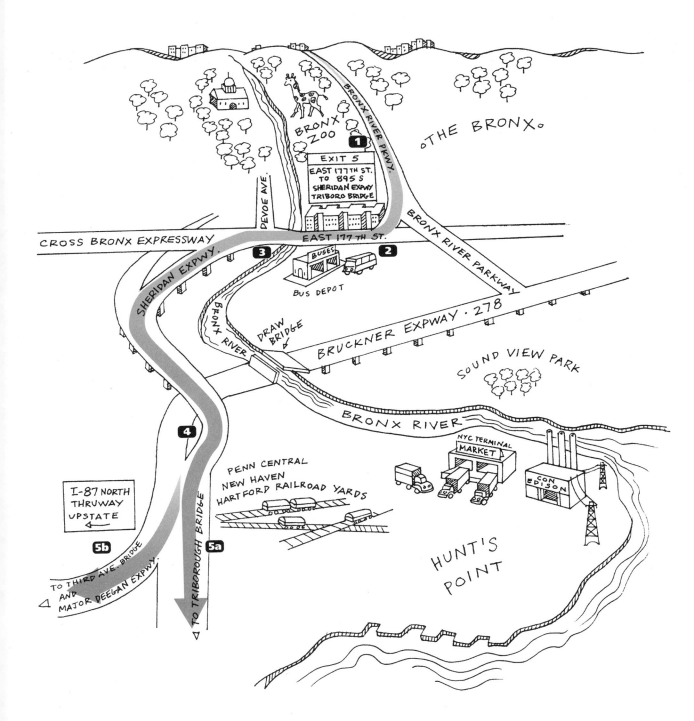

THE BRONX

BRONX ZOO

1

EXIT 5
EAST 177TH ST.
TO 895 S
SHERIDAN EXPWY
TRIBORO BRIDGE

BRONX RIVER PKWY.

DEVOE AVE.

CROSS BRONX EXPRESSWAY

EAST 177TH ST.

3

SHERIDAN EXPWY.

BUSES

BUS DEPOT

2

BRONX RIVER PARKWAY

BRONX RIVER

DRAW BRIDGE

BRUCKNER EXPWAY · 278

SOUND VIEW PARK

4

BRONX RIVER

PENN CENTRAL
NEW HAVEN
HARTFORD RAILROAD YARDS

NYC TERMINAL
MARKET

CON EDISON

I-87 NORTH
THRUWAY
UPSTATE
←

5b

TO THIRD AVE. BRIDGE
AND
MAJOR DEEGAN EXPWY.
◁

5a

TO TRIBOROUGH BRIDGE
◁

HUNT'S POINT

Bypassing the Bruckner Drawbridge

Alternative 2:
Bronx River Parkway to the Triborough or Third Avenue Bridges via Bruckner Boulevard

The East 177th Street alternate route (see previous page) can occasionally become backed up due to construction at the drawbridge. A second alternative involves Bruckner Boulevard, which runs alongside and below the Bruckner Expressway.

1. Exit the Bronx River Parkway southbound at Exit 3 (Westchester Avenue).

2. Turn right on Westchester Avenue and stay in the left lane. In less than a mile you'll cross over the Bronx River and the Sheridan Expressway. (You may encounter some congestion on Westchester Avenue.)

3. At the first traffic signal after crossing the Bronx River, follow the overhead "el" train tracks left onto Whitlock Avenue (there's no sign). You will be riding alongside the Sheridan Expressway.

4. The "el" drops below ground and Bruckner Boulevard merges in on the left. Bruckner is a wide boulevard; the Bruckner Expressway runs overhead.

5. Move into the left roadway. At East 141st Street take the far left lane through the tunnel beneath the Bruckner Expressway.

To get to the Triborough Bridge:

6a. After emerging from the tunnel, make the first right onto St. Ann's Place (there's no sign). Go a block to 134th Street and turn right onto the ramp for the Triborough Bridge.

To get to the Third Avenue Bridge:

6b. Continue on Bruckner Boulevard to Third Avenue and turn left at the bridge approach road. The bridge to Manhattan will be just ahead.

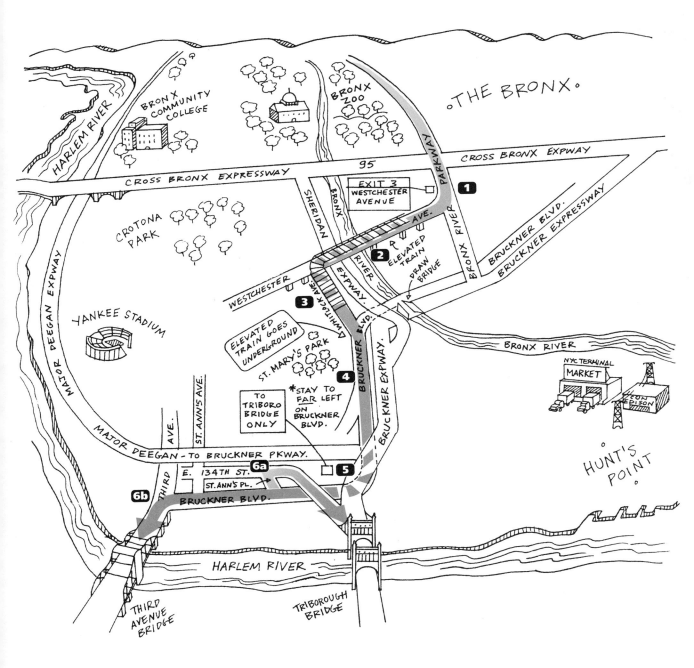

HARLEM RIVER

BRONX COMMUNITY COLLEGE

BRONX ZOO

•THE BRONX•

CROSS BRONX EXPRESSWAY

95

CROSS BRONX EXPWAY

EXIT 3
WESTCHESTER
AVENUE

1

BRONX RIVER PARKWAY

BRUCKNER BLVD.

BRUCKNER EXPRESSWAY

CROTONA PARK

SHERIDAN EXPWAY

BRONX RIVER

ELEVATED
TRAIN
DRAW
BRIDGE

2

WESTCHESTER

3

WHITLOCK AVE.

YANKEE STADIUM

ELEVATED
TRAIN GOES
UNDERGROUND

ST. MARY'S PARK

BRUCKNER BLVD.

4

BRONX RIVER

NYC TERMINAL
MARKET

CON
EDISON

MAJOR DEEGAN EXPWAY

ST. ANN'S AVE.

MAJOR AVE.

TO
TRIBORO
BRIDGE
ONLY

*STAY TO
FAR LEFT
ON
BRUCKNER
BLVD.

BRUCKNER EXPWAY.

HUNT'S
POINT

MAJOR DEEGAN - TO BRUCKNER PKWAY.

THIRD AVE.

E. 134TH ST.

6a

5

ST. ANN'S PL.

6b

BRUCKNER BLVD.

HARLEM RIVER

THIRD
AVENUE
BRIDGE

TRIBOROUGH
BRIDGE

Bypassing the Bruckner Drawbridge

Alternative 3:
Bruckner Expressway to the Bronx River Parkway via the Sheridan Expressway

Going from the Bronx River Parkway to the Sheridan Expressway is a snap, but the reverse is tricky and should be attempted by advanced drivers only.

1.   When traveling east (or north) on the Bruckner Expressway, stay in the right lane. Just before the drawbridge, you'll see signs for Exit 46 (North I-895, Sheridan Expressway). Follow the right lane onto the Sheridan.

2.   Once on the Sheridan, move to the left lane and exit at "E.177 St, E. Tremont Ave." Keep to the far right lane on the ramp to follow the special signal arrow for traffic onto East 177th Street.

3.   Bear right onto 177th Street.

4.   You'll first pass under elevated subway tracks and then cross over the railroad yards. Move into the left lane to pass under the Cross-Bronx Expressway onto Metcalf Avenue.

5.   At the stop sign you'll be faced with a tricky intersection. Make a left onto the service road of the Cross-Bronx Expressway, but keep an eye out over your right shoulder for traffic speeding down the ramp.

6.   Stay in the left lane, but don't get on the ramp located almost immediately to the left; it leads to the Cross-Bronx Expressway.

7.   Instead, take the second left, marked "Bx River Pky North, Cross Bx Expway South, Geo Washngton Br." Follow that road to make a U-turn over the Cross-Bronx Expressway.

8.   Again, when you enter the service road of the Cross-Bronx, be careful. You'll have to weave across a couple of lanes of traffic to get into the right lane, where you'll see the entrance to the Bronx River Parkway northbound on your right.

Note: When the Bruckner Expressway is backed up you can hop onto Bruckner Boulevard instead. Just past Hunts Point Avenue you'll see the entrance to the Sheridan on your right.

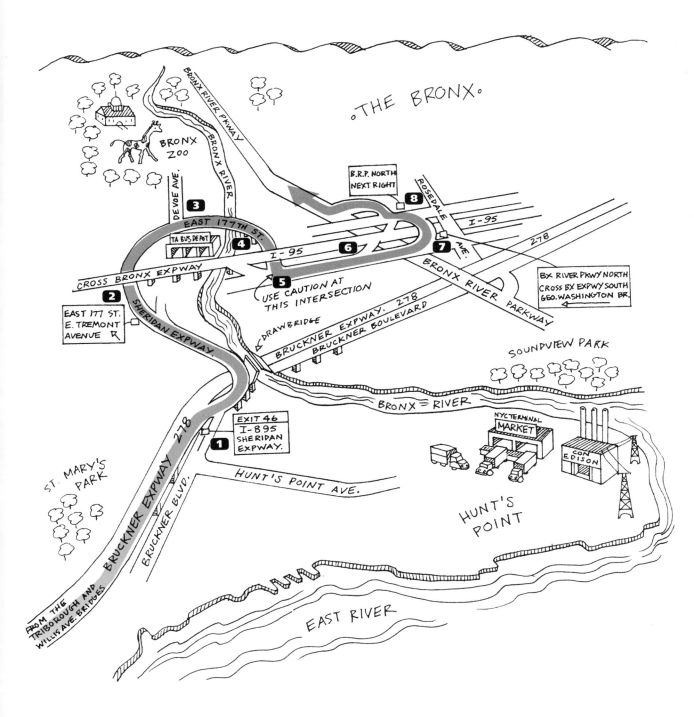

THE BRONX

BRONX RIVER PKWAY

BRONX RIVER

BRONX ZOO

DEVOE AVE.

3

EAST 177TH ST.

TA BUS DEPOT

4

B.R.P. NORTH
NEXT RIGHT

8

ROSEDALE
AVE.

I-95

278

CROSS BRONX EXPWAY

2

I-95

6

7

BRONX RIVER PARKWAY

EAST 177 ST.
E. TREMONT
AVENUE Ⓡ

5

USE CAUTION AT
THIS INTERSECTION

DRAWBRIDGE

BRUCKNER EXPWAY. 278

BRUCKNER BOULEVARD

BX RIVER PKWY NORTH
CROSS BX EXPWAY SOUTH
GEO. WASHINGTON BR.

SHERIDAN EXPWAY.

SOUNDVIEW PARK

BRONX = RIVER

NYC TERMINAL
MARKET

CON
EDISON

ST. MARY'S
PARK

BRUCKNER EXPWAY 278

BRUCKNER BLVD.

1

EXIT 46
I-895
SHERIDAN
EXPWAY.

HUNT'S POINT AVE.

HUNT'S
POINT

FROM THE
TRIBOROUGH AND
WILLIS AVE. BRIDGES

EAST RIVER

Queue Jumping the Backup at the Bronx End of the Throgs Neck Bridge

Occasionally there are major backups at the toll plaza to the southbound Throgs Neck Bridge. There are shortcuts to avoid this, but they lead to the Harding Avenue entrance just before the bridge, which is closed weekdays from 4 PM to 7 PM and weekends from Friday at 4 PM to Monday at 7 AM. At other times, try the following:

1. You can bypass the worst of the jam by hopping off the Cross-Bronx Expressway at Exit 9 (Randall Avenue).

2. Follow the service road of the Cross-Bronx past Hollywood Avenue, where it becomes the Throgs Neck Expressway Extension.

If the Throgs Neck Expressway Extension is clear of traffic:

3a. Take the Throgs Neck Expressway Extension to Harding Avenue and turn left to reach the toll plaza to the bridge.

If the Throgs Neck Expressway Extension is backed up:

3b. Take the Throgs Neck Extension to Throgs Neck Boulevard and turn right.

4b. Go to Harding Avenue and turn left. In just a few blocks you'll reach the toll plaza.

Biggest summons day

The heaviest summons day of the year is the Friday after Thanksgiving. One reason is because it is the busiest shopping day of the year, but the real reason people get caught is they assume holiday rules are in effect. Many people are off from work and the day just feels like a holiday. Tow truck drivers and summons writers amass early on Friday and catch lots of late sleepers who think alternate side parking rules are suspended. Wrong. Every rule remains in effect that day.

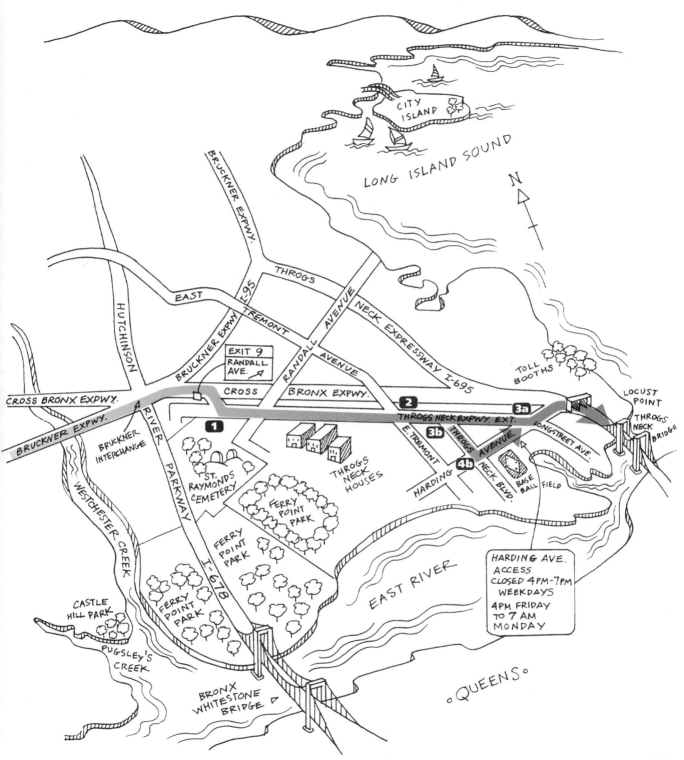

CITY ISLAND

LONG ISLAND SOUND

N

BRUCKNER EXPWY.

HUTCHINSON

EAST

THROGS

I-95

BRUCKNER EXPWY.

TREMONT

RANDALL AVENUE

NECK EXPRESSWAY I-695

TOLL BOOTHS

EXIT 9
RANDALL
AVE.

CROSS BRONX EXPWY.

CROSS

BRONX EXPWY.

2

LOCUST POINT

3a

THROGS
NECK
BRIDGE

BRUCKNER EXPWY.

RIVER

1

THROGS NECK EXPWY. EXT.

E. TREMONT

3b

LONGSTREET AVE.

BRUCKNER
INTERCHANGE

PARKWAY

ST.
RAYMONDS
CEMETERY

THROGS
NECK
HOUSES

4b

THROGS NECK BLVD.

AVENUE

WESTCHESTER CREEK

I-678

FERRY
POINT
PARK

HARDING

BASE
BALL
FIELD

FERRY
POINT
PARK

EAST RIVER

CASTLE
HILL PARK

FERRY POINT
PARK

HARDING AVE.
ACCESS
CLOSED 4PM-7PM
WEEKDAYS
4PM FRIDAY
TO 7 AM
MONDAY

PUGSLEY'S
CREEK

BRONX
WHITESTONE
BRIDGE

QUEENS

When the Bronx River Parkway Floods: Boston Road to 233rd Street Bypass

After heavy rains, it often seems as if the Bronx River runs right down the Bronx River Parkway, especially north of Gun Hill Road. If you are heading north to Westchester after a downpour, here is one way to avoid the flooding:

1. Get off the Bronx River Parkway at Exit 6 (Boston Road north, Bronx Zoo).

2. Make a right at the stop sign onto Boston Road.

3. Go to Bronx Park East, the next intersection, and turn left. You'll still be on Boston Road.

4. Boston Road immediately intersects with Pelham Parkway. Cross Pelham Parkway South and pass the signs for Fordham Road and the Bronx River Parkway southbound. At the far end of this very wide intersection, turn left onto Pelham Parkway North.

5. Take Pelham Parkway North to its end at Bronx Park East; turn right. Bronx Park East runs adjacent to the Bronx River Parkway. After about a mile, Bronx Park East becomes Bronx Boulevard at Burke Avenue.

6. Once you pass 228th Street you'll see the entrance to the Bronx River Parkway northbound on your left. Get back on the Bronx River Parkway here, well north of those stretches of road with poor drainage.

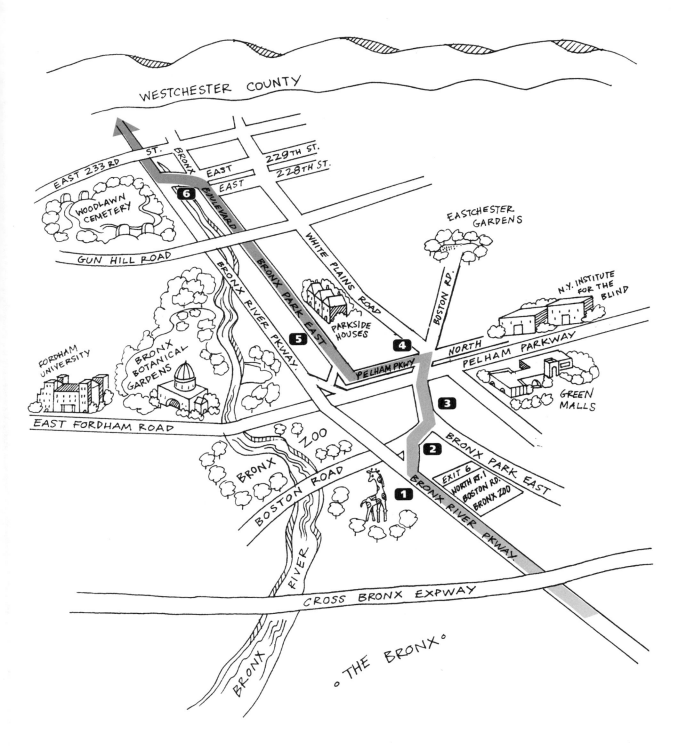

WESTCHESTER COUNTY

EAST 233RD ST.

BRONX

WOODLAWN CEMETERY

229TH ST.
228TH ST.
EAST
EAST

BOULEVARD

6

GUN HILL ROAD

WHITE PLAINS ROAD

EASTCHESTER GARDENS

BOSTON RD.

N.Y. INSTITUTE FOR THE BLIND

BRONX RIVER PKWY.

BRONX PARK EAST

5

PARKSIDE HOUSES

4

PELHAM PKWY.

NORTH

PELHAM PARKWAY

FORDHAM UNIVERSITY

BRONX BOTANICAL GARDENS

GREEN MALLS

EAST FORDHAM ROAD

3

BRONX ZOO

2

BRONX PARK EAST

BOSTON ROAD

1

BRONX RIVER PKWY.

EXIT 6
NORTH RD. 1
BOSTON RD.
BRONX ZOO

CROSS BRONX EXPWAY

BRONX RIVER

° THE BRONX °

Major Deegan Expressway Southbound to the Harlem River Drive via University Heights Bridge

This is one of those "check-the-radio-reports-before-you-try-it" alternatives. The Harlem River Drive is often just as jammed up as the parallel Major Deegan, but if the Deegan is backed up and you hear or see that the Harlem River Drive is okay, then try this:

1.   Exit the Major Deegan Expressway at Exit 9 (Fordham Road).

2.   At the end of the ramp make a right turn and cross over the University Heights Bridge.

3.   Turn left onto Ninth Avenue.

4.   Turn right at 202nd Street and go one block to Tenth Avenue; turn left.

5.   Bear left at the intersection with Dyckman Street; you'll see the entrance to the southbound Harlem River Drive ahead.

What to do at a broken meter?

What do you do when the parking meter is broken? First of all, turn the handle—that's what traffic agents are instructed to do. If the handle is jammed, or there is some other obvious problem other than a bag over a meter (i.e., meter head missing, no lever, etc.), then you may park, but only for the time posted on the nearest sign. If the sign allows for 30-minute parking you may only park up to a half-hour—any longer, and you may be issued a summons. Traffic agents are instructed to note "first observation" at broken or missing meters. They may then return after the posted time period and tag cars still parked at the same meter. If you want to stay longer, move to another meter.

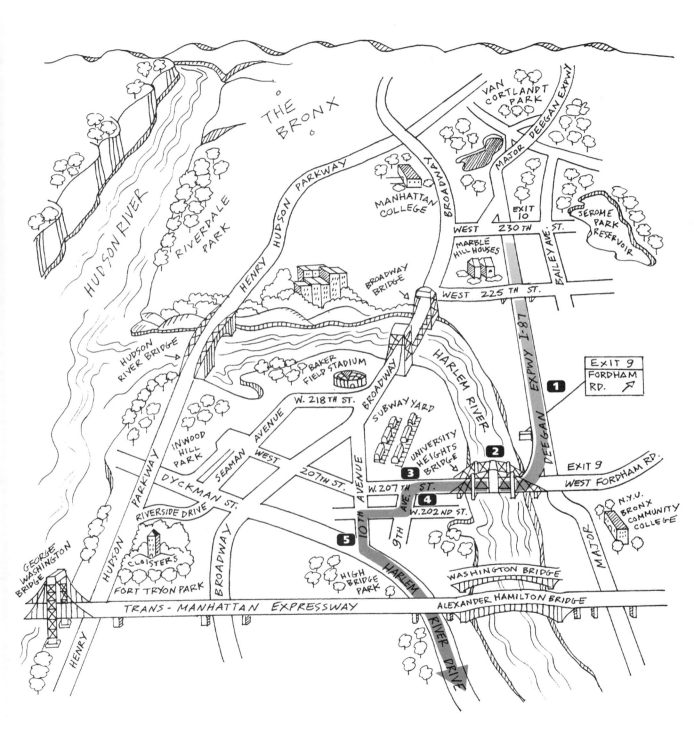

THE BRONX

VAN CORTLANDT PARK

MAJOR DEEGAN EXPWY

MANHATTAN COLLEGE

BROADWAY

EXIT 10

WEST 230TH ST.

BAILEY AVE. ST.

JEROME PARK RESERVOIR

MARBLE HILL HOUSES

HUDSON RIVER

RIVERDALE PARK

HENRY HUDSON PARKWAY

BROADWAY BRIDGE

WEST 225TH ST.

DEEGAN EXPWY I-87

HUDSON RIVER BRIDGE

BAKER FIELD STADIUM

BROADWAY

HARLEM RIVER

EXIT 9
FORDHAM RD. 1

W. 218TH ST.

SUBWAY YARD

INWOOD HILL PARK

SEAMAN AVENUE

WEST

207TH ST.

UNIVERSITY HEIGHTS BRIDGE

2

EXIT 9

WEST FORDHAM RD.

PARKWAY

DYCKMAN ST.

W. 207TH ST.

3

9TH AVE.

4

W. 202ND ST.

10TH AVENUE

N.Y.U. BRONX COMMUNITY COLLEGE

RIVERSIDE DRIVE

GEORGE WASHINGTON BRIDGE

HUDSON

CLOISTERS

FORT TRYON PARK

BROADWAY

HIGH BRIDGE PARK

5

HARLEM RIVER

WASHINGTON BRIDGE

MAJOR

HENRY

TRANS-MANHATTAN EXPRESSWAY

ALEXANDER HAMILTON BRIDGE

RIVER DRIVE

Major Deegan Expressway Southbound to the Henry Hudson Parkway via the Broadway Bridge

The Major Deegan Expressway is often painfully sluggish approaching the George Washington Bridge. If you are heading to Manhattan, you can easily hop off the Deegan north of the George Washington Bridge and follow this alternative route:

1. Take the Major Deegan Expressway southbound and hop off at Exit 10 (West 230th Street).*

2. Stay in the left lane of the exit ramp and make a left turn onto West 230th Street.

3. Move into the right lane of 230th Street. At the second traffic signal turn right onto Bailey Avenue.

4. Make a right turn at the first traffic signal onto 225th Street.

5. Proceed over the Major Deegan to Broadway (you will see the "el" overhead) and turn left.

6. Take the Broadway Bridge over the Harlem River and make the first right onto 218th Street.

7. Go past Columbia University's Baker Field to the stop sign at Seaman Avenue and turn left.

8. Take Seaman Avenue to its end at Riverside Drive and turn right.

9. After about three blocks you will see the entrance to the southbound Henry Hudson Parkway on your left, marked "Downtown Manhattan."

Note: If the 230th Street ramp is closed for construction, exit the Major Deegan at Exit 11 (Van Cortlandt Park South). Turn left onto Van Cortlandt Park South, cross over the Major Deegan, and turn right onto Bailey Avenue. Take Bailey Avenue to 225th Street. Continue following the directions at no. 4, above.

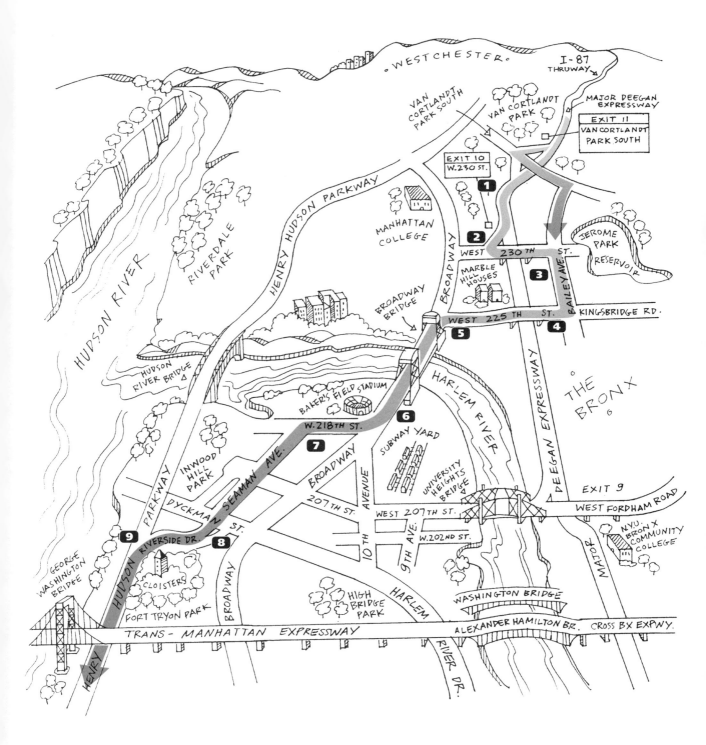

Major Deegan Expressway Southbound to the Harlem River Drive via the Broadway Bridge

If the Major Deegan southbound is moving too slowly for your liking, try this alternate route instead:

1. Take the Major Deegan Expressway southbound and hop off at Exit 10 (West 230th Street).*

2. Stay in the left lane of the exit ramp and make a left turn onto West 230th Street.

3. Move into the right lane of 230th Street. At the second traffic signal turn right onto Bailey Avenue.

4. Make a right turn at the first traffic signal onto 225th Street.

5. Proceed over the Major Deegan to Broadway (you will see the "el" overhead) and turn left.

6. Take the Broadway Bridge over the Harlem River and make the first right onto 218th Street.

7. Go past Columbia University's Baker Field to the stop sign at Seaman Avenue and turn left.

8. Take Seaman Avenue to its end at Riverside Drive and turn left.

9. Go one block to Dyckman Street and turn right.

10. Take Dyckman Street to the entrance of the Harlem River Drive.

Note: If the 230th Street ramp is closed for construction, exit the Major Deegan at Exit 11 (Van Cortlandt Park South). Turn left onto Van Cortlandt Park South, cross over the Major Deegan, and turn right onto Bailey Avenue. Take Bailey Avenue to 225th Street. Continue following the directions at no. 4, above.

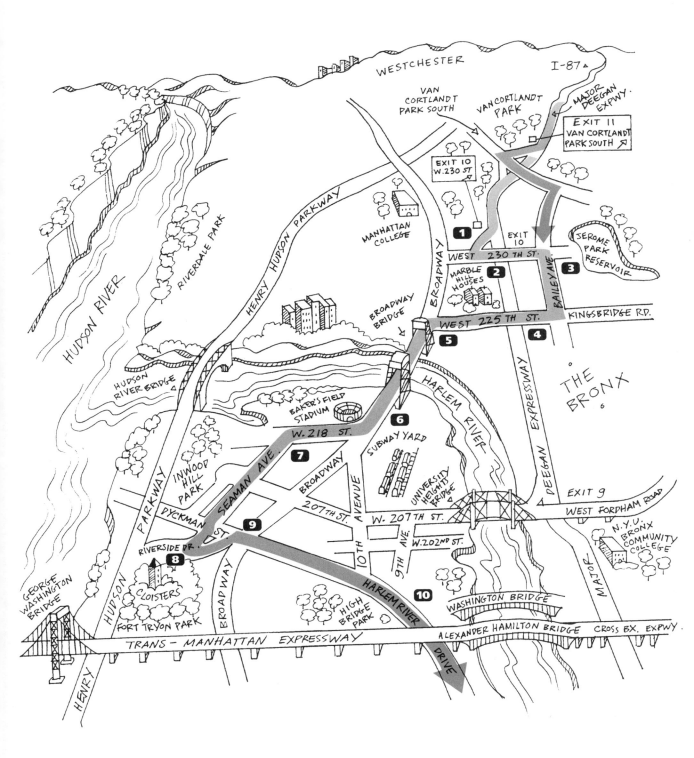

Avoiding the Cross-Bronx Expressway

Alternative 1:
Eastern Westchester or Connecticut to the
George Washington Bridge or West Side Highway

The Cross-Bronx Expressway is the slowest and most uncomfortable road in New York City. You'll spend much of your time here traveling in a narrow concrete trench, with few parallel options to which you can divert once you hit a traffic jam. The key to traveling across the Bronx is to move east–west before you get to the Bronx. If you start out in Westchester, do your east–west traveling on the Cross-County Parkway (sorry, no trucks), the shortest route across Westchester.

1. Take the Hutchinson River Parkway south to Exit 15 (Cross-County Parkway). This exit will put you on the westbound Cross-County Parkway. (Note: If you are on the New York State Thruway southbound or the Bronx River Parkway southbound, you can exit onto the westbound Cross-County as well).

2. Stay on the Cross-County Parkway westbound until it ends, and exit to the left at the exit marked "Saw Mill River Parkway, New York City." Be prepared for a sharp left turn.

3. Follow the Saw Mill River Parkway for less than a mile to reach the toll booths. Stay in the right lane after the toll plaza and follow signs to the Henry Hudson Parkway.

To the George Washington Bridge:

4a. Follow the Henry Hudson Parkway past the Henry Hudson Toll Bridge and bear left to Exit 14–15 (Riverside Drive, George Washington Bridge, Cross-Bronx Expressway). Follow the signs to the George Washington Bridge.

To the West Side Highway:

4b. Follow the Henry Hudson Parkway past the Henry Hudson Toll Bridge and bear right at Exit 14–15 (Riverside Drive, George Washington Bridge, Cross-Bronx Expressway). Continue on the Henry Hudson Parkway, which becomes the West Side Highway south of 72nd Street.

Note: If you are going from the George Washington Bridge or West Side Highway to the Henry Hudson Parkway simply reverse these directions.

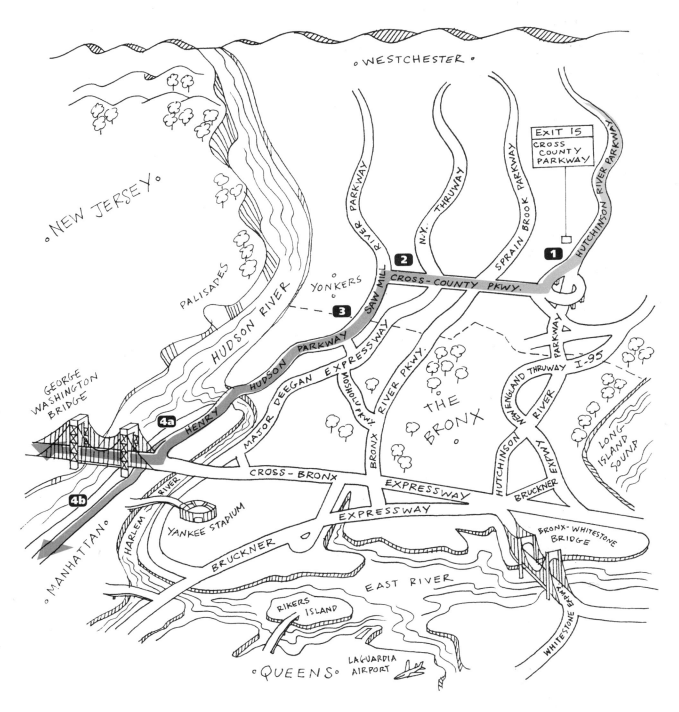

WESTCHESTER

NEW JERSEY

PALISADES

HUDSON RIVER

YONKERS

SAW MILL RIVER PARKWAY

N.Y. THRUWAY

SPRAIN BROOK PARKWAY

HUTCHINSON RIVER PARKWAY

EXIT 15
CROSS
COUNTY
PARKWAY

1

2 CROSS-COUNTY PKWY.

3

HUDSON PARKWAY

MAJOR DEEGAN EXPRESSWAY

BRONX RIVER PKWY.

MOSHOLU PKWY.

THE BRONX

HUTCHINSON RIVER

NEW ENGLAND THRUWAY I-95

LONG ISLAND SOUND

GEORGE WASHINGTON BRIDGE

4a HENRY

4b

MANHATTAN

HARLEM RIVER

YANKEE STADIUM

CROSS-BRONX EXPRESSWAY

EXPRESSWAY

BRUCKNER EXPRESSWAY

BRUCKNER

RIKERS ISLAND

EAST RIVER

BRONX-WHITESTONE BRIDGE

WHITESTONE EXPWY.

QUEENS

LAGUARDIA AIRPORT

Avoiding the Cross-Bronx Expressway

Alternative 2:
Saw Mill River Parkway to the Throgs Neck Bridge

I'm always amazed that people head down the Saw Mill or Major Deegan from Westchester and then head east via the Cross-Bronx Expressway. If you are a masochist then by all means continue to travel along some of the slowest roads in the world. If not, then try this:

1. Take the Saw Mill River Parkway or New York State Thruway to the Cross-County Parkway eastbound.

2. Exit the Cross-County Parkway at Exit 9 (Hutchinson River Parkway southbound, Whitestone Br).

3. Follow the "Hutch" to the Cross-Bronx Expressway eastbound.

4. Follow the signs to the Throgs Neck Bridge.

Most confusing parking signs

My vote for the most confusing parking regulations are the signs installed in the Theater District in 1991. The signs read, "No Standing except Trucks Loading and Unloading 7 AM to 7 PM except Sunday, 6 Hour Meter Parking 7 PM to 1 AM, 6 Hour Meter Parking 8 AM to 7 PM Sundays." Car drivers may park only after 7 PM on Monday through Saturday by activating the meters. They must also activate meters from 8 AM Sunday through 1 AM on Monday.

The runner-up in the most confusing sign category can be found on 47th Street between Fifth and Sixth avenues. The signs read, "No Standing 11 AM to 7 PM except Sunday, No Standing other times except trucks loading and unloading." Do two excepts make it okay to park here on Sunday? Don't even THINK of it.

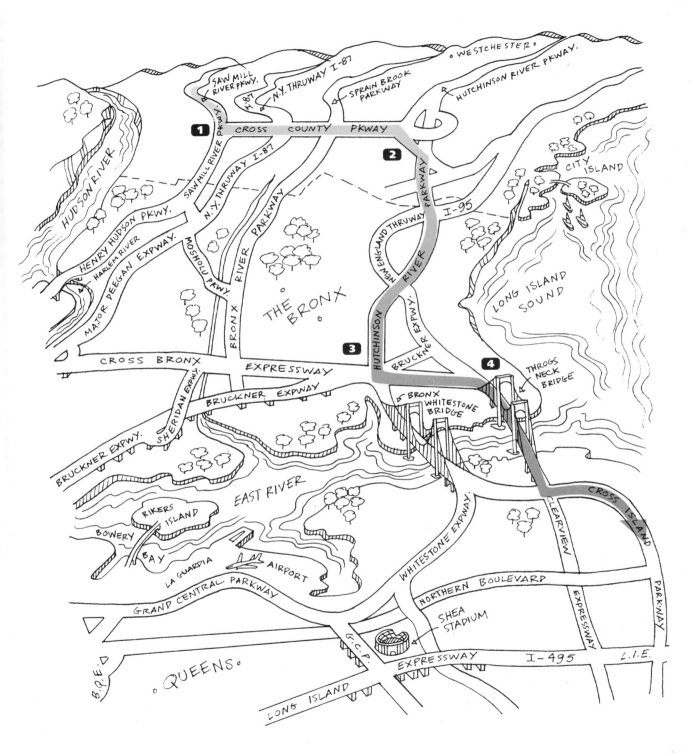

SAW MILL
RIVER PKWY.

I-87

N.Y. THRUWAY I-87

SPRAIN BROOK
PARKWAY

WESTCHESTER

HUTCHINSON RIVER PKWY.

1 CROSS COUNTY PKWAY

2

CITY
ISLAND

HUDSON RIVER

SAW MILL RIVER PKWY.

N.Y. THRUWAY I-87

HENRY HUDSON PKWY.

HARLEM RIVER

MAJOR PEEGAN EXPWAY.

MOSHOLU PKWY.

BRONX RIVER PARKWAY

NEW ENGLAND THRUWAY I-95

HUTCHINSON RIVER PARKWAY

LONG ISLAND
SOUND

THE
BRONX

3

BRUCKNER EXPWY.

4

THROGS
NECK
BRIDGE

CROSS BRONX EXPRESSWAY

SHERIDAN EXPWY.

BRUCKNER EXPWAY.

BRONX
WHITESTONE
BRIDGE

BRUCKNER EXPWY.

EAST RIVER

CLEARVIEW

CROSS ISLAND

RIKERS ISLAND

BOWERY

BAY

LA GUARDIA AIRPORT

WHITESTONE EXPWAY.

EXPRESSWAY

PARKWAY

GRAND CENTRAL PARKWAY

NORTHERN BOULEVARD

SHEA
STADIUM

B.Q.E.

G.C.P.

EXPRESSWAY I-495 L.I.E.

QUEENS

LONG ISLAND

Avoiding the Cross-Bronx Expressway

Alternative 3:
George Washington Bridge to Long Island

The tendency for many heading to Long Island is to take the shortest path—the Cross-Bronx Expressway. While this may be the shortest route with regard to distance, you may find it to be the most time-consuming. Wise motorists listen to radio reports, and when they hear that the Cross-Bronx is crawling, they opt for the following route instead:

1. Cross Manhattan on the George Washington Bridge extension roadway (the Trans-Manhattan Expressway) and exit onto the Major Deegan Expressway southbound.

2. Take the Major Deegan to its southern terminus, bear right, and exit at the Triborough Bridge.

3. Stay in one of the three left lanes as you approach the toll plaza and follow the signs to Queens.

4. At the Queens end, the bridge will feed onto the Grand Central Parkway (GCP)*, which goes to Long Island. The GCP also crosses the Long Island Expressway (I-495), which you can also take east to Long Island.

Note: This well-marked route is entirely reversible. Just take the GCP to the Triborough Bridge to the Bronx and bear left after the toll plaza. At the end of the bridge bear left to the Major Deegan. Follow the signs to the George Washington Bridge.

*Trucks are prohibited on the GCP. At the Queens end of the bridge, truckers should bear right onto Astoria Boulevard, eventually feeding onto the BQE south (west) to the LIE to Long Island.

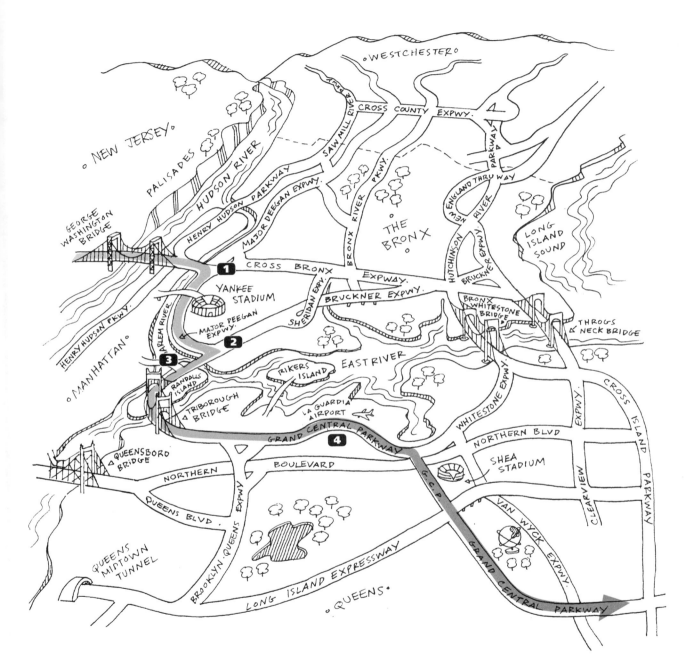

WESTCHESTER

NEW JERSEY

SAW MILL RIVER

CROSS COUNTY EXPWY.

PALISADES

HUDSON RIVER

HENRY HUDSON PARKWAY

MAJOR DEEGAN EXPWY.

BRONX RIVER PKWY.

THE BRONX

NEW ENGLAND THRUWAY

HUTCHINSON RIVER

LONG ISLAND SOUND

GEORGE WASHINGTON BRIDGE

1 CROSS BRONX EXPWAY.

YANKEE STADIUM

HARLEM RIVER

HENRY HUDSON PKWY.

MANHATTAN

SHERIDAN EXPY.

BRUCKNER EXPWY.

HUTCHINSON RIVER PKWY.

BRUCKNER EXPWY.

BRONX WHITESTONE BRIDGE

THROGS NECK BRIDGE

MAJOR PEEGAN EXPWY.

2

3

RANDALLS ISLAND

RIKERS ISLAND

EAST RIVER

TRIBOROUGH BRIDGE

LA GUARDIA AIRPORT

WHITESTONE EXPWY.

GRAND CENTRAL PARKWAY **4**

NORTHERN BLVD

SHEA STADIUM

CROSS ISLAND PARKWAY

QUEENSBORO BRIDGE

NORTHERN BOULEVARD

G.C.P.

CLEARVIEW EXPWY.

QUEENS BLVD.

BROOKLYN-QUEENS EXPWY.

VAN WYCK EXPWY.

GRAND CENTRAL PARKWAY

QUEENS MIDTOWN TUNNEL

LONG ISLAND EXPRESSWAY

QUEENS

Avoiding the Cross-Bronx Expressway

Alternative 4:
George Washington Bridge to the Throgs Neck Bridge or Bronx–Whitestone Bridge

As you may have noticed, most of these alternates for crossing the Bronx involve leaving the borough. If you do want to stay within the Bronx, then try this:

1. Take the George Washington Bridge across Manhattan and exit at the Major Deegan Expressway southbound.

2. Take the Deegan past Exit 1 to the unnumbered exit labeled "I-278 East, East Bronx, New England."

3. Follow the signs to the Bruckner Expressway.

4. Take the Bruckner Expressway past White Plains Road to the exit marked "I-295 South–Throgs Neck Bridge, I-678 South–Whitestone Bridge." Follow the signs to the bridge of your choice.

Complex intersections

Three-phased traffic signals constrict capacity so that traffic slows upstream but moves well downstream past the bottleneck. You will find three-phased signals where three streets cross or where two major streets cross and a special turning signal is provided. For example, at Herald Square, Sixth Avenue crosses Broadway and 34th Street. Sixth Avenue is jammed south of 34th but almost always moves well north of 34th until at least 42nd Street. A smart driver will take advantage of this and enter Sixth just north of Herald Square.

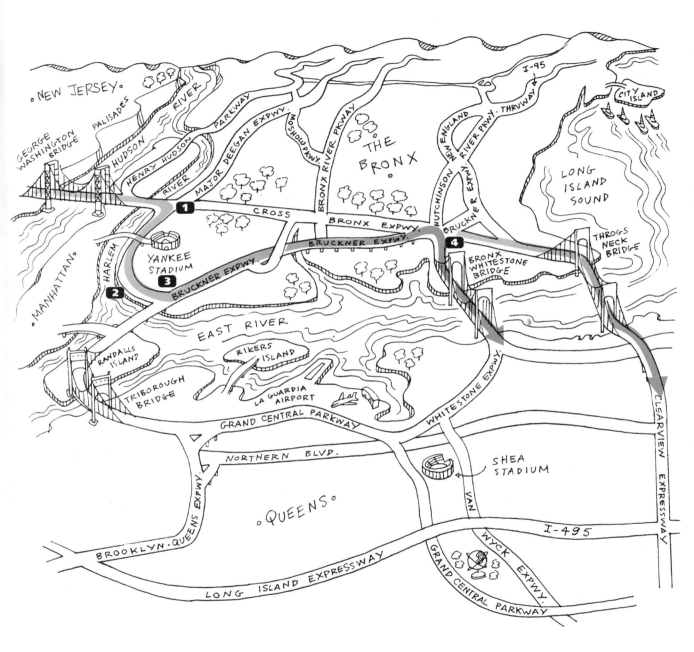

Avoiding the Cross-Bronx Expressway

Alternative 5:
New England Thruway to the George Washington Bridge

The combination of the New England Thruway and the Cross-Bronx Expressway is enough to make anyone stay home. Both roads are constantly under repair; even the police have stopped checking these routes for speeders. Here's a more reliable option:

1. Take the southbound New England Thruway (I-95) to Exit 15 (U.S. Route 1, New Rochelle).

2. Bear right at the yield sign and take Route 1 south to the Hutchinson River Parkway northbound.

3. Proceed on the northbound "Hutch" past the tollbooth to Exit 13 (Cross County Parkway, Saw Mill River Parkway, Yonkers).

4. Stay on the Cross-County Parkway westbound until it ends at the Saw Mill River Parkway exit (less than four miles). The left lane of the Cross-County Parkway will take you onto the southbound Saw Mill River Parkway.

5. The Saw Mill River Parkway leads directly into the Henry Hudson Parkway.

6. Follow the Henry Hudson Parkway past the Henry Hudson Toll Bridge to Exit 14–15 (Riverside Drive, George Washington Bridge, Cross-Bronx Expressway). Follow the signs to the George Washington Bridge.

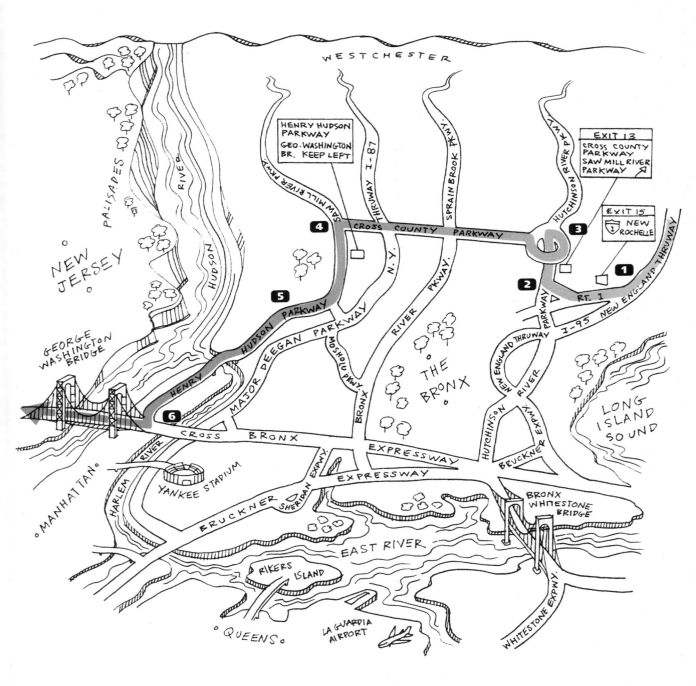

WESTCHESTER

NEW JERSEY

PALISADES

HUDSON RIVER

SAW MILL RIVER PKWY.

HENRY HUDSON
PARKWAY
GEO. WASHINGTON
BR. KEEP LEFT

N.Y. THRUWAY I-87

CROSS COUNTY PARKWAY

SPRAIN BROOK PKWY.

HUTCHINSON RIVER PKWY.

EXIT 13
CROSS COUNTY
PARKWAY
SAW MILL RIVER
PARKWAY →

4

3

EXIT 15
1 NEW
ROCHELLE

5

2

1

RT. 1

I-95 NEW ENGLAND THRUWAY

NEW ENGLAND THRUWAY

HUTCHINSON RIVER

GEORGE
WASHINGTON
BRIDGE

HENRY HUDSON PARKWAY

MAJOR DEEGAN PARKWAY

MOSHOLU PKWY.

BRONX RIVER PKWY.

THE
BRONX

LONG
ISLAND
SOUND

6

CROSS BRONX EXPRESSWAY

BRUCKNER EXPWY.

MANHATTAN

HARLEM RIVER

YANKEE STADIUM

BRUCKNER SHERIDAN EXPWY.

EXPRESSWAY

BRONX
WHITESTONE
BRIDGE

EAST RIVER

RIKERS ISLAND

WHITESTONE EXPWY.

QUEENS

LA GUARDIA
AIRPORT

The George Washington Bridge: New Jersey Approaches

Crossing the George Washington Bridge is something of an art. There are five major approaches to the bridge from New Jersey, but if there is an incident on the bridge itself, all five back-up, though not uniformly. Here is the list of approaches in ascending order of congestion (lightest to heaviest).

1. Palisades Parkway via Fort Lee is usually the lightest approach
2. Routes 1 and 9, and 46
3. Route 4
4. Local lanes of I-80 and I-95
5. Express lanes of I-80 and I-95

The trick to avoiding the worst approaches is to head to Route 46 (which can easily be accessed from the Turnpike, I-95, I-80, and routes 1 and 9). Once on Route 46, try the following:

1.   Take Route 46 east past the exit for routes 1 and 9. Shortly, you'll see a Sunoco gas station on your <u>right</u>. Take the exit ramp just past the Sunoco.

2.   At the second stop sign turn right onto East Brinkerhoff Avenue.

3.   Stay on East Brinkerhoff Avenue for a little more than 1/2 mile. You will go up a steep incline, then down a hill. Turn left at the end onto Anderson Avenue.

4.   Stay to the right; after about 1/2 mile you'll find yourself on Center Avenue.

5.   Continue for another 1/2 mile to Bridge Plaza South. Turn right onto Bridge Plaza South (except weekdays 7 AM—9 AM) and you'll soon see the entrance to the bridge on your left. Weekdays, from 7 AM—9 AM, continue on Center Avenue past Bridge Plaza South and take the entrance to the bridge on the right.

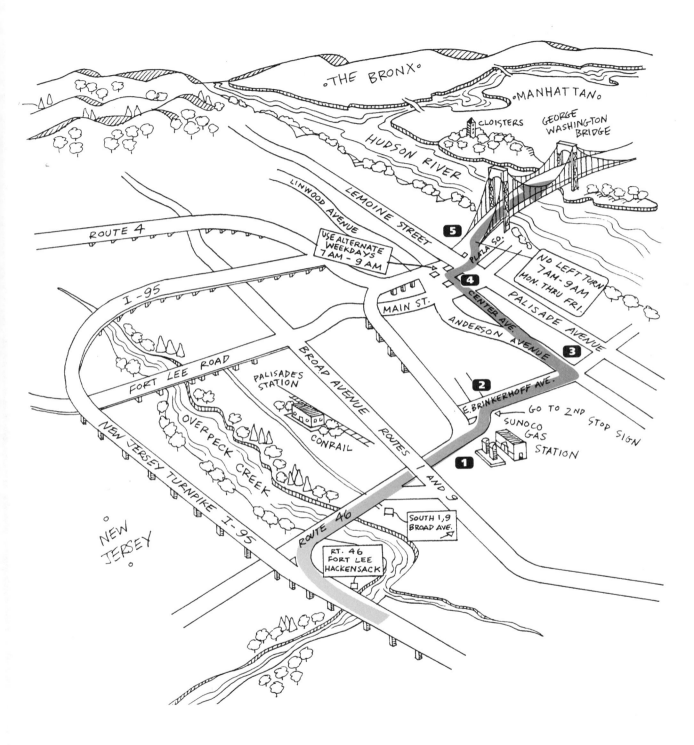

THE BRONX

MANHATTAN

CLOISTERS

GEORGE WASHINGTON BRIDGE

HUDSON RIVER

LINWOOD AVENUE

LEMOINE STREET

ROUTE 4

USE ALTERNATE WEEKDAYS 7 AM - 9 AM

PLAZA SO.

I-95

5

4

NO LEFT TURN 7 AM - 9 AM MON. THRU FRI.

MAIN ST.

CENTER AVE.

ANDERSON AVENUE

PALISADE AVENUE

3

FORT LEE ROAD

PALISADES STATION

BROAD AVENUE ROUTES 1 AND 9

2

E. BRINKERHOFF AVE.

GO TO 2ND STOP SIGN

OVERPECK CREEK

CONRAIL

SUNOCO GAS STATION

1

NEW JERSEY TURNPIKE I-95

ROUTE 46

SOUTH 1,9 BROAD AVE.

NEW JERSEY

RT. 46 FORT LEE HACKENSACK

The George Washington Bridge: New York Approaches

(See pages 6-7, 138-139, 146-147 for approaching the George Washington Bridge from Manhattan, Bronx, Westchester, and Connecticut.)

One of the most frequently used, and therefore most congested, approaches to the George Washington Bridge is the Major Deegan northbound to the Alexander Hamilton Bridge (mistakenly called the Cross-Bronx Expressway by most). Here are a couple of ways to avoid the worst of the jam:

If the northbound Major Deegan is clear to 155th Street:

1a. Take the northbound Major Deegan Expressway to Exit 5 (West 155 St, Stadium, Manhattan).

2a. At the bottom of the ramp follow the signs for "W. 155 St., Manhattan." This will take you to the Macombs Dam Bridge. (Directions continue at no. 3, below.)

When the northbound Major Deegan is jammed:

1b. Take the northbound Major Deegan Expressway to Exit 3 (Grand Concourse, East 138th Street). Take the Grand Concourse to 161st Street and turn left.

2b. Go past Yankee Stadium and follow signs for "Manhattan/155th Street." Go across the Macombs Dam Bridge.

3. At the first traffic light on the Manhattan side of the Macombs Dam Bridge, bear right and go up the hill. Stay on 155th Street until you reach Broadway, then make a right turn.

4. Take Broadway two blocks and turn left onto 157th Street. At the first traffic light turn right.

5. Go one block. At the next intersection you will see three roadways. The center and right roadways are both marked "Riverside Drive." Choose the center roadway.

6. Just past 165th Street you will see the entrance to the George Washington Bridge on the right.

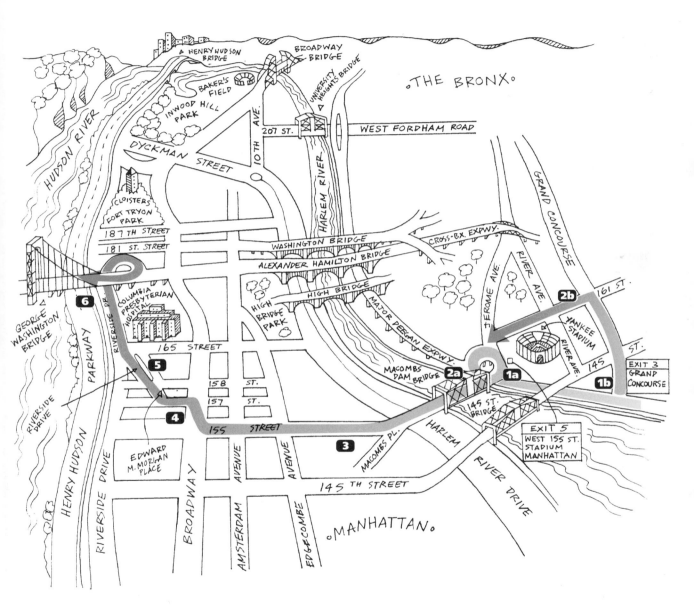

The Lincoln Tunnel:
Bypassing the Helix Inbound

The "helix" approach to the Lincoln Tunnel should be renamed the "stranglehold"; at least, that's what it feels like. It is particularly frustrating to be caught in traffic here, since you can see the skyline of Manhattan just a mile away but you know that it may still take 30–45 minutes to cross the river. Here's a way of shortening the delay.

1. Take I-495 to the last exit before the toll; the sign reads, "Weehawken, Hoboken, Last Exit in New Jersey."

2. This exit will leave you on South Marginal Highway.

3. At the end of South Marginal Highway, bear right at the fork onto John F. Kennedy Boulevard East.

4. Stay in the right two lanes and turn right to the Lincoln Tunnel Plaza.

East to the East River, West to the Hudson River

In 1790, city planners suggested that people "park" their horse carriages so that they face the Hudson River on odd-numbered streets, and the East River on even numbered streets. "Even-numbered streets go east" is a helpful axiom even today, when you're trying to figure out cross-street directions. It follows that odd- numbered streets go west. There are some notable exceptions. To improve traffic circulation around the Queensboro Bridge, engineers reversed 59th and 60th streets. 59th Street is eastbound from Fifth Avenue to the bridge ramp between First and Second avenues. East of that point it is two-way. Sixtieth Street runs west from York Avenue to Central Park. Sixty-fifth and 66th streets were reversed to line up with the transverse roadway in Central Park.

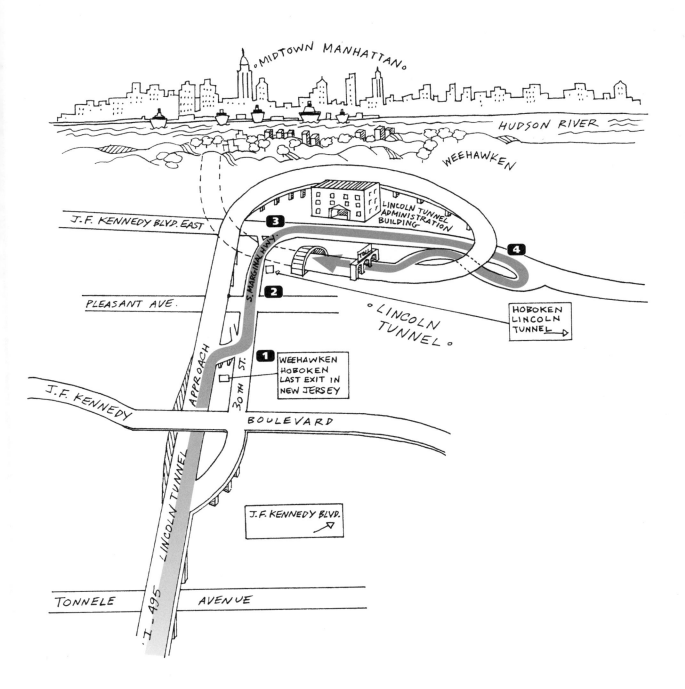

MIDTOWN MANHATTAN

HUDSON RIVER

WEEHAWKEN

J.F. KENNEDY BLVD. EAST

LINCOLN TUNNEL ADMINISTRATION BUILDING

3

S. MARGINAL HWY.

TOLL

4

PLEASANT AVE.

2

LINCOLN TUNNEL

HOBOKEN LINCOLN TUNNEL →

1 WEEHAWKEN HOBOKEN LAST EXIT IN NEW JERSEY

30TH ST.

APPROACH

J.F. KENNEDY

BOULEVARD

J.F. KENNEDY BLVD. ▷

LINCOLN TUNNEL

I-495

TONNELE AVENUE

The Lincoln Tunnel: Manhattan Approaches

Generally, the worst approach to the outbound Lincoln Tunnel is from Ninth Avenue where, night after night, hordes of drivers inch their way down Ninth to the north tube. But there are two other avenues that have entrances to the tunnel, and they usually move better.

From the north:

1. Take 42nd Street across town to Eleventh Avenue. Forty-second Street usually moves quite well between Eighth and Eleventh avenues, so if Ninth is a drag, cut across on 42nd Street instead.

2. Turn left onto Eleventh Avenue and stay to the left. This is where congestion is unavoidable.

3. Go two blocks to 40th Street and turn left. The entrance to the tunnel will be on your right.

From the south:

1a. Take Tenth Avenue to 30th Street and turn right (to the far right, not the immediate right).

2a. Go 1/2 block to the entrance to the tunnel on your left.

OR

1b. Take Eighth Avenue to 31st Street and turn left.

2b. Go 1 1/2 blocks to reach the entrance to the tunnel, on your right.

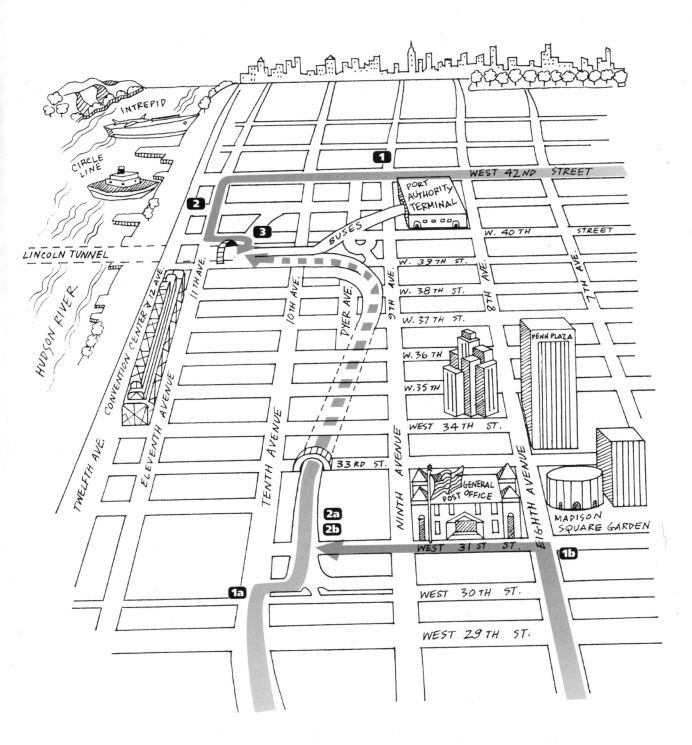

INTREPID

CIRCLE
LINE

LINCOLN TUNNEL

HUDSON RIVER

TWELFTH AVE.

ELEVENTH AVENUE

Convention Center & 12 Ave.

11TH AVE.

10TH AVE.

DYER AVE.

TENTH AVENUE

33RD ST.

9TH AVE.

BUSES

PORT
AUTHORITY
TERMINAL

WEST 42ND STREET

W. 40TH STREET

W. 39TH ST.

W. 38TH ST.

W. 37TH ST.

W. 36TH

W.35TH

WEST 34TH ST.

8TH AVE.

7TH AVE.

PENN PLAZA

NINTH AVENUE

GENERAL
POST OFFICE

EIGHTH AVENUE

MADISON
SQUARE GARDEN

WEST 31ST ST.

WEST 30TH ST.

WEST 29TH ST.

1
2
3
2a
2b
1a
1b

The Lincoln Tunnel Outbound to the New Jersey Turnpike South or Routes 1 and 9 South

Beating "Helix-Lock"

On exiting the Lincoln Tunnel, an observant driver will look to see if the I-495 helix is backed up. If this is the case, the local streets of Hoboken to Routes 1 and 9 or the New Jersey Turnpike Extension are better choices.

1. Emerge from the Lincoln Tunnel and immediately bear right; exit at the sign for Hoboken. This will put you on Willow Avenue heading south.

2. Go approximately two miles through Hoboken to Observer Highway and make a right turn.

3. Follow the road to the left onto Newark Avenue.

4. Just after you pass under the railroad viaduct, turn left onto Jersey Avenue.

5. At the third traffic signal you will come to the wide plaza of the Holland Tunnel exit street. Make a right onto the rising viaduct for the New Jersey Turnpike Extension southbound. Swing wide as you turn right to get to Routes 1 and 9 (the Pulaski Skyway).

What does that solid line mean?
Everybody (I hope) knows that you may not cross a double solid line. You should also know that you may cross a single "skipped" line. But what about a single solid line? The single solid line is advisory only. You may cross it but it is inadvisable. The solid line is often used around curves or where lanes suddenly narrow. Though crossing solid lines is not unlawful, it's best to avoid doing so, for safety sake.

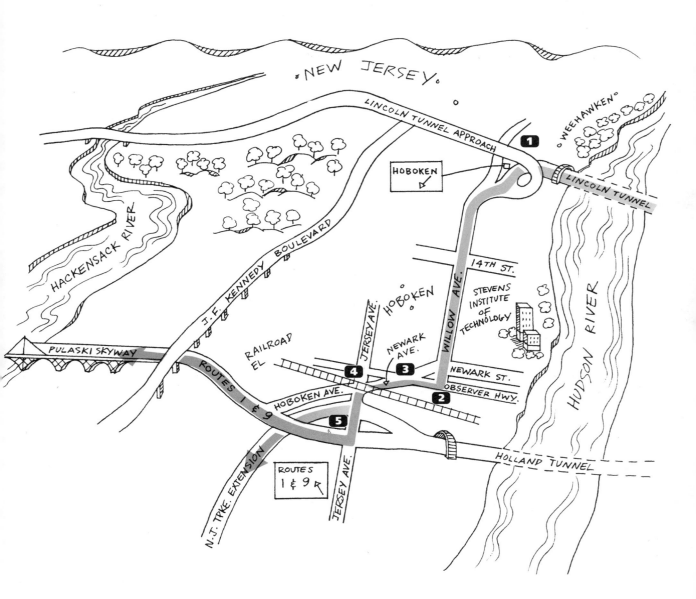

NEW JERSEY

LINCOLN TUNNEL APPROACH

1

WEEHAWKEN

LINCOLN TUNNEL

HOBOKEN

HACKENSACK RIVER

J.F. KENNEDY BOULEVARD

14TH ST.

WILLOW AVE.

STEVENS INSTITUTE OF TECHNOLOGY

HOBOKEN

JERSEY AVE.

RAILROAD EL

NEWARK AVE.

4

3

NEWARK ST.

OBSERVER HWY.

2

PULASKI SKYWAY

ROUTES 1 & 9

HOBOKEN AVE.

5

HUDSON RIVER

HOLLAND TUNNEL

N.J. TPKE. EXTENSION

ROUTES 1 & 9 ↖

JERSEY AVE.

The Lincoln Tunnel: New Jersey Approaches from the New Jersey Turnpike or Routes 78 or 22

Motorists approach the Lincoln Tunnel with dread, awaiting the inevitable bad news from the Shadow Traffic report: "There's an accident on the eastern spur and the western spur is at a standstill." Here's a way of avoiding "spur-lock."

From the New Jersey Turnpike:

1a. Take the New Jersey Turnpike north to Exit 14 (US 1 & 9, I-78, Newark Airport). (Directions continue at no. 2, below.)

From Routes 78 or 22:

1b. Follow the signs for Routes 1 and 9 north, express lanes.

2. Take Routes 1 and 9 north over the Pulaski Skyway.

3. Exit at "Tonnele Avenue, Lincoln Tunnel."

4. Follow the signs to Routes 1 and 9 north to reach Tonnele Avenue.

5. Take Tonnele Avenue approximately 2 1/2 miles. Just after the McDonald's bear left and follow the signs to Route 3.

6. Go past the traffic light and move into the right lane. Turn right at the sign for the Lincoln Tunnel to reach the tunnel's approach road.

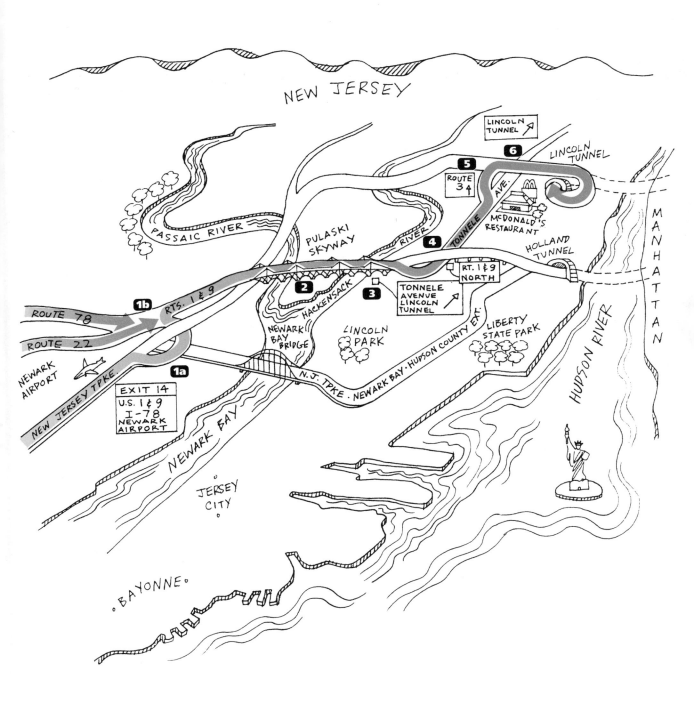

NEW JERSEY

LINCOLN TUNNEL ↗

6 LINCOLN TUNNEL

5 ROUTE 3 ↑

AVE. McDONALD'S RESTAURANT

HOLLAND TUNNEL

PASSAIC RIVER

PULASKI SKYWAY

RIVER

TONNELE

4

RT. 1 & 9 NORTH

TONNELE AVENUE LINCOLN TUNNEL ↗

MANHATTAN

1b RTS. 1 & 9

ROUTE 78

ROUTE 22

2 HACKENSACK

3

LINCOLN PARK

LIBERTY STATE PARK

HUDSON RIVER

NEWARK BAY BRIDGE

NEWARK AIRPORT

1a

N.J. TPKE. · NEWARK BAY · HUDSON COUNTY EXT.

EXIT 14
U.S. 1 & 9
I-78
NEWARK
AIRPORT

NEW JERSEY TPKE.

NEWARK BAY

JERSEY CITY

BAYONNE

The Holland Tunnel:
New Jersey Approach

Alert drivers keep a watchful eye on the viaduct ahead as they approach the Holland Tunnel from the New Jersey Turnpike. At the apex of the viaduct, just before the road curves to the right, stands Dickinson High School. If traffic is backed up that far you know you're in for trouble. The Grand Street exit, 1/2 mile prior to that point, offers your last chance for escaping the jam.

1.   Take the New Jersey Turnpike Extension to Exit 14C (Holland Tunnel).

2.   After the toll booths, stay in the right lane and exit at "Jersey City, Grand Street."

3.   Stay on the service road below the highway to the end at Christopher Columbus Drive.

4.   Turn right on Christopher Columbus Drive and then left on Luis Munoz Marin Boulevard.

5.   The Holland Tunnel will be ahead, less than 1/2 mile away, just past the Newport Centre Mall.

Tickets without a sign
You can receive parking tickets in part of lower Manhattan even if all the signs are missing! The "Blue Zone" was set up because construction workers were taking down parking signs as fast as the city was installing them. The "Blue Zone" regulation makes it illegal to park, signs or no signs, in the area south of the Brooklyn Bridge and east of Broadway from 7 AM to 7PM, Monday through Friday.

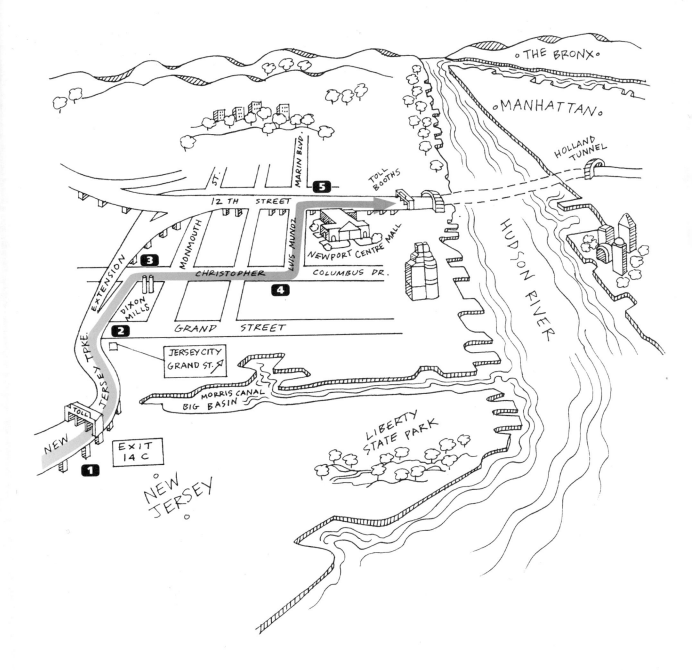

THE BRONX

MANHATTAN

HOLLAND TUNNEL

HUDSON RIVER

TOLL BOOTHS

5

12TH STREET

MARIN BLVD.

ST.

NEWPORT CENTRE MALL

LUIS MUNOZ

MONMOUTH

3

CHRISTOPHER

COLUMBUS DR.

4

EXTENSION

DIXON MILLS

2

GRAND STREET

JERSEY CITY GRAND ST. ↗

MORRIS CANAL BIG BASIN

LIBERTY STATE PARK

NEW JERSEY TPKE.

TOLL

NEW

EXIT 14 C

1

NEW JERSEY

The Holland Tunnel: Manhattan Approaches

The best route for reaching the Holland Tunnel during peak traffic times is to take Washington Street to Spring Street. Washington Street is northbound between Hubert Street and Spring Street, and southbound between 14th Street and Spring Street. At Spring Street all traffic is forced east. Here's how to use Washington Street from the north or south:

From the north:

1a. Take 14th Street westbound to Washington Street and turn left.

2a. Take Washington Street to Spring Street, and turn left.
(Directions continue at no. 3, below.)

From the south:

1b. Take Hudson Street to Laight Street and turn left. Don't worry if Laight Street looks congested; almost all the drivers are heading to West Street.

2b. Turn right onto Washington Street, zip all the way up to Spring Street, and turn right.

3. Take Spring a few blocks to Varick Street and turn right.

4. Move into the right lanes of Varick Street. You'll soon see the entrance to the Holland Tunnel on your right.

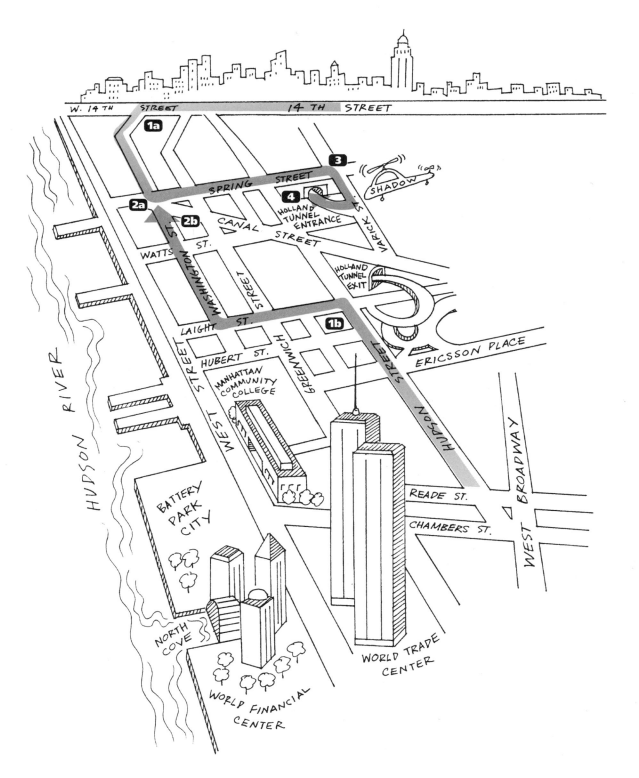

Approaching the Outerbridge Crossing from New Jersey

Ever try taking the Outerbridge Crossing on Thanksgiving, Mother's Day, or any weekend afternoon in the summer? Forget about it! You can sit for 30 minutes or longer waiting on Route 440 to get to the bridge. Here's a way to bypass about 20 minutes of that congestion.

1. Exit Route 440 at "Route 35, Amboy Avenue, Perth Amboy."

2. Take the left fork from the service road.

3. Go past the traffic signal and take the right fork, marked "Amboy Avenue."

4. Shortly you will see a tall water tower on your right. The next intersection with a traffic light is Amboy Avenue.

5. Cross Amboy Avenue and bear left, following the sign marked "Route 440 North, Staten Island."

6. Move into one of the two left lanes to reach the approach road to the Outerbridge Crossing.

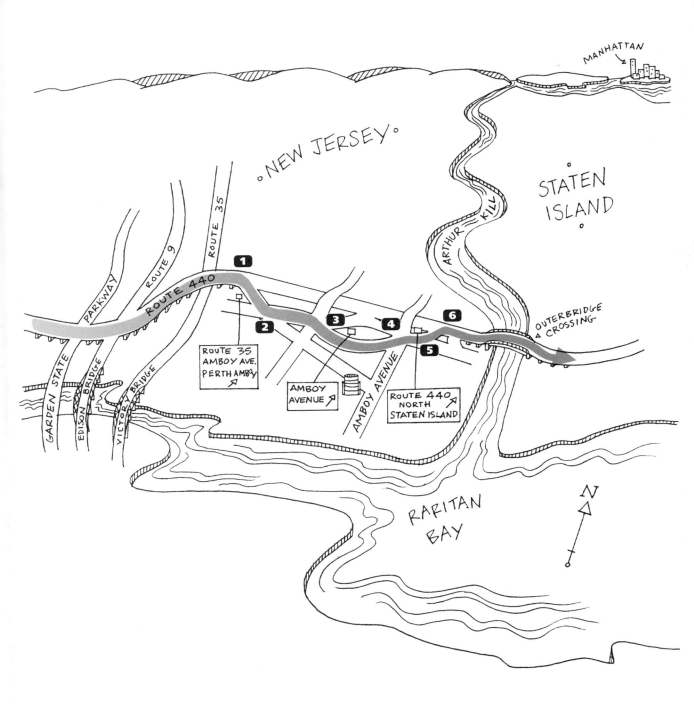

MANHATTAN

NEW JERSEY

STATEN ISLAND

ARTHUR KILL

GARDEN STATE PARKWAY

ROUTE 9

ROUTE 35

ROUTE 440

EDISON BRIDGE

VICTORY BRIDGE

OUTERBRIDGE CROSSING

1

2

3

4

6

5

ROUTE 35
AMBOY AVE.
PERTH AMBOY

AMBOY
AVENUE

AMBOY AVENUE

ROUTE 440
NORTH
STATEN ISLAND

RARITAN BAY

N

Trips to the airports can be some of New York City's most stressful drives—one jammed highway and you've missed your flight. In planning your route to the airport it's best to choose a consistently reliable route with many options, rather than what is traditionally considered the "fastest" route. Here are a few tips on getting to and from the airports.

From the Bronx to Kennedy Airport: Avoiding the Van Wyck Expressway

Bronxites and others coming from the north dread the trip to Kennedy Airport because it involves taking the southbound Van Wyck Expressway. Here's relief for those days when the Van Wyck is creeping along at a snail's pace.

1. Take the Bronx–Whitestone Bridge to the southbound Whitestone Expressway.

2. Head toward the Van Wyck southbound, but exit at Exit 8 (Union Turnpike west). Follow the signs to Union Turnpike.

3. Move into the left lanes as you go west on Union Turnpike. Turn left at Woodhaven Boulevard, which will become Cross Bay Boulevard south of Liberty Avenue.

4. Look for the sign, "East 878 Nassau Expressway, East 27 S. Conduit Avenue, Kennedy Airport." Turn left at South Conduit Avenue.

5. Keep to the right at the fork, and follow the signs to Lefferts Boulevard.

6. Continue straight past Lefferts Boulevard. Follow the signs for "Kennedy Airport, Van Wyck Expressway" to the airport entrance.

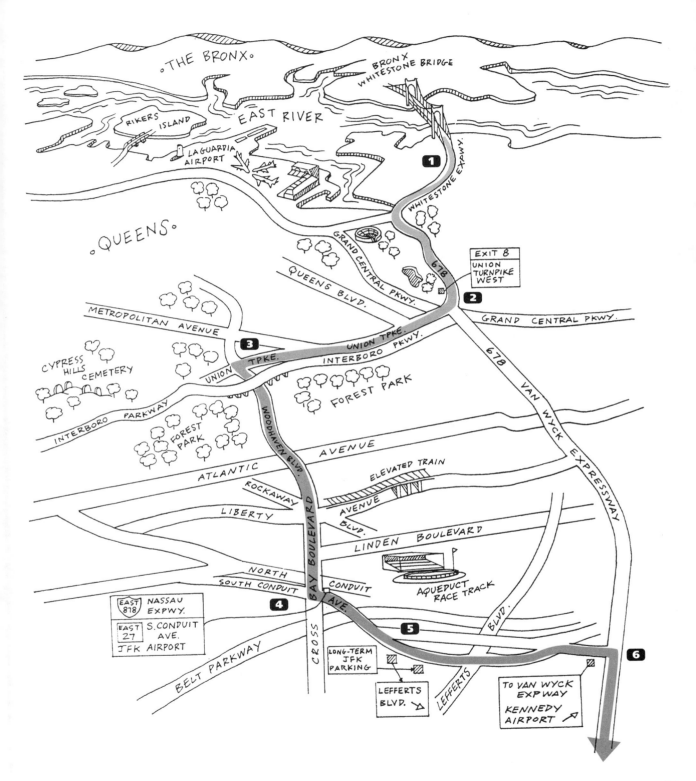

THE BRONX

BRONX WHITESTONE BRIDGE

EAST RIVER

RIKERS ISLAND

LA GUARDIA AIRPORT

QUEENS

1

WHITESTONE EXPWY.

GRAND CENTRAL PKWY.

678

EXIT 8
UNION TURNPIKE WEST

2

GRAND CENTRAL PKWY.

QUEENS BLVD.

METROPOLITAN AVENUE

3

UNION TPKE.

UNION TPKE.

INTERBORO PKWY.

678

VAN WYCK EXPRESSWAY

CYPRESS HILLS CEMETERY

INTERBORO PARKWAY

FOREST PARK

FOREST PARK

WOODHAVEN BLVD.

ATLANTIC AVENUE

ROCKAWAY

ELEVATED TRAIN

AVENUE BLVD.

LIBERTY

LINDEN BOULEVARD

AQUEDUCT RACE TRACK

NORTH
SOUTH CONDUIT

BAY BOULEVARD

CONDUIT AVE.

EAST 878 NASSAU EXPWY.

EAST 27 S. CONDUIT AVE. JFK AIRPORT

4

5

BLVD.

6

CROSS BAY BOULEVARD

LONG-TERM JFK PARKING

LEFFERTS BLVD. ↘

LEFFERTS

TO VAN WYCK EXPWAY
KENNEDY AIRPORT ↗

BELT PARKWAY

From Manhattan to Kennedy Airport: Avoiding the Van Wyck Expressway

Just about everyone is familiar with the traditional highway routes from Manhattan to Kennedy. From Midtown, you can take the LIE into the Van Wyck south to the airport.
From lower Manhattan, either take one of the lower East River Bridges to the BQE to the LIE to the Van Wyck, or take the Gowanus to the Belt and follow it around southern Brooklyn to the airport. However, all the highways—the LIE, Belt Parkway, BQE, and Van Wyck—are extremely unreliable. So rather than taking a gamble that may leave you sitting in a seemingly interminable traffic jam, try one of these alternatives:

From Midtown:

1a. Take the Queens–Midtown Tunnel to the LIE.

2a. Exit at Exit 19 (Woodhaven Blvd, Rockaways, Queens Blvd). Turn right at the traffic light onto Woodhaven Boulevard, which becomes Cross Bay Boulevard south of Liberty Avenue.

3a. Look for the sign marked, "East 878 Nassau Expressway, East 27 S. Conduit Avenue, JFK Airport." Turn left at South Conduit Avenue. (Directions continue at no. 5, below.)

From lower Manhattan:

1b. Take the Brooklyn Bridge to Adams Street, which becomes Boerum Place.

2b. From Boerum Place turn left onto Atlantic Avenue.

3b. A little more than a mile past Pennsylvania Avenue, at Fountain Avenue, the road curves to the right. At the fork, take the right leg to Conduit Boulevard, which leads into South Conduit Avenue.

4b. Continue on South Conduit Avenue, passing under Cross Bay Boulevard.

5. Bear right at the fork and follow the signs to Lefferts Boulevard. Continue straight past Lefferts Boulevard. Follow the signs for "Kennedy Airport, Van Wyck Expressway" to the airport entrance.

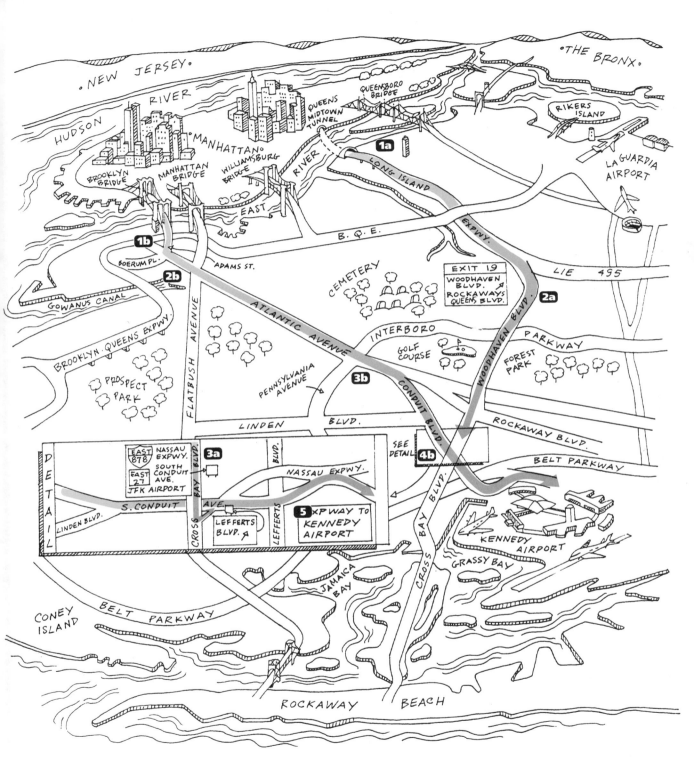

From Brooklyn to Kennedy Airport: Avoiding the Belt Parkway

Brooklyn has such a shortage of highways that nearly everyone assumes the only way to reach Kennedy Airport is via the Belt Parkway. For many it is the best alternative, but since the Belt is a "ring road" around Brooklyn it is often congested. Also, if the Belt's Mill Basin Bridge is raised you can forget about making your flight on time. For many in the interior of Brooklyn there are two reasonable alternatives to the Belt.

Via Linden Boulevard:

From Bay Ridge, Borough Park, Flatbush, and East Flatbush, the better alternative is via Fort Hamilton Parkway/Caton Avenue/Linden Boulevard. They are all conveniently marked "Route 27."

1a. Take Linden Boulevard to the very end, where all traffic will be forced to turn right onto South Conduit Avenue. (Directions continue at no. 2, below.)

Via Atlantic Avenue:

From Downtown Brooklyn, Bedford-Stuyvesant, and Crown Heights, you'll be better off taking Atlantic Avenue.

1b. Take Atlantic Avenue a little more than a mile past Pennsylvania Avenue. Follow the road as it curves to the right at Fountain Avenue. Take the right leg of the fork onto Conduit Boulevard, which leads into South Conduit Avenue.

2. Continue on South Conduit Avenue under Cross Bay Boulevard.

3. Bear right at the fork and follow the signs to Lefferts Boulevard. Continue past Lefferts Boulevard, following the signs for "Kennedy Airport, Van Wyck Expressway" to the airport entrance.

Note: This works well in reverse. Exit Kennedy Airport via the JFK Expressway. Follow signs for the Belt Parkway west, which will lead to North Conduit Avenue. Stay left for Linden Boulevard, right for Atlantic Avenue.

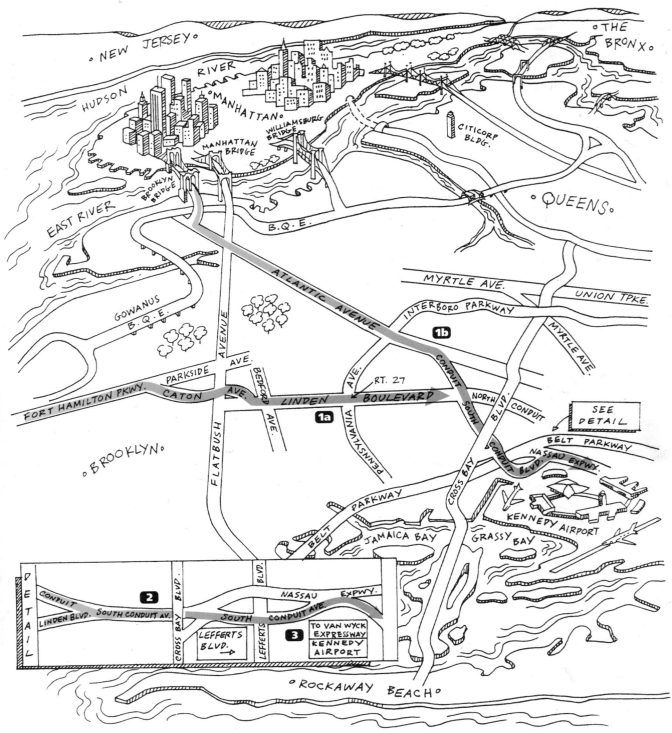

NEW JERSEY

THE BRONX

HUDSON RIVER

MANHATTAN

CITICORP BLDG.

WILLIAMSBURG BRIDGE

MANHATTAN BRIDGE

BROOKLYN BRIDGE

EAST RIVER

QUEENS

B.Q.E.

MYRTLE AVE.

UNION TPKE.

GOWANUS B.Q.E.

ATLANTIC AVENUE

INTERBORO PARKWAY

1b

MYRTLE AVE.

AVENUE

PARKSIDE AVE.

BEDFORD AVE.

AVE.

RT. 27

CONDUIT

SEE DETAIL

FORT HAMILTON PKWY. CATON AVE. LINDEN BOULEVARD

NORTH

BLVD. CONDUIT

1a

SOUTH

BELT PARKWAY

BROOKLYN

FLATBUSH AVE.

PENNSYLVANIA AVE.

CONDUIT BLVD.

NASSAU EXPWY.

CROSS BAY

KENNEDY AIRPORT

BELT

PARKWAY

JAMAICA BAY

GRASSY BAY

DETAIL

CONDUIT

LINDEN BLVD. SOUTH CONDUIT AV.

CROSS BAY BLVD.

BLVD.

NASSAU EXPWY.

2

SOUTH CONDUIT AVE.

LEFFERTS BLVD.

LEFFERTS

3 TO VAN WYCK EXPRESSWAY KENNEDY AIRPORT

ROCKAWAY BEACH

From Kennedy Airport to Manhattan via the Cross Island Parkway

Galileo's Theory for reaching Manhattan from Kennedy Airport

Galileo said that the world was round and you can get to the west by going east. Frank Katz, a veteran New York City cabby, uses the same principle when going to Manhattan from Kennedy; he advises drivers to "Go east, young man." Here's what he means:

At times the northbound Van Wyck Expressway and westbound Belt Parkway are so jammed that you end up spending more time on the ground than you've spent in the air. You'll find less resistance getting on the Belt Parkway heading in the wrong direction (eastbound). (This longcut is quite circuitous and should only be used when the alternative routes are bumper-to-bumper.)

1. As you exit the airport, follow signs for the Belt Parkway and eastern Long Island. Exit onto the eastbound Belt.

2. Stay to the left after Exit 23 to head north on the Cross Island Parkway.

3. Move into the right lanes after Exit 24B to remain on the Cross Island Parkway.

4. At the approach to the Throgs Neck Bridge, bear left.

5. At the approach to the Whitestone Bridge, bear left again and follow the sign marked, "Whitestone Expwy, NY Airports, Stay Left."

6. Take the Whitestone Expressway southbound, following the signs for "Grand Central Pkwy West, La Guardia Airport, Triborough Bridge."

7. The Grand Central Parkway westbound will take you to the Triborough Bridge, and on to Manhattan.

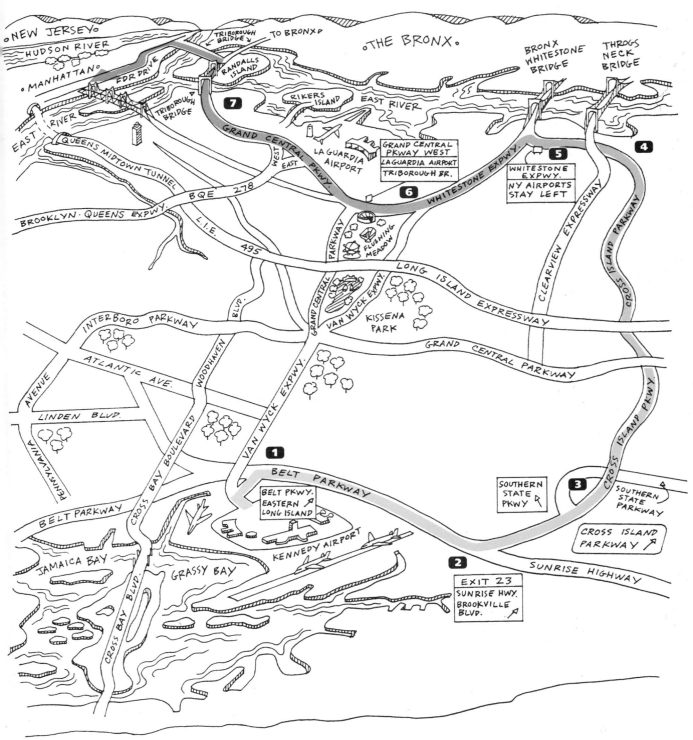

NEW JERSEY

HUDSON RIVER

TRIBOROUGH BRIDGE
TO BRONX

THE BRONX

BRONX WHITESTONE BRIDGE

THROGS NECK BRIDGE

MANHATTAN

FDR DRIVE

RANDALLS ISLAND

7

RIKERS ISLAND

EAST RIVER

EAST RIVER

TRIBOROUGH BRIDGE

GRAND CENTRAL PKWY.

LA GUARDIA AIRPORT

GRAND CENTRAL PKWAY WEST
LAGUARDIA AIRPORT
TRIBOROUGH BR.

5

WHITESTONE EXPWY.

WHITESTONE EXPWY.
NY AIRPORTS
STAY LEFT

4

QUEENS MIDTOWN TUNNEL

BQE 278

BROOKLYN·QUEENS EXPWY.

L.I.E. 495

WEST East

6 WHITESTONE EXPWY.

PARKWAY

FLUSHING MEADOW

CLEARVIEW EXPRESSWAY

CROSS ISLAND PARKWAY

LONG ISLAND EXPRESSWAY

GRAND CENTRAL

VAN WYCK EXPWY.

KISSENA PARK

INTERBORO PARKWAY

GRAND CENTRAL PARKWAY

BLVD.

AVENUE

ATLANTIC AVE.

WOODHAVEN

VAN WYCK EXPWY.

LINDEN BLVD.

PENNSYLVANIA

CROSS BAY BOULEVARD

CROSS ISLAND PKWY.

1

BELT PARKWAY

BELT PKWY.
EASTERN
LONG ISLAND

3

SOUTHERN STATE PKWY.

SOUTHERN STATE PARKWAY

CROSS ISLAND PARKWAY

BELT PARKWAY

KENNEDY AIRPORT

JAMAICA BAY

CROSS BAY BLVD.

GRASSY BAY

2

SUNRISE HIGHWAY

EXIT 23
SUNRISE HWY.
BROOKVILLE BLVD.

173

Parking at La Guardia Airport

There are three different parking options at La Guardia Airport: Some drivers elect to park on the street near the airport, others use nearby hotel lots, while the majority use the designated airport lots and garages.

You may actually find parking on Ditmars Boulevard, which runs parallel to the Grand Central Parkway, and on the side streets perpendicular to the GCP. If this is the case, you'll need to be aware of a few things. First, check to make sure that a restrictive parking rule doesn't "kick in" while you are gone. Secondly, be aware of the obscure traffic regulation prohibiting on-street parking for more than 24 consecutive hours on any city street. While this regulation is rarely enforced, the police will use it when residents complain.

The hotels and motels near La Guardia allow travelers to use their parking lots and provide shuttle service to all terminals. The rates are about $10 per day. Just pull up in front of the hotel and check with the doorman.

If you're parking at La Guardia's main terminal, there is a simple way to avoid having to drive to the front of the terminal:

From Manhattan:

1a. From the eastbound Grand Central Parkway take the exit prior to the airport, Exit 6 (94th Street).

2a. Turn left onto 94th Street. (Directions continue at no. 3, below.)

From Long Island:

1b. Take the westbound Grand Central Parkway to Exit 7 (94 St, La Guardia Airport).

2b. Stay on the service road and follow the signs to 94th Street. Turn right onto 94th Street.

3. You will see a sign marked, "Parking Garage Only." This route will take you to the garage in front of the main terminal.

4. After you park, go to Level 4 to find the bridge across the terminal's roadway.

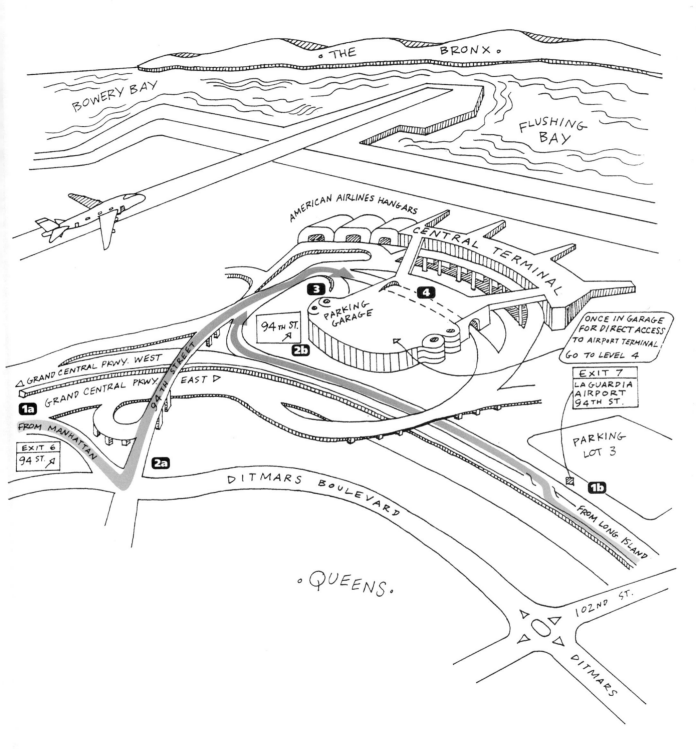

THE BRONX

BOWERY BAY

FLUSHING BAY

AMERICAN AIRLINES HANGARS

CENTRAL TERMINAL

3

4

PARKING GARAGE

94TH ST.

2b

ONCE IN GARAGE FOR DIRECT ACCESS TO AIRPORT TERMINAL GO TO LEVEL 4

△ GRAND CENTRAL PKWY. WEST

GRAND CENTRAL PKWY. EAST ▷

94TH STREET

1a

FROM MANHATTAN

EXIT 6
94 ST. ↗

EXIT 7
LA GUARDIA
AIRPORT
94TH ST.

PARKING
LOT 3

1b

2a

DITMARS BOULEVARD

FROM LONG ISLAND

∘ QUEENS ∘

102ND ST.

DITMARS

From Manhattan to La Guardia Airport by Taxi

More than 60% of the passengers flying out of La Guardia come from Manhattan; many are business people who find themselves in the back of a taxi at the mercy of their cabdriver. If this sounds like you, don't feel helpless. Let the cabby know that you've read Gridlock Sam's book of shortcuts and remind him or her of the city regulation requiring cabbies to follow passengers' recommended alternatives. Don't use this route if you have a lot of luggage, since you will have to walk a short distance to the terminal.

1. Tell the driver to exit the eastbound Grand Central Parkway at Exit 6(94th Street) and turn left toward the airport.

2. When you see the Amoco gas station on your left, bear left, following the gray sign marked "Marine Air Terminal, Delta Shuttle, Rental Cars."

3. You'll immediately see a sign marked, "Walkway to Main Terminal." Bear right at this sign.

4. You can hop out at the sign or wait for the signal to change (it's a long one) and get out in the taxi queuing area. You'll be at the main terminal in less than a minute. This is especially good for United, American, TWA, and Continental. (Don't use this route for the shuttles, Northwest, US Air, or Delta.)

Note: A good way to save time and money when leaving the central terminal at La Guardia is to head toward the American Airlines hangar instead of trying to get a cab directly in front of the terminal. Turn right when you exit the building for the brief walk to the edge of the terminal. Cabs are usually plentiful and they can exit the airport more quickly from here.

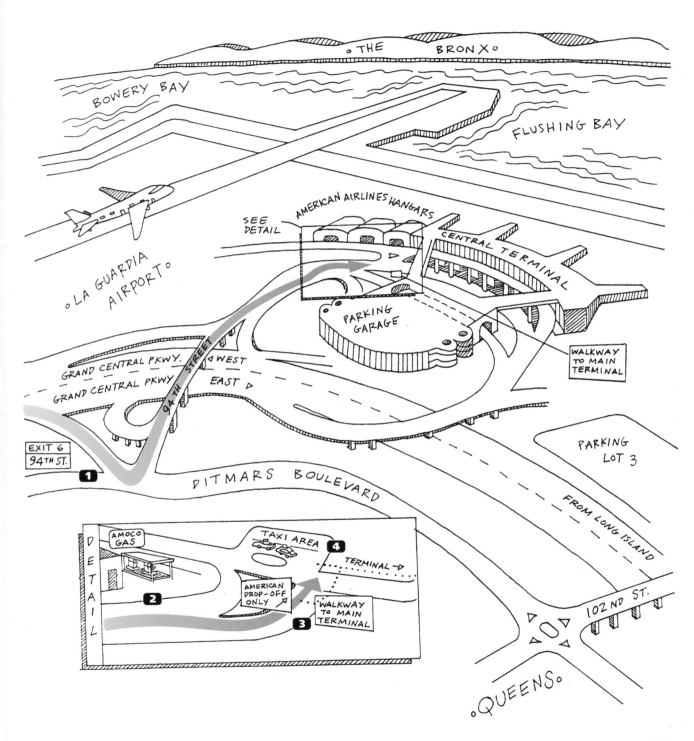

THE BRONX

BOWERY BAY

FLUSHING BAY

AMERICAN AIRLINES HANGARS

SEE DETAIL

CENTRAL TERMINAL

LA GUARDIA AIRPORT

PARKING GARAGE

WALKWAY TO MAIN TERMINAL

GRAND CENTRAL PKWY. WEST

GRAND CENTRAL PKWY. EAST

94TH STREET

EXIT 6 94TH ST.

1

DITMARS BOULEVARD

PARKING LOT 3

FROM LONG ISLAND

DETAIL

AMOCO GAS

TAXI AREA

4

TERMINAL →

AMERICAN DROP-OFF ONLY

WALKWAY TO MAIN TERMINAL

2

3

102 ND ST.

QUEENS

177

From La Guardia to Manhattan by Local Streets

There are plenty of times when the GCP or BQE is out of commission for one reason or another. You say you just don't know what to do? Never fear, Gridlock Sam is here.

1. When exiting the airport, head west on the GCP but get off at the first exit, Exit 5 (Steinway Street, Marine Air Terminal).

2. Turn right onto Ditmars Boulevard.

3. Follow Ditmars Boulevard about two miles to 21st Street and turn left.

4. Take 21st Street a little more than a mile to Broadway. You'll first pass under the Triborough Bridge and then cross Astoria Boulevard. Turn right onto Broadway.

5. Go a few blocks to the end and turn left onto Vernon Boulevard. (Be careful not to turn onto 11th Street, which intersects with Broadway about 50 feet before Vernon Boulevard.)

6. You'll soon pass under the Queensboro Bridge. Turn left immediately past the bridge and take the 11th Street entrance ramp, on your left, to the bridge's upper level.

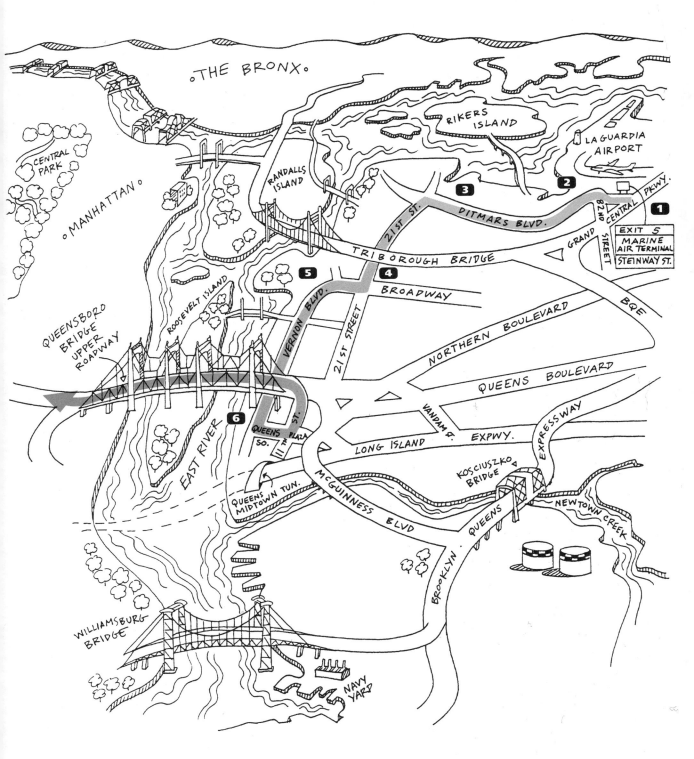

THE BRONX

CENTRAL PARK

MANHATTAN

RIKERS ISLAND

LA GUARDIA AIRPORT

RANDALLS ISLAND

3

21ST ST.

DITMARS BLVD.

2

82ND STREET

GRAND CENTRAL PKWY.

1

EXIT 5
MARINE
AIR TERMINAL
STEINWAY ST.

TRIBOROUGH BRIDGE

BQE

5

4

BROADWAY

ROOSEVELT ISLAND

VERNON BLVD.

21ST STREET

NORTHERN BOULEVARD

QUEENS BOULEVARD

QUEENSBORO BRIDGE UPPER ROADWAY

VANPAM ST.

LONG ISLAND EXPWY.

EXPRESSWAY

6

QUEENS PLAZA

SO.

EAST RIVER

KOSCIUSZKO BRIDGE

NEWTOWN CREEK

QUEENS MIDTOWN TUN.

McGUINNESS BLVD

BROOKLYN · QUEENS

WILLIAMSBURG BRIDGE

NAVY YARD

La Guardia Airport: The Secret Drop-off Areas in the Garage

On busy days the drop-off area can get stacked up with cars and you can lose precious minutes just a few hundred feet from your terminal. If you are traveling light and you're in a taxi or someone is dropping you off, you'll do better using the alternate drop-off area. Here's what to do:

1. Follow signs to the central terminal's departure roadway.

2. Keep to your left when you first get on the departure roadway.

3. Before you reach the terminal you will see a road to the left with a sign marked "Alternate drop-off area." This will take you through the garage (no charge).

4. If you are heading to Continental or TWA, stop at the first escalator on your right, behind the elevators, as you enter the garage. For American and United, go to the escalator at the other end of the garage, also found behind the elevator.

5. The escalators will leave you on Level 4, where the pedestrian bridges lead directly into the terminal.

Heaviest traffic days
The heaviest traffic days of the year are the two Fridays before Christmas and the Wednesday before Thanksgiving. The traffic jams on the Fridays center around Midtown tourist areas (especially the tree at Rockefeller Center) and shopping districts throughout town. Herald Square should be avoided at all costs on those days. On the Wednesday before Thanksgiving, the longest back-ups occur on the "get-away" routes between 4 PM and 7 PM. At 5 PM the lines at the George Washington Bridge will usually be five miles in both directions. It's also the peak day of the year at most airports.

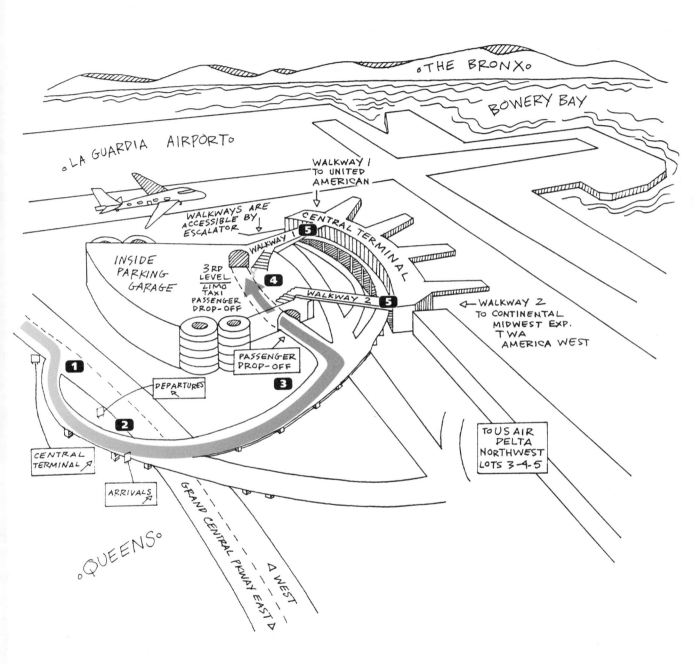

THE BRONX

BOWERY BAY

LA GUARDIA AIRPORT

WALKWAY 1
TO UNITED
AMERICAN

WALKWAYS ARE
ACCESSIBLE BY
ESCALATOR

CENTRAL TERMINAL

WALKWAY 1

5

INSIDE
PARKING
GARAGE

3RD
LEVEL
LIMO
TAXI
PASSENGER
DROP-OFF

4

WALKWAY 2

5

WALKWAY 2
TO CONTINENTAL
MIDWEST EXP.
TWA
AMERICA WEST

PASSENGER
DROP-OFF

1

DEPARTURES

3

2

TO US AIR
DELTA
NORTHWEST
LOTS 3-4-5

CENTRAL
TERMINAL

ARRIVALS

GRAND CENTRAL PKWAY EAST ▷

◁ WEST

QUEENS

From Midtown to Newark Airport via the Lincoln Tunnel

Even veteran New Yorkers tend to treat Newark Airport as if it were located on Mars; unfairly, since it is as close as La Guardia (time-wise) and far more accessible than Kennedy. Newark has its share of drawbacks too, however, including the Lincoln Tunnel (especially the helix) and the New Jersey Turnpike. Here's how to avoid the helix and much of the Turnpike.

1. Upon exiting the Lincoln Tunnel, immediately bear right and exit following the sign to Hoboken. You will be heading south on Willow Avenue.

2. Go a little under two miles through Hoboken to the end of Willow Avenue and make a right turn onto Observer Highway.

3. Follow the road to the left onto Newark Avenue.

4. Just after you pass under the railroad viaduct, turn left onto Jersey Avenue.

5. At the third traffic signal you will come to the wide plaza of the Holland Tunnel exit street. Make a right* onto the rising viaduct for the New Jersey Turnpike Extension southbound.

6. Take the Turnpike Extension to Exit 14 (Newark Airport). For quicker access to the airport (and a few extra cents), go one more exit to Exit 13A (also Newark Airport).

Note: If the Turnpike Extension is jammed, swing wide as you turn right at the Holland Tunnel Plaza to get to Routes 1 and 9 (the Pulaski Skyway), which leads directly to the airport.

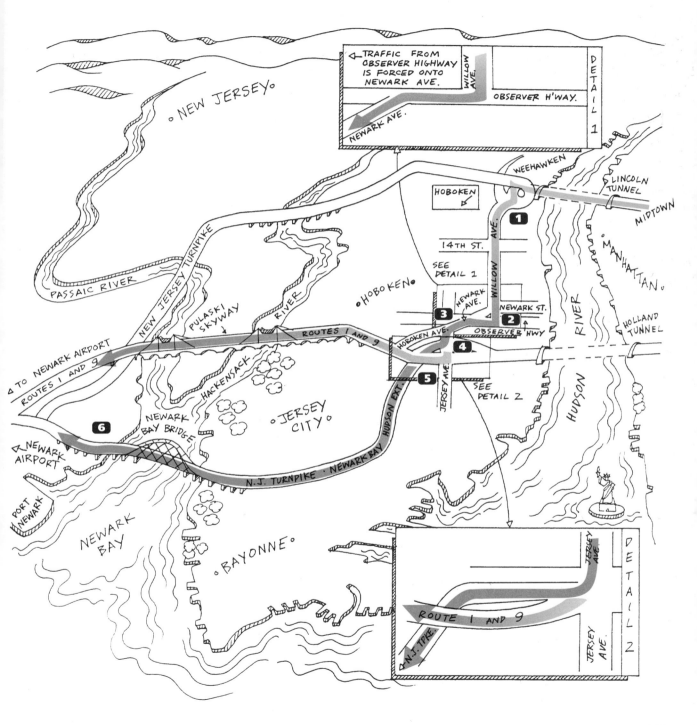

NEW JERSEY

TRAFFIC FROM OBSERVER HIGHWAY IS FORCED ONTO NEWARK AVE.

WILLOW AVE.

OBSERVER H'WAY.

NEWARK AVE.

DETAIL 1

WEEHAWKEN

LINCOLN TUNNEL

HOBOKEN

1

14TH ST.

SEE DETAIL 1

WILLOW AVE.

MIDTOWN

MANHATTAN

PASSAIC RIVER

NEW JERSEY TURNPIKE

HOBOKEN

NEWARK AVE.

3

NEWARK ST.

2

OBSERVER HWY

HUDSON RIVER

HOLLAND TUNNEL

PULASKI SKYWAY

RIVER

ROUTES 1 AND 9

HOBOKEN AVE.

4

TO NEWARK AIRPORT

ROUTES 1 AND 9

5

JERSEY AVE.

SEE DETAIL 2

HUDSON EXT.

HACKENSACK

6

NEWARK BAY BRIDGE

JERSEY CITY

NEWARK AIRPORT

PORT NEWARK

NEWARK BAY

N.J. TURNPIKE · NEWARK BAY

BAYONNE

DETAIL 2

JERSEY AVE.

ROUTE 1 AND 9

N.J. TPKE.

JERSEY AVE.

183

From Brooklyn to Newark Airport

When a Brooklynite needs to catch a plane, Kennedy or La Guardia naturally spring to mind. Newark, New Joisey is just too fah. Well, fellow Kingsmen and women, have I got news for you! You don't have to sit in northbound BQE or eastbound Belt traffic to get to an airport. By flying out of Newark you can take these same roads in the opposite, less congested, directions. Here's how:

1.   Take the Verrazano–Narrows Bridge to the Staten Island Expressway.

2.   Take the Staten Island Expressway to the Goethals Bridge.

3.   Once across the Goethals Bridge, follow the signs to the New Jersey Turnpike northbound.

4.   Take the Turnpike one exit to Exit 13A (Newark Airport, Elizabeth Seaport). This ramp will take you directly to the airport.

> **Radar can be inexact**
> Speeders often get trapped by radar. But a fair number of non-speeders also get trapped because radar "guns" can be inexact. The radar gun sends out a radar beam that bounces off an object and returns to the gun. The speed is calculated by the difference between the original beam and the reflected beam. The radar gun emits not just one beam, but a spray of beams; if there's more than one vehicle traveling at the time in either direction, it's impossible to be sure which vehicle was hit. If you were traveling with a group of vehicles and were stopped for speeding, you may have a case for dismissal.

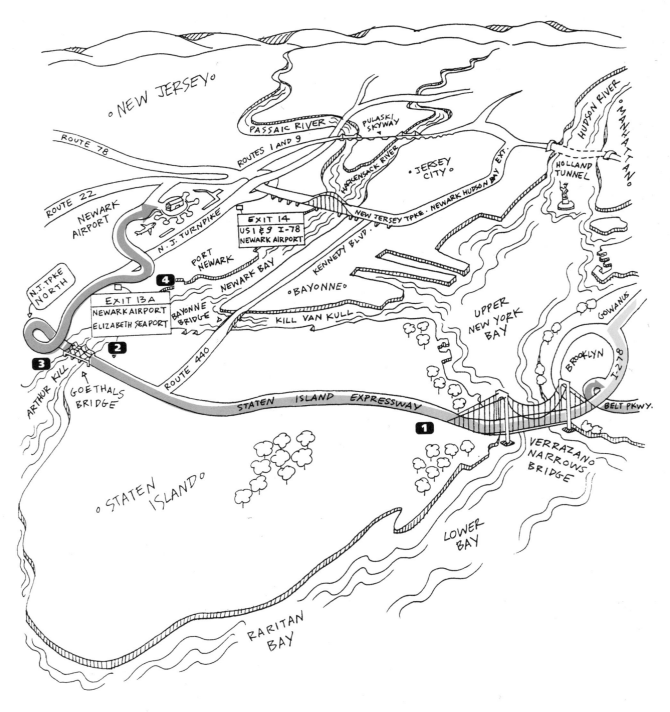

NEW JERSEY

PASSAIC RIVER

PULASKI SKYWAY

HUDSON RIVER

MANHATTAN

ROUTE 78

ROUTES 1 AND 9

HACKENSACK RIVER

JERSEY CITY

HOLLAND TUNNEL

ROUTE 22

NEWARK AIRPORT

N.J. TURNPIKE

EXIT 14
US 1 & 9 I-78
NEWARK AIRPORT

NEW JERSEY TPKE · NEWARK HUDSON BAY EXT.

N.J. TPKE NORTH

4 PORT NEWARK

NEWARK BAY

KENNEDY BLVD.

BAYONNE

UPPER NEW YORK BAY

GOWANUS

EXIT 13A
NEWARK AIRPORT
ELIZABETH SEAPORT

BAYONNE BRIDGE

KILL VAN KULL

BROOKLYN

I-278

2

3 ARTHUR KILL

GOETHALS BRIDGE

ROUTE 440

STATEN ISLAND EXPRESSWAY

BELT PKWY.

1

VERRAZANO NARROWS BRIDGE

STATEN ISLAND

LOWER BAY

RARITAN BAY

185

JFK International Airport

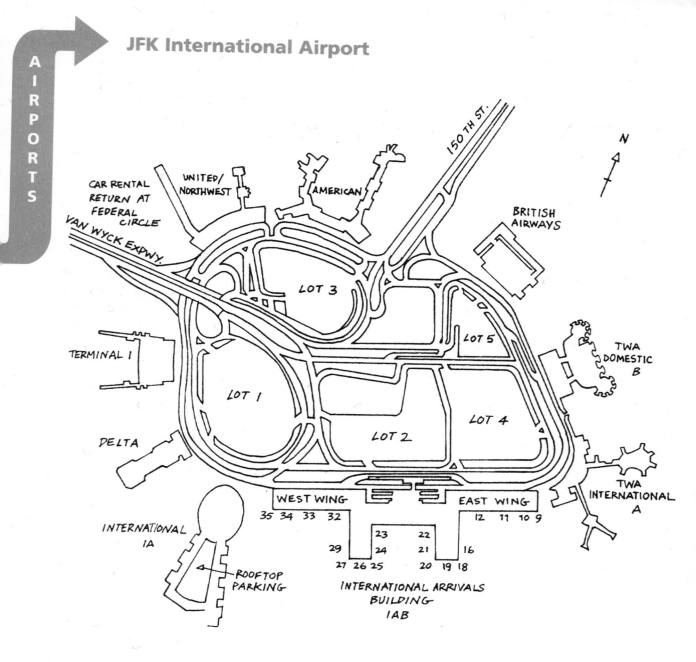

N

150 TH ST.

CAR RENTAL RETURN AT FEDERAL CIRCLE

VAN WYCK EXPWY.

UNITED/ NORTHWEST

AMERICAN

BRITISH AIRWAYS

LOT 3

LOT 5

TERMINAL 1

TWA DOMESTIC B

LOT 1

LOT 4

DELTA

LOT 2

TWA INTERNATIONAL A

INTERNATIONAL 1A

ROOFTOP PARKING

WEST WING

35 34 33 32

EAST WING

12 11 10 9

29

23
24

22
21

16

27 26 25

20 19 18

INTERNATIONAL ARRIVALS BUILDING 1AB

La Guardia Airport

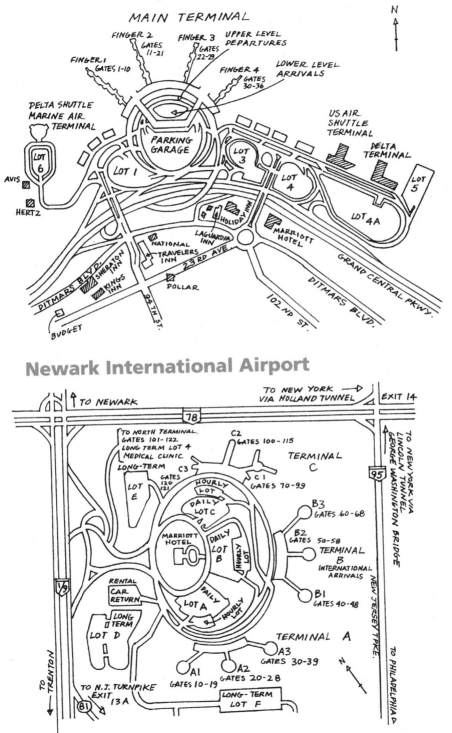

MAIN TERMINAL

FINGER 2
GATES 11-21

FINGER 3
GATES 22-29

UPPER LEVEL
DEPARTURES

FINGER 1
GATES 1-10

FINGER 4
GATES 30-36

LOWER LEVEL
ARRIVALS

N

DELTA SHUTTLE
MARINE AIR
TERMINAL

US AIR
SHUTTLE
TERMINAL

DELTA
TERMINAL

PARKING
GARAGE

LOT 6

LOT 1

LOT 3

LOT 4

LOT 5

AVIS

LOT 4A

HERTZ

HOLIDAY INN

MARRIOTT
HOTEL

NATIONAL
TRAVELERS
INN

LAGUARDIA
INN

SHERATON
INN

23 RD AVE.

KINGS
INN

DOLLAR

GRAND CENTRAL PKWY.

PITMARS BLVD.

94 TH ST.

102 ND ST.

DITMARS BLVD.

BUDGET

Newark International Airport

TO NEWARK

TO NEW YORK
VIA HOLLAND TUNNEL

EXIT 14

78

TO NORTH TERMINAL
GATES 101-122
LONG TERM LOT 4
MEDICAL CLINIC

C2
GATES 100-115

TERMINAL
C

95

LONG-TERM
LOT E

C3
GATES
120
121

HOURLY
LOT

C1
GATES 70-99

DAILY
LOT C

B3
GATES 60-68

MARRIOTT
HOTEL

DAILY
LOT
B

HOURLY
LOT

B2
GATES 50-58

TERMINAL
B
INTERNATIONAL
ARRIVALS

RENTAL
CAR
RETURN

DAILY
LOT A

HOURLY
LOT

B1
GATES 40-48

I/9

LONG
TERM

LOT D

TERMINAL A

A3
GATES 30-39

TO
TRENTON

A1
GATES 10-19

A2
GATES 20-28

N

TO PHILADELPHIA

81

TO N.J. TURNPIKE
EXIT 13A

LONG-TERM
LOT F

NEW JERSEY TPKE.

TO NEW YORK VIA
LINCOLN TUNNEL
GEORGE WASHINGTON BRIDGE

Getting to the Hamptons

The two most common routes to the Hamptons are NY Route 27 (Sunrise Highway), which leads directly to the Hamptons, and I-495 (the Long Island Expressway) to Exit 70 (County Route 111), which then connects with NY Route 27. What sounds like a simple drive is often marred by heavy traffic, and many a vacation has been ruined by the torturous drive to and from the Hamptons. In the next few pages I've tried to offer some relief, but keep in mind the following axioms from veteran Manhattan-to-Hamptons commuter and traffic engineer, Bill Hirsch:

A.   From April to November, the worst time to leave Manhattan for the Hamptons is Friday between 2 PM and 8 PM.

B.   From June through September, avoid starting the return trip between 3 PM and 9 PM on Sunday.

C.   If it's snowing, avoid the LIE between exits 68 and 70 (a.k.a. "The Devil's Playground").

D.   The advisory message signs on the LIE and Northern State Parkway really do work.

I avoid the LIE as much as possible, opting instead to take the Grand Central Parkway to the Northern State Parkway. Exit 37A on the parkway leads directly to the LIE; by this point you'll have already put a good bit of distance between you and Manhattan.

Bypassing the jam at LIE Exit 70:

Traffic on the LIE flows reasonably well until Exit 70, where it seems that just about everybody is exiting. To avoid joining the crowd, try one of the following alternates:

1a.   Take the LIE eastbound to Exit 68 (Shirley, Wading River).

2a.   Once on the service road, follow signs marked "Shirley, Route 46 south."

3a.   Route 46 south becomes William Floyd Parkway. Follow this for 2 1/2 miles to Route 27 east.

If heading east of Hampton Bays:

1b.   Go past LIE Exit 70 to Exit 71 (NY Route 24).

2b.   From the exit, turn right onto Route 24 and take this south to Route 27 east.

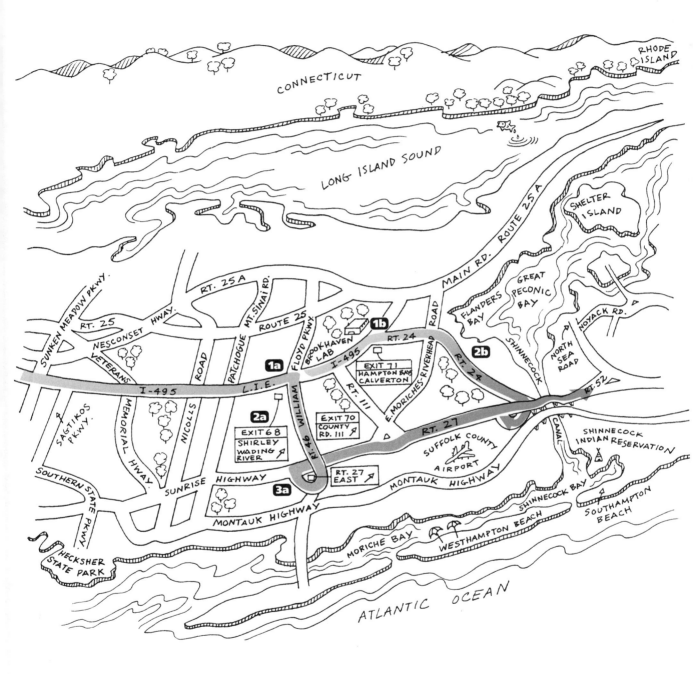

CONNECTICUT

RHODE ISLAND

LONG ISLAND SOUND

SHELTER ISLAND

MAIN RD. ROUTE 25 A

GREAT PECONIC BAY

FLANDERS BAY

NOYACK RD.

RT. 25 A

MT. SINAI RD.

ROUTE 25

FLOYD PKWY.

1b

BROOKHAVEN LAB

RT. 24

NORTH SEA ROAD

SUNKEN MEADOW PKWY.

RT. 25

NESCONSET HWAY.

VETERANS

PATCHOGUE ROAD

E. MORICHES RIVERHEAD ROAD

SHINNECOCK

RT. 52

1a

I-495

2b

RT. 24

I-495   L.I.E.

WILLIAM

RT. 111

SAGTIKOS PKWY.

MEMORIAL HWY.

NICOLLS

2a

EXIT 71
HAMPTON BAY
CALVERTON

RT. 27

SUFFOLK COUNTY AIRPORT

SHINNECOCK CANAL

SHINNECOCK INDIAN RESERVATION

EXIT 68
SHIRLEY
WADING
RIVER

RT. 46

EXIT 70
COUNTY
RD. 111

SUNRISE HIGHWAY

3a

RT. 27
EAST

MONTAUK HIGHWAY

SHINNECOCK BAY

SOUTHAMPTON BEACH

SOUTHERN STATE PKWY.

MONTAUK HIGHWAY

WESTHAMPTON BEACH

HECKSHER STATE PARK

MORICHE BAY

ATLANTIC OCEAN

Leaving the Hamptons

Just in case you don't follow Hirsch's Axioms (*see* page 188) and do attempt to leave the Hamptons on a Sunday afternoon, here are a couple of alternative routes. Typically, the westbound backup occurs between Exit 62 and County Route 111. Here are two ways around the jam.

1a. Take NY Route 27 past Exit 62 to Exit 58N (William Floyd Parkway, Wading River).

2a. Follow the William Floyd Parkway north to the LIE westbound.

OR,

1b. Stay on NY Route 27 to Exit 51 (Rt. 97, Stony Brook). From the service road, follow signs to Route 97 north.

2b. Route 97 is Nicolls Road. Take this north for a few miles to the LIE westbound. The signs for the LIE are sloppy; you can easily mistake the exit for the LIE eastbound with the westbound exit, so be careful.

On weekends, pay the toll

Weekend drivers are far less savvy than their commuter counterparts. During the weekday rush hours, nearly all bridges and tunnels are filled to capacity. But on the weekends the toll-free bridges are often jammed while the toll bridges are relatively empty. The Brooklyn, Manhattan, and Williamsburg Bridges are often disasters on Saturdays and Sundays. The nearby Brooklyn–Battery Tunnel and Queens–Midtown Tunnel are usually free flowing. So, weekend drivers, think carefully if that extra 15–30 minutes of torturous smog-filled driving is worth the $3 you saved by avoiding the toll.

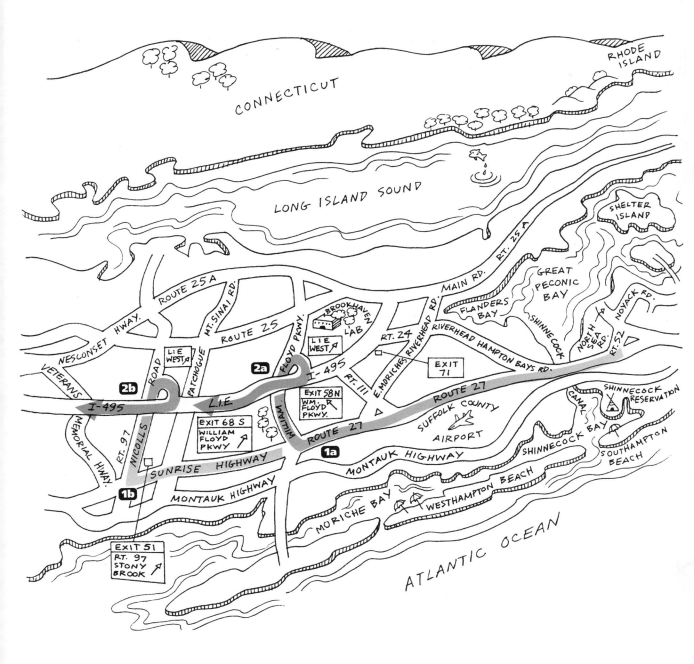

CONNECTICUT

RHODE ISLAND

LONG ISLAND SOUND

SHELTER ISLAND

RT. 25 A

GREAT PECONIC BAY

MAIN RD.

ROUTE 25 A

MT. SINAI RD.

ROUTE 25

BROOKHAVEN LAB

FLOYD PKWY.

LIE WEST

RT. 24

FLANDERS BAY

RIVERHEAD

SHINNECOCK

NORTH SEA RD.

NOYACK RD.

RT. 52

NESCONSET HWAY.

PATCHOGUE ROAD

LIE WEST

I-495

RIVERHEAD HAMPTON BAYS RD.

E. MORICHES RIVERHEAD RD.

EXIT 71

SHINNECOCK RESERVATION

VETERANS

2b

I-495

L.I.E.

2a

EXIT 58 N
WM. FLOYD PKWY.

RT. 111

ROUTE 27

SUFFOLK COUNTY AIRPORT

CANAL

MEMORIAL HWY.

RT. 97

NICOLLS

EXIT 68 S
WILLIAM FLOYD PKWY

WILLIAM FLOYD PKWY

1a

ROUTE 27

MONTAUK HIGHWAY

SHINNECOCK BAY

SOUTHAMPTON BEACH

1b

SUNRISE HIGHWAY

MONTAUK HIGHWAY

MONTAUK HIGHWAY

WESTHAMPTON BEACH

EXIT 51
RT. 97
STONY BROOK

MORICHE BAY

ATLANTIC OCEAN

191

Bypassing NY Route 27 in the Hamptons

The main traffic congestion in the Hamptons begins just east of the Shinnecock Canal. About two miles past the canal, NY Route 27 narrows from a four-lane expressway to a two-lane local road with traffic lights. On Friday evenings and Saturdays the traffic crawls along this local road for nearly twenty miles to East Hampton. Remember this general rule of thumb: if there is slow moving traffic west of South Hampton, it will only get worse as you travel east through the other villages. This calls for a shortcut (actually a "longcut," but much faster).

1. Take Route 27 about three miles past the start of the narrowed section to Exit 8 (North Sea, Noyack) and turn left.

2. At the next traffic light, after about a mile, turn left onto Route 38 (North Sea Road).

3. Go about 1 1/2 miles to Noyack Road (the continuation of Route 38) and turn right.

4. Stay on Noyack Road for just over eight miles and bear left at the fork onto Brick Kiln Road.

5. Turn left onto Main Street (you'll see Mashashimuet Park on the far right corner).

6. Continue on Main Street about 1/2 mile to Union Street (just past the library) and turn right.

7. Go two blocks to Hampton Street (NY Route 114) and turn right.

8. Bear left to continue on Hampton Street (NY Route 114), which, after six miles, becomes Buells Lane. Buells Lane intersects with Route 27.

Note: This shortcut is reversible.

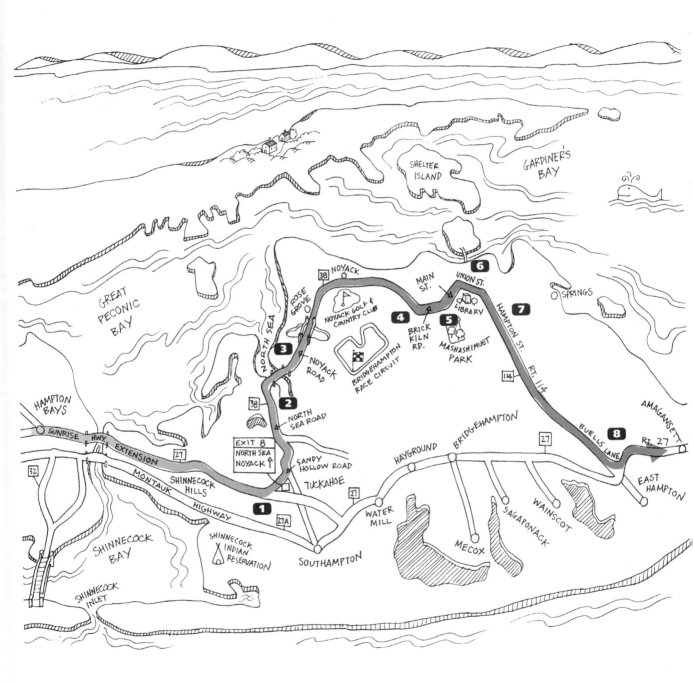

GREAT
PECONIC
BAY

SHELTER
ISLAND

GARDINER'S
BAY

NOYACK
38
ROSE
GROVE
NOYACK GOLF &
COUNTRY CLUB
NORTH SEA
3
NOYACK
ROAD
38
2
NORTH
SEA ROAD
BRIDGEHAMPTON
RACE CIRCUIT

MAIN
ST.
UNION ST.
6
SPRINGS
LIBRARY
4
BRICK
KILN
RD.
5
MASHASHIMUET
PARK
7
HAMPTON ST.
RT. 114
114

HAMPTON
BAYS
SUNRISE   HWY
EXTENSION
27
32
MONTAUK
HIGHWAY
SHINNECOCK
HILLS
EXIT 8
NORTH SEA
NOYACK ↑
SANDY
HOLLOW ROAD
1
27A
TUCKAHOE
27
WATER
MILL
HAYGROUND
BRIDGEHAMPTON
27
BUELLS LANE
8
AMAGANSETT
RT. 27
EAST
HAMPTON

SHINNECOCK
BAY
SHINNECOCK
INDIAN
RESERVATION
SOUTHAMPTON
MECOX
SAGAPONACK
WAINSCOT

SHINNECOCK
INLET

The Jersey Shore: Garden State Parkway to Route 18 (Asbury Park to Point Pleasant)

The Garden State Parkway is the traditional route to the Jersey Shore—just stay on the parkway until you spot signs for your destination. But if you're making this trip on a Friday afternoon or Saturday morning with the rest of the masses, the parkway can be a real pill. Avoid the mess by taking the recently improved Route 18, which can zip you past the get-away crowd.

1.   Take the New Jersey Turnpike to Exit 11 (Garden State Parkway southbound).

2.   Continue on the Garden State Parkway to Exit 105. After the toll stay to the right and follow the signs to Route 18 south.

3.   Route 18 intersects the east–west routes to the shore. Choose one of the following to your destination:

- Route 66 east for Asbury Park

- Route 33 east for Ocean Grove, Bradley Beach, Avon-By-The-Sea

- Route 138 east for Belmar, Spring Lake, Sea Girt, and Manasquan

- Route 34/35 south for Point Pleasant/Bay Head

Can I make a U-turn on a New York City street?
U-turns are prohibited on two-way streets if indicated by a sign, and on any street in a business district. A business district is defined in the Vehicle and Traffic Law as, "the territory contiguous to and including a highway when within any six hundred feet along such highway there are buildings in use for business or industrial purposes... which occupy at least three hundred feet of frontage on one side or three hundred feet collectively on both sides of the highway."

In layman's terms, if there are stores or businesses, U-turns are prohibited. If there are only residential dwellings, U-turns are permitted (unless signed otherwise).

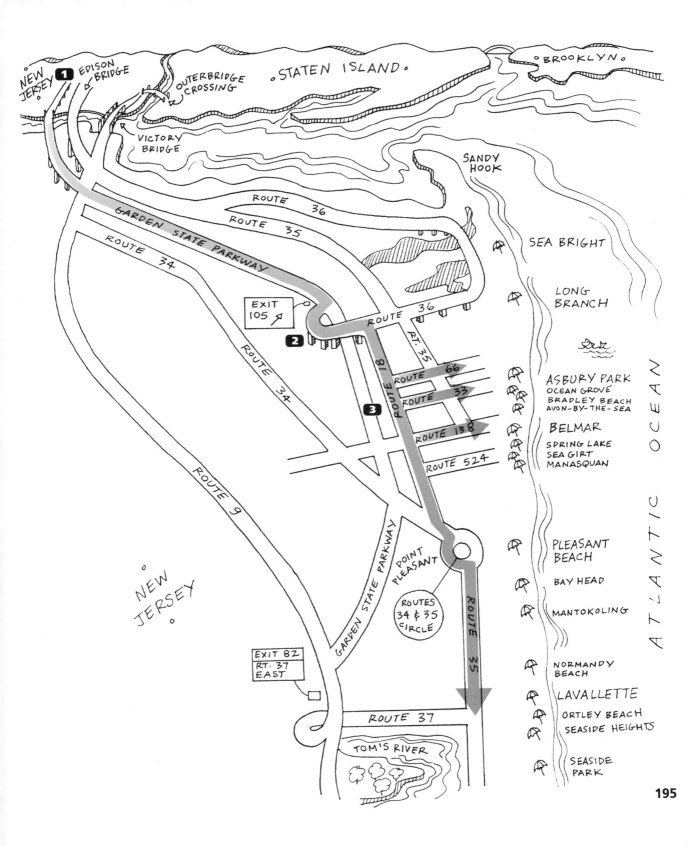

The Jersey Shore from Sandy Hook to Seaside Park: Avoiding the Turnpike and the Garden State Parkway

The most direct route to the Jersey Shore from New York City is the New Jersey Turnpike southbound to Exit 11 (the Garden State Parkway). The Garden State Parkway has exits for a variety of shore destinations.

However, during the peak periods (Friday afternoons and evenings, Saturday mornings) the turnpike may be backed up from exits 13 through 11, and the Garden State Parkway could be jammed from the turnpike to Exit 120, and again at the Asbury and Toms River tolls. Choose one of the five alternate routes listed below, depending on your destination. (Routes 1 and 9 are easily accessed from the Lincoln and Holland tunnels.)

A. Sandy Hook and Seabright

1a. Take Route 9 south to Route 35.

2a. Take Route 35 south about ten miles to Route 36 eastbound. Route 36 leads to Sandy Hook and Sea Bright.

B. Long Branch, Asbury park, Ocean Grove, and Bradley Beach

1b. Take Route 9 to Route 35 south. Continue for about 20 miles, until you see signs for your destination.

C. Belmar

1c. Head south on Route 9 for about five miles past the Edison Bridge. Move into the left lane and take Route 34 south.

2c. Continue on Route 34 for some 20 miles, then take Route 138 east to Belmar.

D. Point Pleasant, Manasquan, Mantoloking, and Normandy Beach

1d. Head south on Route 9 about five miles past the Edison Bridge. Move into the left lane and take Route 34 south.

2d. Continue on Route 34 for about 25 miles, then take Route 35 south to your destination.

E. Seaside Heights, Seaside Park, Lavallette, and Ortley Beach

1e. Head south on Route 9 for about 35 miles past the Edison Bridge. Route 9 will merge with the Garden State Parkway.

2e. Take Exit 82 to Route 37 east, which will take you directly to the shore.

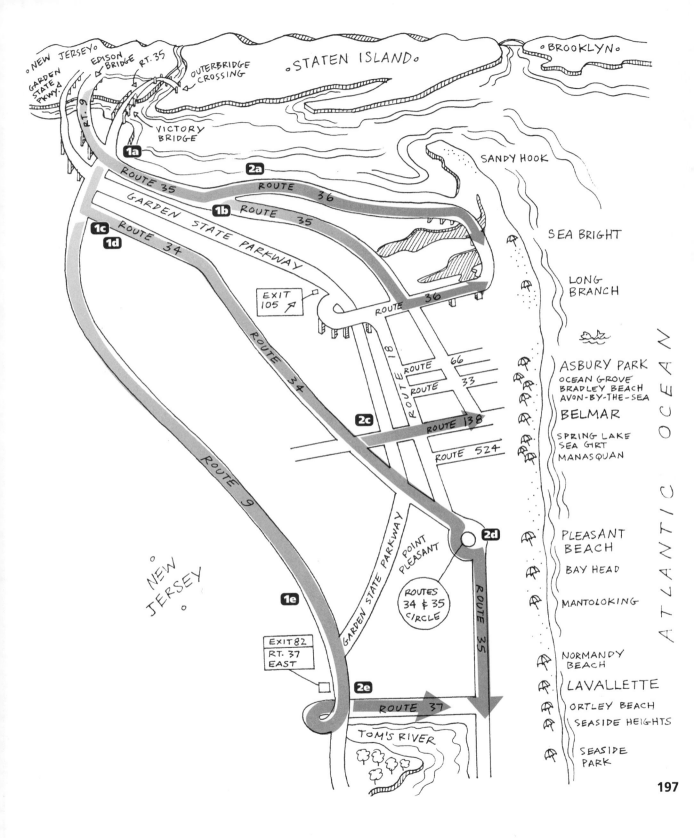

Away to the Catskills

New Yorkers have been escaping to the Catskills Region for recreation for over a half-century. The traditional route leads across the George Washington Bridge and northwest via Route 4 into Route 17, or on the New York Thruway over the Tappan Zee Bridge to Route 17. But just getting across the George Washington Bridge and traveling on congested New Jersey roads has gotten many a vacation off to a bad start. The Tappan Zee Bridge and the thruway can be a drag as well. When nothing seems to be working, the following alternative is a far more scenic and relaxing drive that's almost always trouble-free. It works just as well in reverse, and the tolls are cheaper, too.

From the west side of Manhattan:

1a. Take the Henry Hudson to the Saw Mill River Parkway.

2a. Take the Saw Mill River Parkway to Exit 26 (Taconic Parkway, Albany). Directions continue at no. 3, below.

From the east side of Manhattan:

1b. Take the Triborough Bridge to the Bruckner Expressway.

2b. Take the Bruckner to the Bronx River Parkway northbound, which leads directly into the Taconic State Parkway.

3. Continue on the Taconic State Parkway to northern Westchester and exit at the Bear Mountain Parkway exit.

4. This segment of the Bear Mountain Parkway will end after one mile at Route 202. Turn right onto Route 202.

5. On a Friday afternoon you will encounter a backup on Route 202, but it should only last 5–7 minutes. Take Route 202 about two miles and you will see signs to the next segment of the Bear Mountain Parkway on your right. Take the Bear Mountain Parkway for just under four miles to the intersection with routes 6, 9, and 202. Turn right toward Route 6.

6. Go across the Jan Peek Bridge. At the traffic circle, follow the signs to Route 6 West, Bear Mountain Bridge. This will take you along one of the most scenic winding roads this side of the Mississippi River.

7. Cross over the Bear Mountain Bridge; at the traffic circle follow the signs for Route 6 West.

8. Route 6 merges with the Palisades Interstate Parkway. Continue to Exit 18 (Route 6, Central Valley, Seven Lakes Drive).

9. Route 6 will lead directly into Route 17 West (the Quickway) to the Catskills Region.

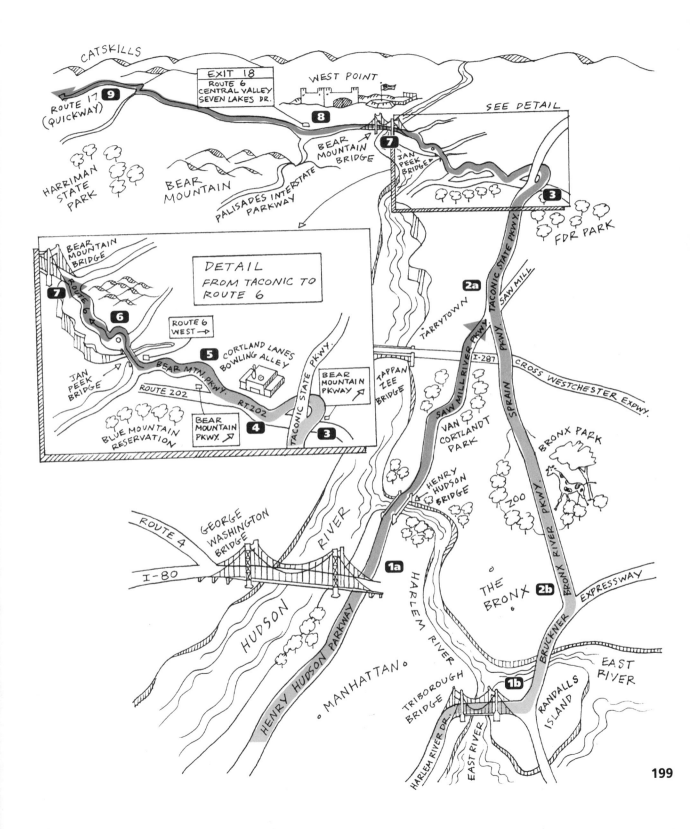

CATSKILLS

EXIT 18
ROUTE 6
CENTRAL VALLEY
SEVEN LAKES DR.

WEST POINT

SEE DETAIL

ROUTE 17
(QUICKWAY) **9**

8

BEAR
MOUNTAIN
BRIDGE

7

JAN PEEK BRIDGE

3

HARRIMAN
STATE
PARK

BEAR
MOUNTAIN

PALISADES INTERSTATE
PARKWAY

FDR PARK

DETAIL
FROM TACONIC TO
ROUTE 6

BEAR
MOUNTAIN
BRIDGE

7

ROUTE 6

6

ROUTE 6
WEST →

CORTLAND LANES
BOWLING ALLEY

5

2a

TARRYTOWN

TACONIC STATE PKWY.

SAW MILL

JAN
PEEK
BRIDGE

BEAR MTN. PKWY.

ROUTE 202

RT. 202

4

BEAR
MOUNTAIN
PKWY.

TACONIC STATE PKWY.

3

BEAR MOUNTAIN
PKWY.

TAPPAN
ZEE
BRIDGE

I-287

SAW MILL RIVER PKWY.

CROSS WESTCHESTER EXPWY.

SPRAIN PKWY.

BLUE MOUNTAIN
RESERVATION

VAN
CORTLANDT
PARK

BRONX PARK

ROUTE 4

GEORGE
WASHINGTON
BRIDGE

I-80

HENRY
HUDSON
BRIDGE

ZOO

HUDSON RIVER

1a

HARLEM RIVER

THE
BRONX

2b

BRONX RIVER PKWY.

BRUCKNER EXPRESSWAY

EAST
RIVER

HENRY HUDSON PARKWAY

MANHATTAN

TRIBOROUGH
BRIDGE

HARLEM RIVER DR.

EAST RIVER

1b

RANDALLS
ISLAND

199

Getting to Shea Stadium or the Flushing Meadow Tennis Center

I'll let you in on a little secret. When I was the city's traffic commissioner I wrote a special World Series computer program that would allow me to work late and still make it to Shea Stadium in time for the game. The program is still used today whenever there's a big game at Shea. Here's how it works: Since Shea can be reached easily from Northern Boulevard, about an hour before game-time traffic signals on Northern Boulevard from the Queensboro Bridge eastbound are timed to favor traffic heading toward the stadium. Similarly, westbound traffic signals toward Shea from the Queens–Nassau County line are favored. After the game, the signals all favor traffic away from Shea Stadium.

A. From northern midtown:

Take the Queensboro Bridge, lower level, to Queens Plaza to Northern Boulevard. Just stay to the left as you exit the bridge. Take Northern Boulevard all the way to Shea Stadium.

B. From southern midtown:

Take the Queens–Midtown Tunnel to the LIE. Exit at the BQE eastbound and take the BQE to Exit 38 (Route 25A, Northern Boulevard). At the traffic signal at the end of the ramp, turn right. You'll be on Northern Boulevard at 68th Street.

C. From Brooklyn:

Take the BQE eastbound to Exit 38 (Route 25A, Northern Boulevard). At the traffic signal at the end of the ramp, turn right onto Northern Boulevard.

D. From the Bronx and Westchester:

Take the southbound Bronx River Parkway, Hutchinson River Parkway, or New England Thruway to the Bruckner and follow this over the Triborough Bridge onto the Grand Central Parkway. Stay in the right lane after the roadway dips below ground level and take the first exit, Exit 4 (Bklyn-Qns Expwy, Verrazano Bridge). Move into the right lane to exit at Exit 38 (Route 25A, Northern Boulevard). At Northern Boulevard turn left.

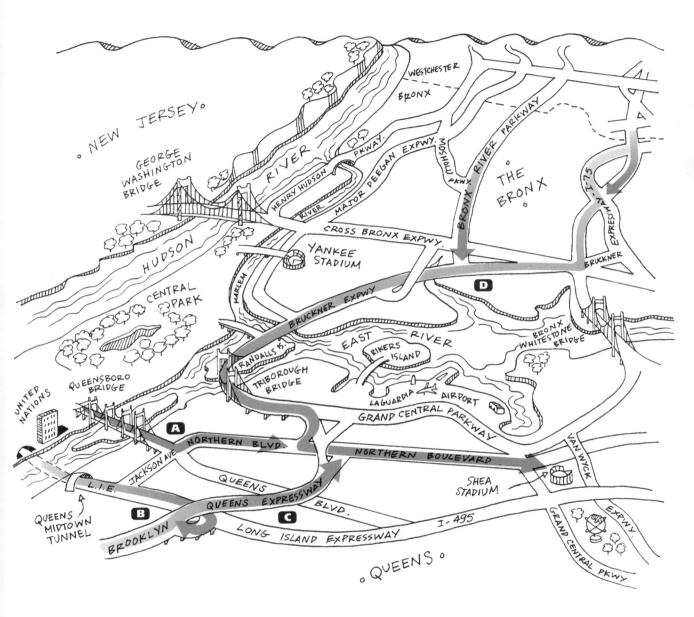

S
T
A
D
I
U
M
S

Yankee Stadium

People heading to Yankee Stadium seem to think that the Major Deegan Expressway is the only way to get there. Also, they tend to follow the directions given on signs posted along the way—not necessarily the best advice. For example, if you are heading northbound on the Deegan, the first stadium sign you will encounter is at Exit 4 (East 149 St, Stadium). Most people get off at that exit, but those in the know go one more stop to Exit 5 (West 155 St, Stadium, Manhattan). As long as you arrive a half-hour early and the game is not sold out, this exit will save you time and lead you directly to the parking garage.

If you are coming from the north or New Jersey, take the Harlem River Drive southbound in lieu of the Major Deegan:

1. Take the George Washington Bridge to the southbound exit for the Harlem River Drive (*see* pages 28-29, 132-133, 136-137... for other ways to access the Harlem River Drive from the Major Deegan or Henry Hudson Parkway).

2. Go less than a mile to Exit 23 (W. 155 St.).

3. From the exit go up the hill and make a left at the first light onto 155th Street.

4. Proceed across the Macombs Dam Bridge and, at the Bronx end, follow the signs to the parking areas at Yankee Stadium. (Use only designated stadium parking areas, to avoid potential vandalism and/or parking tickets.)

Stadium Traffic

For major sports or entertainment events you should always assume that a high percentage of first-timers, and even those that have been there before, know just one way to get to the arena. These people almost always stay on what appears to be the most direct highway route. For a poorly attended game this is fine, but when there's a sellout—forget it! You can easily miss an inning or two sitting on an expressway. If you're familiar with the local streets, you'll find that these little-known routes move surprisingly well.

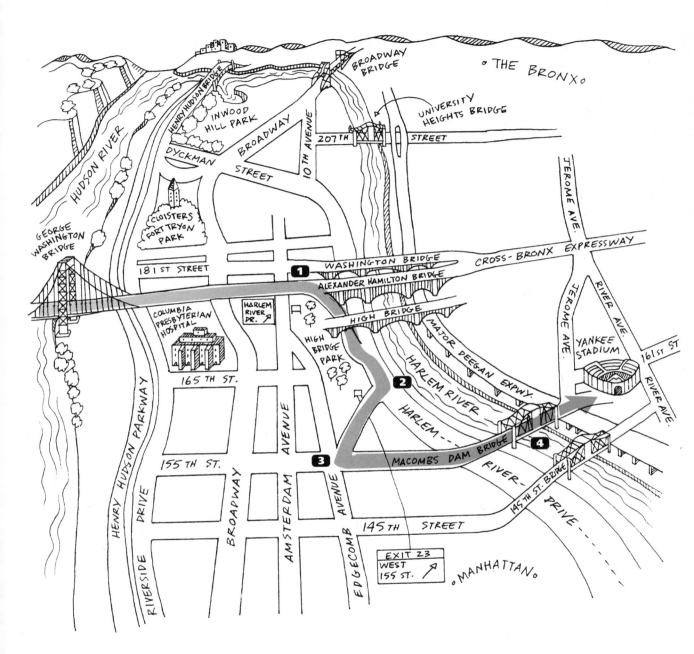

THE BRONX

HUDSON RIVER

HENRY HUDSON BRIDGE

INWOOD HILL PARK

BROADWAY BRIDGE

DYCKMAN STREET

BROADWAY STREET

10TH AVENUE

207TH STREET

UNIVERSITY HEIGHTS BRIDGE

JEROME AVE.

GEORGE WASHINGTON BRIDGE

CLOISTERS FORT TRYON PARK

181ST STREET

WASHINGTON BRIDGE

CROSS-BRONX EXPRESSWAY

1 ALEXANDER HAMILTON BRIDGE

JEROME AVE.

RIVER AVE.

COLUMBIA PRESBYTERIAN HOSPITAL

HARLEM RIVER DR.

HIGH BRIDGE

YANKEE STADIUM

161ST ST.

HIGH BRIDGE PARK

2

MAJOR DEEGAN EXPWY.

HARLEM RIVER

RIVER AVE.

165TH ST.

155TH ST.

BROADWAY

AMSTERDAM AVENUE

3

MACOMBS DAM BRIDGE

4

RIVER-

145TH ST. BRIDGE

HENRY HUDSON PARKWAY

RIVERSIDE DRIVE

EDGECOMB AVENUE

145TH STREET

DRIVE

EXIT 23
WEST
155 ST.

MANHATTAN

The Meadowlands Complex

The Meadowlands Complex (Giants Stadium, Brendan Byrne Arena, and Meadowlands Race Track) differs from other stadiums because it caters to a much wider variety of events. Different events require different driving strategies. For example, college basketball and football games cause far more congestion than professional games drawing equal-size crowds. College fans come from a greater distance and are less familiar with the local roads than their "pro" counterparts. Since most people attending professional events have season tickets, they are familiar with the roads and are more likely to know alternative routes.

The main route for the majority of fans is the New Jersey Turnpike, which allows direct access from its western spur. Consequently, nearly everybody takes the western spur—and that's why you should take the eastern spur. The following are alternates from every direction.

A. From the south:

Take the New Jersey Turnpike north to the eastern spur. Take Exit 16E(NJ 3, Lincoln Tunnel, Secaucus). Follow the signs to Route 3 west, which will lead to the complex.

B. From the north:

Take the New Jersey Turnpike's eastern spur south and exit at Exit17 (NJ 3, Lincoln Tunnel, Secaucus). Follow the signs to Route 3 west, which will lead to the complex.

C. From the west:

Take Route 46 east to Route 17 south. Continue on Route 17 south to Route 120 south, Paterson Plank Road, Sports Complex. Take Route 120 south, Paterson Plank Road, east to the complex.

D. From the George Washington Bridge:

Take I-95 south to Route 46 west. Continue for about two miles and turn left onto Liberty Street. The Liberty Street sign is tiny and easy to miss. Liberty Street is the first intersection with a traffic light after Grand Street. Liberty Street becomes Moonachie Avenue (Route 503), then Washington Avenue (still Route 503), and then Route 120. Route 120 goes between the arena and the stadium.

E. From the Lincoln Tunnel:

Take Route 3 west straight to the complex.

F. From the Holland Tunnel:

Follow the signs to routes 1 and 9. At the Tonnele Circle follow the signs for routes 1 and 9 north. Head north on Tonnelle Avenue for about two miles and follow the signs to Route 3 west to the complex.

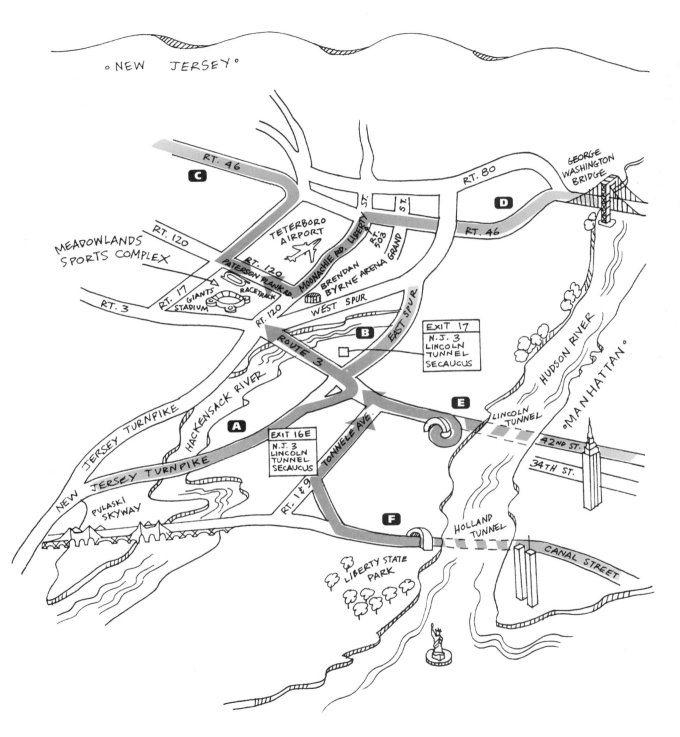

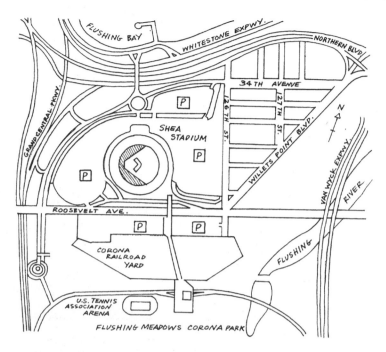

Shea Stadium and the U.S.T.A. Tennis Center

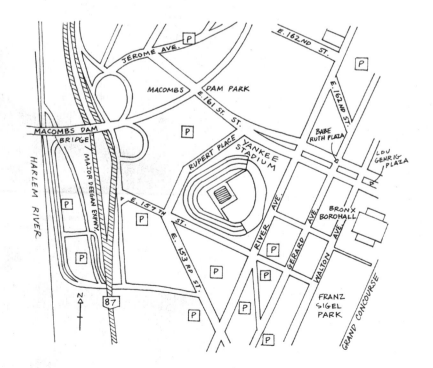

Yankee Stadium

Meadowlands Complex

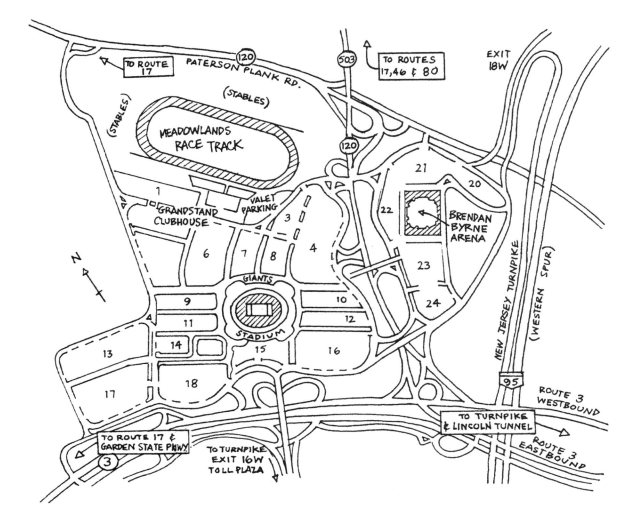

"Making" the "Key" Traffic Signal

This may come as a surprise to many drivers, but somebody actually thinks about how to time the traffic signals! A group of traffic engineers studies traffic volume, congestion levels, and speeds and tries to minimize system delay. That is, they look at a whole area and decide how to time the signals so that traffic flows as smoothly as possible with minimal stops—not an easy task. Once you understand the logic used by the engineers you'll be able to spot "key" signals and reduce your own travel time. By the time you get through this chapter you will have earned three credits in Gridlock Sam's School of Traffic Science. But first, you'll need to learn some "lingo."

Signal Terminology

phase: each signal has a green period, a yellow period, and a red period; these are called "phases." A signal may also have a phase for a turning movement, an all-red phase for pedestrians, and even a phase for bicycles (i.e., Herald Square).

cycle length: a signal goes through a green phase, a yellow phase, and a red phase. Then it all starts over again with a green phase. The time it takes the signal to go through all the phases is called the cycle length.

green time: just what it sounds like—the length of the green phase.

The Simple Single Signal

The "simple" intersection has two roads crossing at approximately 90 degree angles. For the purpose of timing the signals, one road is called the "major" street, the other, the "minor" street. The major street typically carries more traffic, is usually more significant (i.e., carries buses, is a truck route, etc.), and is often wider. The minor street is typically a low volume local street and often does not go "through" great distances.

The traffic engineer studies the volume and congestion levels and then decides the amount of green time to give each approach. If a heavily traveled bus and truck route passes a little used local street, the engineer is likely to set the heavy street's green phase at 70% or more of the cycle length. If the difference between the streets is less pronounced, then a 55/45 split is more likely.

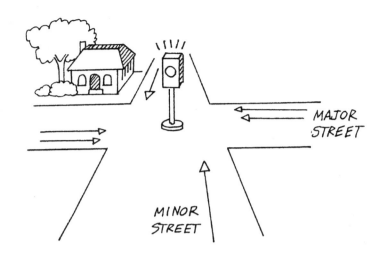

Every intersection has a major and minor street. The major street gets more green time than the minor street.

MAJOR STREET

MINOR STREET

Often a major street becomes a minor street where it crosses an even more significant street at an intersection. For example, Church Avenue in Brooklyn is a pretty significant street. It carries buses and trucks and is heavily used. When Church Avenue intersects with East 18th Street or Argyle road, Church is the major street and is given a greater percentage of green time. However, when Church Avenue crosses an even more major street, Flatbush Avenue, Church becomes the minor street. So how could knowing this help you save time?

First of all, if you're traveling a long distance, you're almost always better off taking a major street over a minor street. When you are traveling on the major street be aware of any significant or more major streets that you are crossing. Each time you approach a significant or more major cross street you're likely to have less green time. If you are approaching the intersection well after the start of the green phase, you are more likely to be stopped at the significant or more major streets than at the minor ones. In these situations you may decide to change lanes or accelerate safely to "make" the signal. A few examples: If you're on Church Avenue you'll have less green time at Flatbush Avenue than at other intersections. If you're traveling southbound on Fifth Avenue you may comfortably make the signals at 44th and 43rd streets but you may have to scoot to make the light at 42nd Street. **The key signals are the major crossings.**

The Three–Phased Signal

Most traffic signals have a green phase for the major street, followed by a green phase for the minor street, and then a return to the major street green phase. However, at complex intersections like Herald Square, three streets intersect. Each street has it's own green phase. At others, like Northern Boulevard at 33rd Street or Ocean Parkway at Avenue J, specially dedicated phases for turning vehicles have been installed. These intersections are referred to by traffic engineers as "three-phased." (Some intersections are four-phased, but these are very rare.)

At a two-phased intersection the major street may get 50 seconds of green time and the minor street 40 seconds. However, at a three-phased intersection the 90–second signal cycle must be shared three ways. The most major street may get 40 seconds, the next most major street 30 seconds, and the minor street just 20 seconds. Say you're traveling on a major street and you're 40 seconds into the green phase. In our example the major street gets 50 seconds of green time. Well, you should have no problem making the light because you've got 10 seconds to spare. However, if you're approaching a three-phased intersection with just 40 seconds of major street green time, you'll be cutting it close.

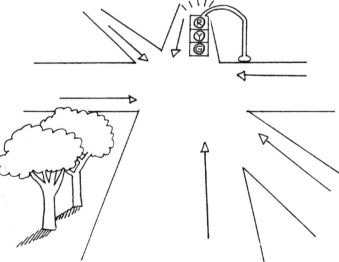

Multi-phased intersections are often key signals to make.

This is a three-phased intersection where three streets meet and must share the cycle length.

Herald Square is the intersection of 34th Street, Broadway, and Sixth Avenue. Broadway and Sixth Avenue are major streets at almost all intersections. Thirty-fourth Street is on a par with most streets it crosses. However, at Herald Square these three big roads must share a 90-second cycle. Sixth Avenue may get just 35 seconds, Broadway just 30 seconds, and 34th Street only 25 seconds. This is why Herald Square is almost always congested. It also explains why Sixth Avenue between 34th and 42nd streets almost always moves well. Sixth approaching 34th Street gets just 35 seconds of green. But Sixth between 35th and 41st streets averages 50 seconds of green! Traffic is constricted south of 34th Street, enabling traffic north of 34th Street to move better. This raises three axioms:

- **The key signal is often at the three-phased intersection.**

- **If you can avoid a three-phased intersection, do so.**

- **Once past a three-phased intersection, traffic usually moves well.**

Where special turn signals are provided, the intersection is multiphased.

Traffic Signal Patterns

Until now we've been discussing traffic signals at individual intersections. But in Long Island City, at the Traffic Bureau's headquarters, there are master computers that look at the system of signals and control them centrally. This is why, when you're traveling on Northern Boulevard, the Grand Concourse, or Flatbush Avenue, you'll notice the signals are "staggered" toward Manhattan in the morning rush hour and away from Manhattan in the evening. The computer in Long Island City has decided to favor the dominant flow. A "staggered" or progressive pattern is just one of many used in New York City. The four patterns that you will most likely encounter are described below:

Progressive or "Staggered" Signal Patterns

The only way to accurately determine what pattern you're in is to study the signals at the start of the green phase. Trying to determine patterns from the start of the red phase could be misleading.

In a progression, the signal nearest you turns green first, followed by the next signal, and in sequence each signal after that. When traveling First Avenue in Manhattan you'll notice that once the signal at 42nd Street turns green, the signal at 43rd Street will change about six seconds later, and the signal at 44th Street will change about six seconds after that. Every six seconds or so the next intersection signal will turn green. The pattern is set so that in light or moderate conditions you should be able to travel great distances without stopping. The block lengths in Manhattan are short, so that six seconds is about the time it takes a car to travel a block at the speed limit. If the distances between signals was longer the offset time would be longer as well.

The key is to travel at or near the beginning of the green phase. If you're late in the green phase (you can usually tell if the pedestrian signals are flashing "DON'T WALK"), you're likely to be stopped at a major cross street or almost certainly at a three-phased intersection.

Let's say you're traveling on Northern Boulevard toward Manhattan at 7 AM. The signals are in progression and you're breezing along. You pass Shea Stadium with no problem and the signals are changing just three or four blocks ahead of you. When you pass 80th Street you notice that the signals are now changing six or seven blocks ahead, and as you pass 75th Street

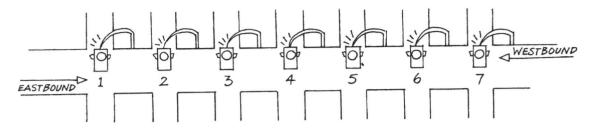

In an eastbound progression, signal 1 turns green first. A few seconds later, signal 2 turns green; then signals 3, 4, 5...in sequence. Eastbound vehicles traveling with the progression should travel great distances between stops. Westbound vehicles face a reversed progression, and will be forced to stop every few blocks.

you spot the "DON'T WALK" sign flashing. Your key signal ahead is the three-phased intersection with the BQE service road at 68th Street. If you tarry you'll probably be stopped. If you make the light at the BQE service road you should make the next ten intersections and, under favorable conditions, reach Queens Plaza without stopping.

The axioms are:

- **Under light or moderate conditions (especially in the early morning peak period), progressions are terrific. Under those conditions always choose a street with a progressive pattern in the direction you're traveling.**

- **The key signals to watch for are the three-phased intersections and the more major streets.**

- **When you've passed the three-phased or more major intersection, relax—you're certain to make the next series of lights.**

- **If the DON'T WALK lights are flashing, don't tarry or you'll be stopping soon.**

Reversed Progressions

It's just what it sounds like; you're traveling opposite a progression.   The way to spot it is if you notice green lights coming toward you. That is, a signal two blocks away turns green, then one a block away, and then your signal changes. Chances are there's a progressive pattern, but you're traveling the wrong way. When you're going opposite a progression you'll hit a red signal every few blocks.

For example, if you're heading north on Riverside Drive in the morning (when most people are traveling south), you'll be stopped every few blocks. You would be better off one block east on West End Avenue, which doesn't have such a pattern in the morning (because it has yet to be hooked up to the computer, a project scheduled for late 1994).

Consequently, my advice is:

- **Reversed progressions should be avoided at all costs.**

- **If that's not possible, relax and resign yourself to stopping every few blocks.**

The Alternate Group Pattern

During midday, at night, and on weekends many streets have a "balanced" pattern that treats traffic equally in both directions. One of the most widely used patterns is the alternate group. Essentially, the signals are timed so that approximately half (by distance) will be green and the other half red. Groups are typically strings of two to five (though they could be as few as one or as many as eight).

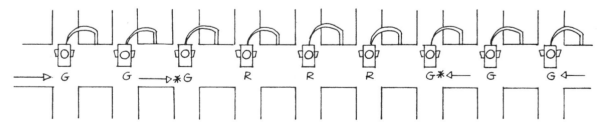

A typical alternate group pattern has a string of green lights, followed by a group of red lights. The key signal to make is the last green. If you make it, you'll easily make the next few signals. If you don't, you'll be stopped twice.

Say you're at an intersection and your signal turns green. The next two signals turn green simultaneously. But looking farther ahead you see that the three signals beyond that are red (often they turn red a few seconds after your signal turns green). A bird's eye view would show three green signals, followed by three red , followed by three green, and so on. If you make the last signal in your group you'll be approaching the red group. Just as you reach the first signal in the red group it will turn green (as will the next two signals). This pattern repeats itself, so theoretically you should be able to travel great distances without stopping.

But there's a downside. If the last of the three signals turns red before you get there you'll be stopped both there and at the following signal! While you're stopped the first time the next three lights will be turning green. Shortly after your signal turns green (and just before you arrive at the next signal), the next group will turn red. Our rules for driving in an alternate group are:

- **The key signal in an alternate group pattern is the last in a string of "greens."**
- **If you get stopped at a signal in an alternate group pattern, you may as well relax and drive slowly to the next signal group, where you'll surely be stopped again.**

The Simultaneous Pattern

The simultaneous pattern is the easiest to understand and the easiest to spot. All the signals turn green at the same time. However, not all the signals turn red at the same time. At each crossing with a major street or a multi-phased intersection the red is likely to come on earlier than at the other intersections. **The key signal in a simultaneous pattern is the major cross street or three-phased intersection.**

When you're traveling in a simultaneous pattern and the cross streets' pedestrian signals are flashing "DON'T WALK," you know you're late in the green phase. At this point you may as well relax; there's not much you can do since nearly all the signals will be turning red at about the same time. The best you can "squeeze out" from a simultaneous pattern is 1/2 to 3/4 mile per green phase.

SHADOW TRAFFIC

The Shadow Traffic Broadcast Center is the source of traffic information for a region encompassing thirteen thousand square miles. Right in the center of this region is New York City, which has fifteen river crossings spewing a million cars in and out of the city by bridge and tunnel daily.

The roadways of Metropolitan New York have major limitations. With a crumbling infrastructure and many single-lane arteries, the city is incapable of handling the traffic that overwhelms it daily. The inability of these arteries to meet today's demands is not a matter of debate. It is a fact of life. There is just no room to expand. The only option available to drivers today is to learn more about the streets on which they drive, pinpoint problem locations, and learn alternative routes.

Sam Schwartz, former Chief of the New York City Traffic Bureau, and Shadow Traffic have combined efforts to lift some of the burden imposed upon you, the driver, with recommended shortcuts and alternate routing. Shadow began to gather and disseminate traffic information more than fifteen years ago. Since then, its facilities have been upgraded to the point where a highly technical software program now delivers intricate details about the flow of traffic through the maze of city streets, avenues, and highways.

This information is upgraded minute-by-minute through the use of five fixed-wing airplanes and two jet helicopters tracing the same routes that you travel daily. Shadow is also electronically connected both to road sensors designating the exact flow of traffic on certain highways and strategically positioned cameras scanning heavily trafficked locations, enabling technicians to actually look at problems while Shadow is reporting them. There are six hundred stringers on "The Shadow Road Team"— people with cellular phones who call in around the clock with details of traffic problems they are witnessing. Often they broadcast on a radio station right from the scene of the problem.

Shadow's main operation center is located in Rutherford, New Jersey. In-house personnel are also stationed in bureaus—mini-versions of the main center—strategically located on the outskirts of the city to provide localized information about traffic through all the gateways into and out of the city.

All this information is filtered through Shadow's in-house system and delivered to the public through the sixty radio stations that Shadow serves. The information is often accompanied by recommended alternate routes, many of which are described in this book.